# The Laughing Policeman

## Policing in Norfolk 1966 – 1981

### By Chris Clark

# The Laughing Policeman

## Policing in Norfolk 1966 – 1981

### By Chris Clark

The Laughing Policeman - Policing in Norfolk 1966 – 1981. This book was first published in Great Britain in paperback during June 2016.

The moral right of Chris Clark is to be identified as the author of this work and has been asserted by him in accordance with the Copyright, Designs and Patents Act of 1988.

All rights are reserved and no part of this book may be produced or utilized in any format, or by any means, electronic or mechanical, including photocopying, recording or by any information storage or retrieval system, without prior permission in writing from the publishers – Coast & Country/Ads2life. ads2life@btinternet.com

All rights reserved.

ISBN-13: 978-1534691476

Copyright © June 2016 Chris Clark

## "The Laughing Policeman" By Charles Penrose 1922

*I know a fat old policeman, he's always on our street*

*Fat jolly red-faced man, he really is a treat.*

*He's too kind for a policeman, he's never known to frown*

*And everybody says he is the happiest man in town.*

*He laughs upon point duty, he laughs upon his beat*

*He laughs at everybody while he's walking down the street*

*He never can stop laughing, he says he never tried*

*Well; once he did arrest a man and laughed until he cried.*

*His jolly face it wrinkled and then he shut his eyes*

*He opened his great mouth, it was a wondrous size*

*He said I must arrest you, but he didn't know what for*

*And then he started laughing until he cracked his jaw.*

*So if you chance to meet him, when walking round the town*

*Just shake him by his fat old hand and give him half a crown*

*His eyes will beam and sparkle, he'll gurgle with delight*

*And he'll start laughing with all his blessed might.*

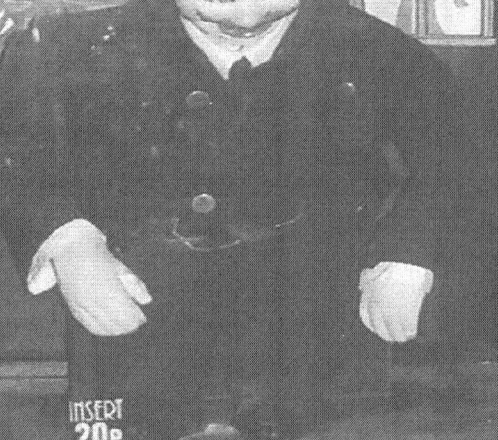

## CONTENTS

                                                                                        Page

Prologue ............................................................................... i

The Author .......................................................................... iii

**Chapter One**

"Early Life" ............................................................................. 1

**Chapter Two**

"The End Of An Era" 1966 -1967 ......................................... 21

**Chapter Three**

"From Heartbeat To Z Cars" 1968 – 1973 ............................ 115

**Chapter Four**

"Into The Light" 1974 ........................................................ 224

**Chapter Five**

"By Royal Appointment" .................................................... 248

**Chapter Six**

"Pastures New" ................................................................... 287

In this first part autobiography I have included various funny and sometimes 'black humour' events which occurred during my personal journey through life and eventual police career and into retirement. The following 'warts and all' account interjected with my own thoughts illustrates how humour and laughter can get oneself through the harshness's of life. On occasions to protect the guilty identifiable names have been omitted changed or abbreviated.

Chris Clark June 2016.

## Prologue

This is a book which I never thought I would get completed before I fell off the perch, but here some 50 years from when I joined here is the first part.

### *This book is dedicated to a number of people*

Firstly to all of my colleagues who served on 'B' Relief Kings Lynn from 1967 to 1987 where I served on as man and boy for 16 of those 20 years and who I kept a close contact with for the missing years 1978 to 1981 through my first wife Therese being in my place on the Relief. Some are mentioned some not and to countless other serving police officers of all ranks who were in Kings Lynn Division from April 1967 until my enforced early retirement in August 1994 after some twenty eight and a half years; including colleagues on "D" Relief from 1991 to 1994. It was a pleasure to serve you all and to serve with you.

Secondly to Therese to whom I spent twenty five years with as a partner some happy and some sad including some eight years as a colleaugue; as well as raising two children together. Thank you for those years and the memories.

Thirdly to the memory of Superintendent Robin 'Bob' Humphrey who sadly died very prematurely in office from cancer he was instrumental in me starting off a scrap book in August1986 of my first 20 years police service up until then, ready for the 150th anniversary of King's Lynn Police Force; this formed the skeleton of my work.

**Lastly and most importantly to my Wife Jeanne who some ten years after my retirement gave me the love encouragement and inspiration to eventually pick up my pen and to start this account of my life in the police and eventually to correspond with former colleagues. Without your continual support and love I would not have survived until now let alone have had the strength and courage to sit**

down and tell my story of Norfolk Constabulary and its changes. Thank you Darling from the bottom of my heart! You have stood by me steadfastly through the bad times and into the good and Darling I know that I have said this before but you are the wind beneath my wings.

You raise me up so I can stand on Mountains

My Love Always.

## *The Author*

Chris Clark, formerly Police Constable 409 of Norfolk Constabulary came into the world on Christmas Day 1945 the eldest child of Tom and Stella Clark. Dad had joined the Royal Air Force in June 1939 when he was still seventeen. WW2 started in the September and in 1940 he was posted to Bircham Newton in Norfolk where he met my Mum in nearby Stanhoe. The war interrupted their courtship until March 1945 when they were reacquainted and were married at Fakenham Register Office on 13th August with Mum carrying a noticeable bump! It was a few months after the end of the war when I made my appearance and the United Nations Organisation had just been born it was also the start of the trials of Nazi Germans at Nuremberg.

I was eventually one of eight children and because of Dad's postings, educated at various schools in Norfolk, Berkshire, Oxfordshire, Cambridgeshire, Wiltshire and Singapore. We eventually settled in 1955 at "Excelsior" Brook Road in the village of Dersingham close to Sandringham this is where I completed my education at St George's Secondary Modern at age fifteen. By then I had seen the insides of nine different assorted primary junior and secondary modern schools. After a number of labouring jobs I eventually joined Norfolk Constabulary as a Police Constable in March 1966 and had many diverse roles within the Uniform Branch until my retirement during August 1994.

## *Chapter One*

## *"Early Life"*

I was born on Christmas Day 1945 in a tithe cottage belonging to Church Farm on Burnham Road, Stanhoe opposite Stanhoe duck pond. This was the home of my maternal Grandparents John (Jack) and (Florence) Florrie Stringer. At the time my Parents Tom and Stella were officially living in rented accommodation in Redman's Yard off the Market Place, Burnham Market however Dad, Flight Lieutenant Tom Clark RAF was a Signaller on 271 Squadron flying Dakotas long haul to India to bring back time-expired troops and repatriated ex Far East prisoners of war therefore Mum my elder half Brother Trevor Stringer and I lived with Jack and Florrie for the best part of the first three years of my life. Obviously I remember little of the first three years of my young life other than two incidents which occurred whilst we lived with my Grandparents; which I probably remember because of the effect that they had on me.

The first occasion was whilst carrying a jam jar full of tadpoles into the house I tripped over the raised wooden threshold door step and fell onto a quarry stone floor smashing the jar in the process and receiving cuts to my lip, palm of my hands and knees. I still bear these scars after over sixty years the tadpoles fared less favourably as they never got to be frogs.

This incident set the trend for my future clumsy escapades which portrayed that I was a bit of Norman Wisdom and Frank Spencer rolled into one; Dad summed it up when he called me *"ham fisted."*

The second occasion was the first of a series of injuries inflicted upon me by Trevor who was some seven years old than I. Trevor was a failed Actor at heart and on this occasion he must have been to Docking Cinema to see the 1930 film *"Moby Dick"* the White Whale; this was an adaptation from an 1851 novel and was later released in 1956 with Gregory Peck and Sir Bernard Miles. Anyhow Trevor an adventure seeking ten year old rigged up our tin bath which was kept on the gable end when not in use got a large sharp ended steel poker out of the hearth and tied a length of rope through the *"eye"* of the poker handle to a handle of the tin bath and climbed in and became *"Captain Ahab"* the main character

(Mum) Stella Clark     (Dad) Tom Clark
and The Author age 18 months in 1947

Guess who I was to be yes none other than *"Moby Dick."* Trevor then enacted the scene where *"Moby Dick"* is harpooned by *"Ahab"* and he got me to swim (trot) past the ship (bath) whereupon he flung the poker as his harpoon, straight into the back of my left leg behind the knee with the resulting effect of my arterial blood suddenly spurting everywhere! I cannot remember precisely what happened apart from Mum carrying me into the house stopping the flow of blood and my nasty wound being treated and being bandaged. This episode should have been the turning point in his behaviour towards me but it was only the first in a number of future *"incidents."*

***The Author and Brother Trevor***

During autumn of 1949 and through to June 1950 we lived in Married Quarters firstly at Waterbeach in Cambridgeshire where Dad was briefly with 10 and 24 VIP Squadron's and then on to Crowmarsh in Berkshire which is near to Wallingford, Oxon when he was on his second posting to The King's Flight at Benson from June 1950 until October 1952; Crowmarsh is where I first went to School and where I spent my first two and a half years education.

*Crowmarsh School photo 1951*

During this period I recall yet another episode of Trevor's bizarre *"games"* when I was on the receiving end, on this occasion he was aged about fourteen and me seven. He used to carry a large hunting knife in a sheath and we were walking down a lane in Crowmarsh Wood when he pulled the knife out and said *"Run away as fast as you can and I'll try to hit you."* Obediently I ran off and hadn't got very far when I felt a sharp blow and the blade of the knife stuck into my back near to the left shoulder blade. On yet another occasion around this time Trevor had got himself a long-bow and arrows set he took aim not at a target but vertical to the sky and fired off one of the arrows. The arrow flew high until its upward motion was halted by the earth's gravity whereupon it stopped and about turned and came plunging back to Terra Firma. Luckily for me it came tail first as I stood innocently gazing skyward and it embedded itself into the bottom of my eye; just missing completely blinding me. After this episode I had to wear spectacles for some time at Primary School and in later life.

In October 1952 Dad was posted to the Far East Transport Wing VIP Flight and based at FEAF Headquarters at Changi in Singapore and spent most of his time during the next two and a half years flying the Commander In Chief around the various Bases of Command including Kai Tak in Kowloon Hong Kong during the end of the Korean War and during the Malaya Emergency. During this time we again went to live with my Grandparents Jack and Florrie Stringer who in the meantime had moved to No. 4 Ramp Row Cottages, Bircham Road, Stanhoe. Goodness knows how we all fitted in this small two up one down cottage, as there were three adults and by now five children, with a sixth on the way. I remember that downstairs was an open plan lounge kitchen and dining area.

Rationing was still in force so wild rabbit caught from Major Ralli's Farm was the mainstay of our existence; another favourite being rabbit braised in the oven with onions and gravy or jugged hare. Rationing had continued after the end of the war. In fact it became stricter after the war ended than during the hostilities. Bread was on ration from 1946 until 1948 potato rationing began in 1947 sweet rationing continued until February 1953 and sugar until September 1954; with meat and other food rationing continuing until July 1954.

The toilet at Stanhoe was in a little shed at the end of the garden an original *"thunder box"* fitted out with a wooden bench seat with a hole cut out for one's bottom and underneath was a large metal bucket which had *"Elsan"* toilet disinfectant in it the bucket was to catch the *"number ones and number two's"* and there would be newspaper cut into squares on a hook for toilet paper. When the bucket was nearly full Granddad would dig a pit and empty the contents of the bucket into it, cover it with soot and ashes then refill it; at night time we had a porcelain potty under the bed which was taken down in the morning and emptied.

*My Grandparents John (Jack) and Florence (Florrie) Stringer 1952*

This leads me onto washing during the rest of the week we had to make do with washing our face, hands, armpits and privates in that order at the sink located in the scullery. On Friday evenings the tin bath was hauled in and filled with steaming water from the kettle and saucepans from the fire. One by one each of us had a bath in the same water and was then towelled down in front of the fire.

Stanhoe being only some few miles from the North Norfolk coast was in the teeth of the vicious hurricane force winds whipped up on the night of the 31st of January 1953 when the East Coast Floods occurred and during that night I lay in bed petrified hearing the wind screaming and the windows rattling and the roof threatening to come off. That night there was also a different wailing noise my youngest Sister was born amidst the storm; there were now six of us siblings to be fed and clothed.

I went to Stanhoe Primary School and on June the 2nd 1953 the day of HM The Queen Elizabeth 11 Coronation, along with the other pupils I was presented with a Coronation Mug and New Testament Bible. I don't know what happened to the mug but I still have my Bible.

*Stanhoe School photo 1953*

The next stage of my childhood was the most exciting that any young person could hope to experience and nowadays with our modern clinical concrete world would be impossible to fully achieve. Dad as previously mentioned was on Far East duty with the RAF and at the start of January 1954 we were to join him in Officer's Married Quarters in Singapore; some third of the World in distance away. He flew home to collect us and we travelled as a family by car through the night to Southampton Docks and we were loaded on board the SS "Empire Trooper". Our cabins were located on the water line on the outside of the vessel and all we could see through the thick portholes was the sea and we set off on a month long cruise of some 8,000 miles it was at times exciting, frightening or wondrous an unforgettable experience. In those days apart from the very rich and service personnel families no trip of this magnitude was the norm, just travelling from one end of England to Scotland was an epic journey.

*SS Empire Trooper*

We arrived in Singapore at the end of February 1954 having traversed the Bay of Biscay in a force 12 storm, across the tranquil Mediterranean Sea through the Suez Canal which divides Africa from Asia, into the Red Sea and across the Indian Ocean. The Island was then a paradise full of exotic flowers, insects and snakes and unlike the concrete jungle it is today as is Hong Kong. Little shops and markets sold all manner of things both Oriental and Western. Little had changed on the Island since the Japanese occupation and the end of World War 11 some nine years previous it still bore many fresh scars of that terrible time.

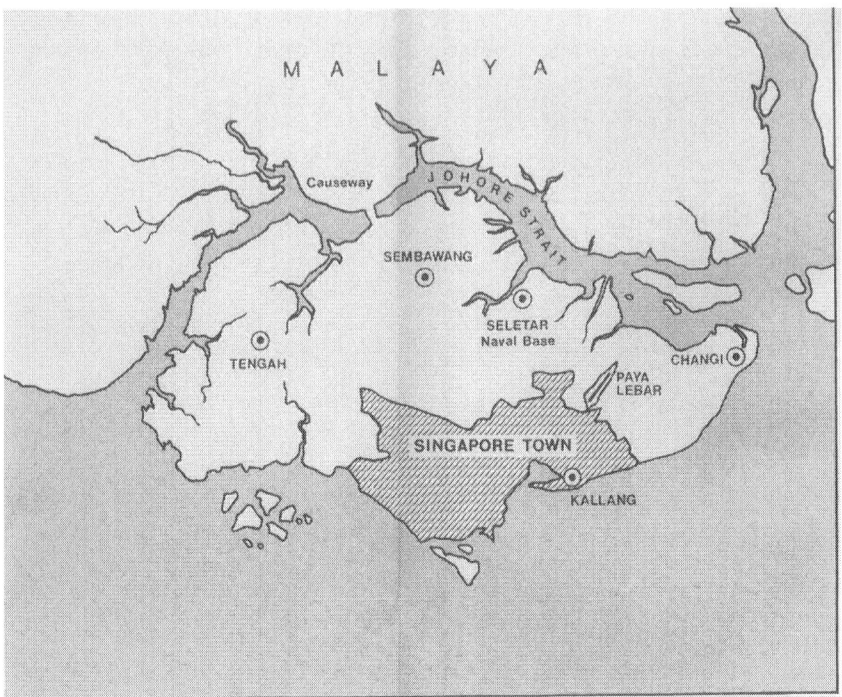

Lloyds Leas the RAF Married Quarters estate where we lived was a complex of recently built bungalows all fitted with the latest mod cons of that era including fully functional kitchens with electric cookers fridge/freezer and a separate laundry room with washing machine. Bathrooms and toilets had mains water hot and cold taps and flush toilets. Outside there were modern styled concrete street lamps tarmac roads with footpaths and drains which led to enormous monsoon drains. The whole style of modern living was advanced and vastly superior to what we had left behind in England. Lloyd Leas was on a hill overlooking deep jungle and the infamous Changi Jail was about half a mile away in a clearing.

*The Author at Changi Beach*

This idyllic lifestyle came to a sudden end some 14 months later on *"Good Friday"* during April 1955 when my beloved Grandfather *"Jack"* Stringer died suddenly of a heart attack back in England some six months short of his seventieth birthday and was later buried in Stanhoe Churchyard; Granny had three months to get out of the tithe cottage which had been her home for some ten years. During early May 1955 we as a family flew home from Singapore in a four propeller Handley Page Hermes aircraft which carried 50 passengers like a flying bus; it had a cruising speed of 270mph and a range of just under 2,000miles. This flight took three days to complete with overnight stops at Delhi in India, Karachi in West Pakistan and Rome in Italy and additional landings at Rangoon, Calcutta, Basra and Cairo. It was some long haul journey when you compare it to nowadays jet aircraft doing it in ten hour flights with one refuelling stop. Going over places like Afghanistan and the Arabian Desert the aircraft flying at 11,500feet would hit an air pocket and plummet a thousand feet the engines would falter and then we would regain height; whilst we were scared witless and being air sick into brown paper bags or chewing on boiled sweets to make our ears pop. This part of our flight was every bit as bad as the sea crossing of Biscay. Three days after setting out from Singapore we landed at Blackbushe Airport on the Surrey/Hampshire border as our original destination in London was fog-bound we then caught the train back to Norfolk.

*A Hermes at Blackbushe Airport*

On arrival back in England Dad took compassionate leave and was then posted to RAF Swanton Morley as an Air Electronics Officer and we moved into temporary Officer's Married Quarters whilst Mum and Dad started looking for a permanent new home to accommodate them and their six soon to be seven Children; with baby number seven being due at the end of the year. So it was during the summer of 1955 that we moved into *"Excelsior"* Brook Road, Dersingham bought at a princely sum of £3,500.

I started school at Dersingham Primary by this time I had been in over six different primary schools with different teaching methods including the time in Singapore when education was sparse and I only excelled in Geography .This wasn't a surprise for this *"boy in a suitcase"* needless to say I failed my *"Eleven Plus"* and didn't get into Grammar School; but my final position of 8th out of 24 wasn't bad considering the length of time that I had been settled there. Remarks on my school report read *"Conduct Good. Works steadily."* In the meantime another Brother had arrived on the scene having been born during May 1957.

During this period as on other occasions through my young life Dad was away a lot doing his job in the RAF; Trevor was an apprentice Game Keeper at Sandringham and it would fall to me to be *"Mum's Little Helper."* I used to do all of the shopping at Milton Butchers, Playford

Bakers and Parker's Grocery and Drapery shop, the latter situated on Manor Road at the corner with Sandringham Hill. I would carry all of the family shopping home in a cardboard box and at home I would help mum prepare the vegetables and mash the potatoes when the meal was cooked.

Later I had after school and Saturday jobs at Milton's, Playford's and Handford Grocery Store where I rode a trade bike and delivered groceries to elderly and housebound customers; these jobs brought in a nice amount of pocket money.
I left Dersingham Primary in July 1957 and started at St George's Secondary Modern that September. I was only at St George's for a matter of months before Dad was posted this time to RAF Hullavington in Wiltshire I started school at Bremilham School during the winter term of 1957 and I often had to trek through snowdrifts on the long walk to Stanton St Quinton to catch the bus to Malmesbury and then the reverse trek at the end of the school day.

I re-started the Autumn Term on Monday 8th September 1958, and by that November I was back at St George's Dersingham for the rest of the autumn and winter Terms as Dad had been posted to RAF Watton in Norfolk.

I continued at St George's into the Spring and Summer Terms of 1959 in Form 2 George with Eric Norton my Form Master with Geography, Science and Gardening being my best subjects and my final class position in July was a poor 27th out of 38.

Upon leaving school in July 1961 having excelled only in Science, Geography and Gardening I obtained a place as a Student Worker on a one year's course at Burlingham Horticultural Station near Acle in Norfolk. It took three separate trains to travel from Dersingham Station to Lingwood Station with my cycle on board in the Guard's Van, where I boarded with a retired schoolteacher Mrs Mingay in the village of

Lingwood together with a fellow student from Ipswich.

***The local Hunstanton to King's Lynn train leaving Lynn Station***

For breakfast I had half a fried egg each and one rasher of rancid bacon. For lunch we were invariably packed up with one ham sandwich which again was rancid with loads of fat and a cheese one on alternative days. I used to toast mine by opening the flap to the large coal fired boiler at work. There used to be a daily vehicle delivering pop crisps and sausage rolls and we would buy from it to supplement our meagre lunchbox. Our evening meals were also insufficient for two hard working young men and we would go to the local pub where we would purchase snack food. At our Lingwood lodgings I remember that we did not have a flush toilet but a *"thunder box"* in an outhouse attached to the kitchen/scullery. This had to be emptied once a week it was however better than the one mentioned before that we had at our grandparents that one was down the bottom of the garden and you had to go out in all weathers to use it.

At Burlingham I studied all theory and practical aspects of growing crops flowers plants etc. I completed the course at the end of August

1962; my only excitement during this time apart from the local hostelry was watching the *"Black Arrows"* Hawker Hunters the original Royal Air Force flying display team going through their paces at nearby RAF Coltishall.

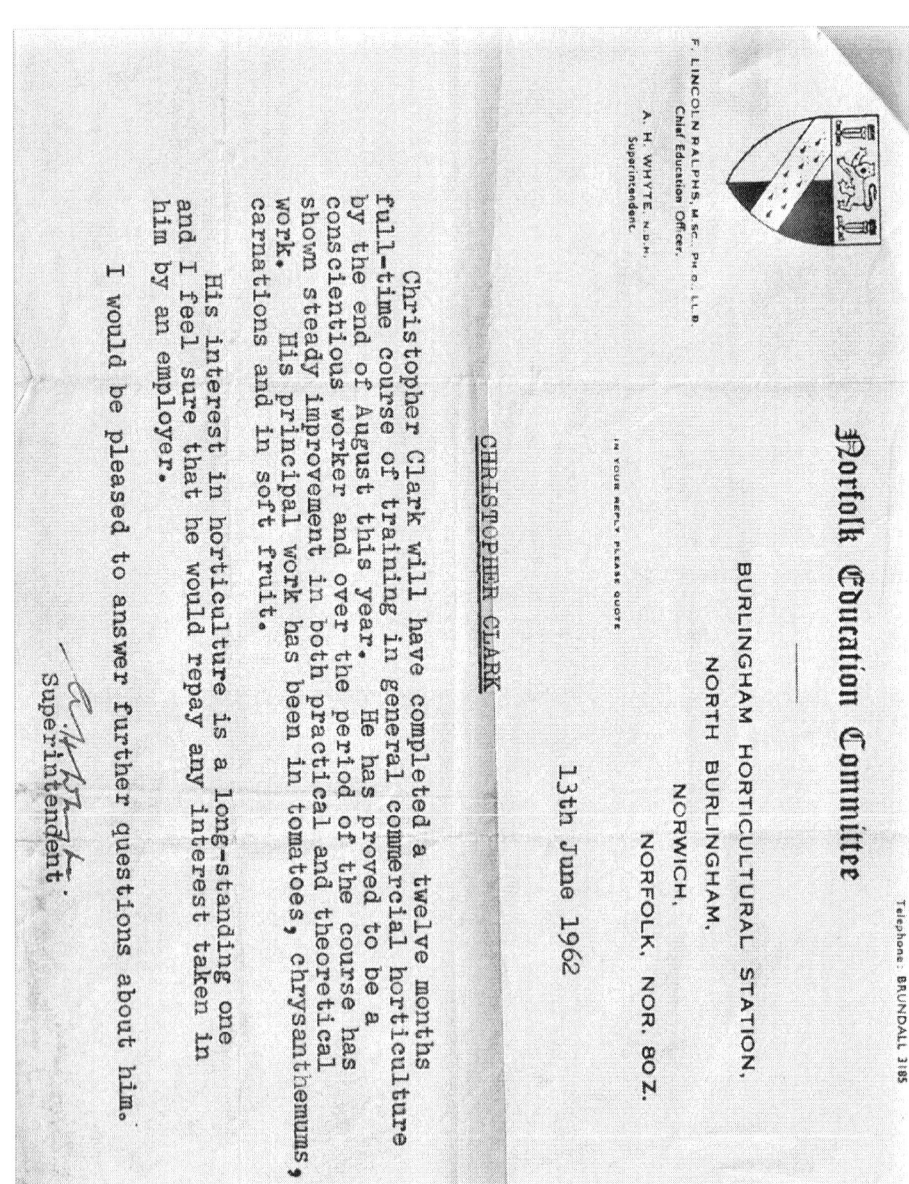

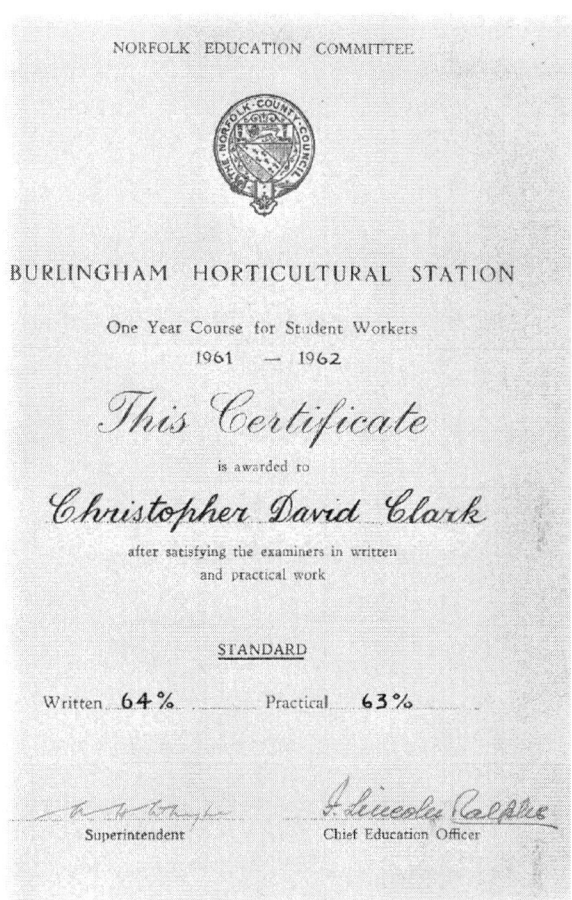

***"I was a Pig man before I became A Pig"***

From 1962 to 1964 I had two years employment on a pig and poultry farm at Home Cloisters Farm in Roydon near Kings Lynn, where I cycled five miles each way, before and after work. It was during this time that I experienced the worst winter of my life, which started abruptly during the end of December 1962 and gave the first White Christmas since 1938. There was a predominate biting easterly wind which came from Siberia. This weather continued for over three months and it was the coldest winter on record since 1740, there was still frozen snow on the ground in mid April. And during this winter the North Sea in The Wash at Hunstanton froze beyond The Pier (this has now gone) and at home the 4" outside stench pipe which carried the first floor toilet flushes froze solid and Dad on several occasions with the aid of a ladder and blowlamp tried to unblock it. We also had ice which formed on the inside of the windows and were grateful that Dad had several RAF greatcoats which we put on our beds and these supplemented our blankets.

*Digging deep: Rail workers brave the elements winter 1962/3*

Having over 500 herd of pigs and 2000 chickens to feed, water and muck out as well as frequent deliveries of animal feed was a particularly taxing task at the best of times. On one occasion rushing back from emptying my large muck barrow to my next room service the barrow stopped but I didn't and I went headlong into the barrow like Superman on speed and the fingers of my ungloved hands stuck into the jagged metal holes my muck fork had made in the barrow. I then had to extricate myself somewhat painfully with bleeding fingers from this shitty mess!

## *"By Royal Appointment"*

During 1964 I became a kitchen gardener to HM Queen Elizabeth 2$^{nd}$ at Sandringham where I grew fruit flowers vegetables and mushrooms for the royal table as well as commercially for Covent Garden in London.

An aerial view of the Royal Kitchen Gardens at Sandringham showing the range of greenhouses and *"The Bothe"* to the left and in the centre of the picture. *"Loppy"* Parsons the Head Gardener's house. Sandringham House can just be seen at the foot of the photo.

I lived in *"The Bothe"* the single men's quarters at the gardens which had an enclosed dormitory where I had a good sized oak panelled room.

Some of my single men colleagues were Peter Bradshaw, Ray Allington, Arthur Savage and Jim Forbes.

A workmate of mine, Ray Allen, told me a story when he had started working there a few years previously. At Christmas all of the estate workers lined up in the ballroom at Sandringham to receive a boxed Christmas pudding from HM The Queen. Ray was a very small chap and would easily have been mistaken for a jockey, he stood there in line very nervous and intent waiting for his turn to be introduced and listened to what the royal party said to other workers and their reply. Basically The Queen and Prince Phillip said *"Merry Christmas and a Happy New Year"* and the resulting reply was *"The same to you Maam/Sir"* When Prince Phillip spotted Ray he said *"You're a little one aren't you?"* Ray not really hearing for being nervous stammered out *"and the same to you Sir"* whereupon the royal party collapsed into laughter.

One lunchtime I borrowed Pete Bradshaw's racing cycle which had drop handlebars and raced off down to see Mum in Dersingham, by the time she had made lunch and I had eaten it I realised that I was going to be late back for work and raced off. When I got onto the rough hoggen road which leads onto the kitchen gardens I failed to negotiate a sharp right hand bend and came off in a by now time honoured fashion; what is it about me and Superman? Having slid along the road using the palms of my hands as brakes I found when I got up the skin of both hands was hanging like parchment paper and all of the capillary veins were bleeding like good ones. A quick trip to the Doctors with *"Loppy"* and bandaging before he put me on *"light duties"* for the rest of the day consisting of turning the racks of apples, eventually bound for the royal table in the purpose built store.

Two workmates, Arthur Savage and Fred Rix had both been special constables and they knew that I was looking for a challenge in life and between them suggested a career in the police. I had originally intended joining the RAF but was under qualified and didn't have 20 – 20 vision for flying.

## Chapter Two

## *"The End of an Era 1966 – 1967"*

## 1966

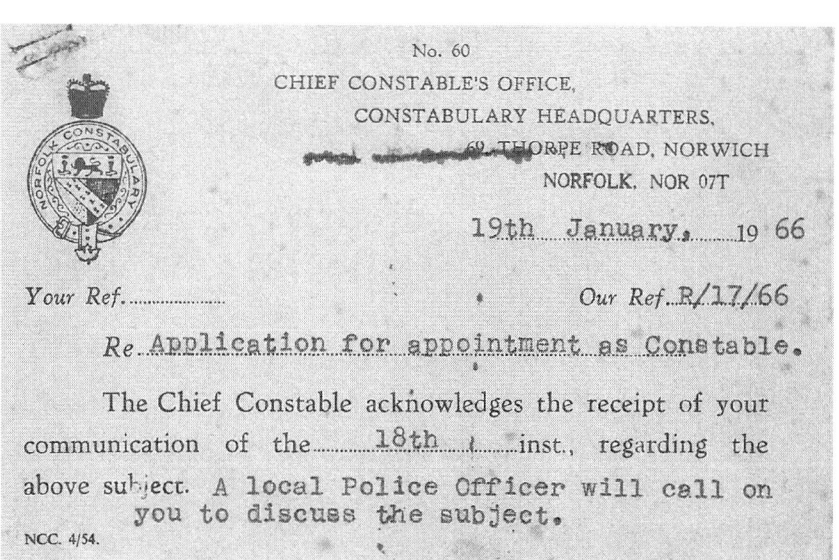

A Sergeant at Dersingham Police Station called and discussed my application to join Norfolk Constabulary. I later at the police station sat an examination consisting of an English essay, mathematics and general knowledge somehow with several different schools and teaching methods behind me I scraped through.

CHIEF CONSTABLE'S OFFICE,
COUNTY CONSTABULARY,
69, THORPE ROAD,
NORWICH, NORFOLK
NOR 07T

TELEPHONE: NORWICH 21234/5.
(2 LINES)
ALL OFFICIAL COMMUNICATIONS SHOULD
BE ADDRESSED TO
"THE CHIEF CONSTABLE OF NORFOLK."
REF. NO.

1st February, 1966.

Mr. C. D. Clark,
The Bothe,
Sandringham Gardens,
Sandringham,
Norfolk.

Dear Sir,

    With reference to your application for appointment as a Constable in this Force I should be glad if you would call at this office at 9.30 a.m. on Monday, 7th February, 1966 for an interview with the Chief Constable and for a medical examination. You will be required to remain in Norwich until approximately 4.30 p.m.

    Please acknowledge receipt of this letter and state whether or not you will be able to keep this appointment.

Yours faithfully,

Inspector
for Chief Constable.

On Monday 7th February I travelled to Norwich for an interview with The Chief Constable and a medical examination which took place at the old Police Headquarters situated at 69 Thorpe Road the medical examination was the easiest part as I had been a labourer for the previous five years and lifting anything up to 2cwt (about 100 kg) was child's play (I wonder how I would have got on with the medical now!) it was a bit embarassing though standing undressed having to touch my toes and then cough!

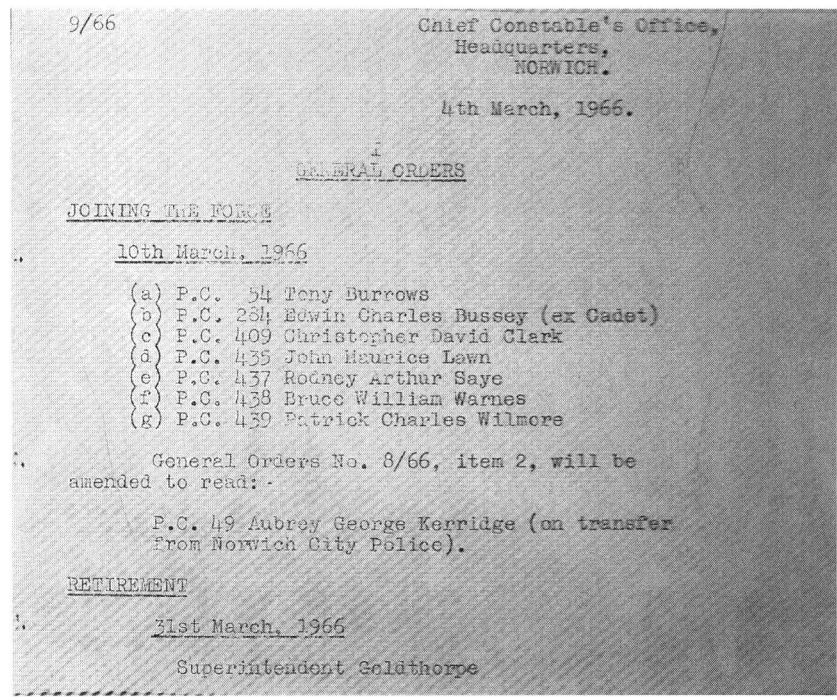

On Thursday the 10th of March 1966 came my big day I caught an early morning train from Kings Lynn to Norwich travelling together with another from Kings Lynn who was also joining that day.

We got to Headquarters a tiny cramped hole of a place I distinctly remember the worn brown cracked lino flooring and the darkness of the place it was quite oppressive and foreboding. I was kitted out with various items of uniform including a cape, some of it was second hand cast from previously serving officers who had either retired or left the force for some reason.

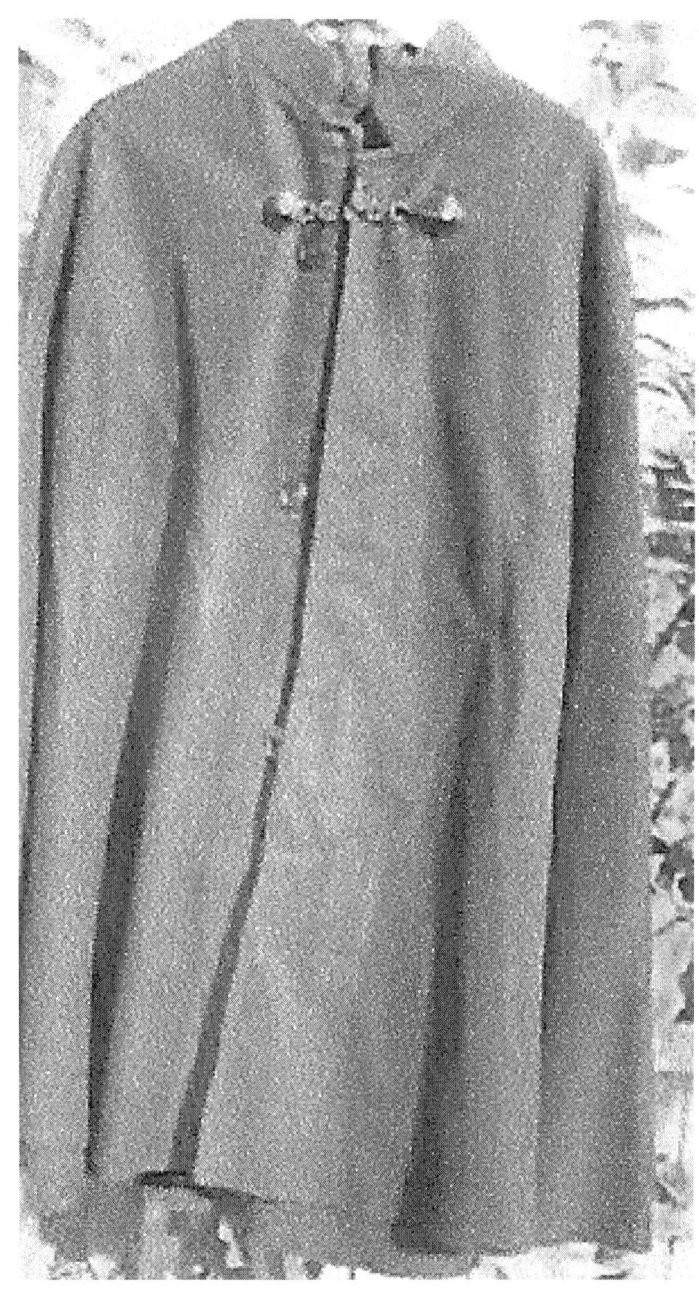

*A Police Cape*

One item I would have preferred to have had second-hand was a brown leather pocket book holder. The replacements being cheap looking black plastic ones they looked like what you would get nowadays in a children's boxed police/spy kit and they were crap! They fell to bits in no time and mine finished up being left in a drawer. The handcuffs were the type with a butterfly screw to tighten the metal cuff you only see these in museums and they needed both hands to operate them and a model prisoner to put them on. This really defeated the purpose behind them to restrain a violent struggling prisoner or potential escapees.

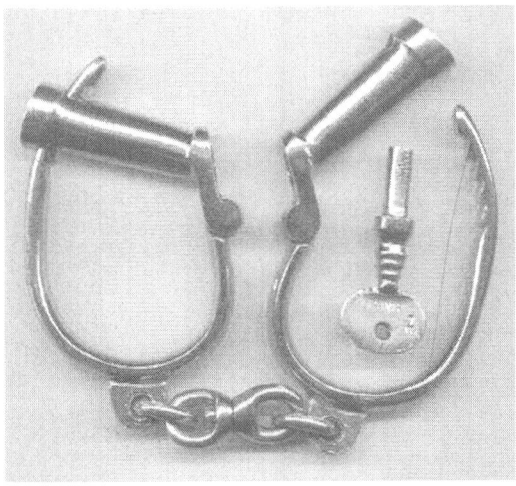

However we were proud as guardsmen with this sorry array of uniform and equipment which included whistle and truncheon the latter carried in a special sleeve sewn into the inside right leg of uniform trousers; tough shit if you were left handed!
Then quick as a flash we were transported by the force Recruiting Sergeant in the pride of the headquarters fleet of vehicles through the streets of Norwich to the Shire Hall Magistrates Court in wait for it – A Hillman Husky! Having been sworn in by Norwich Magistrates I was now Constable 409 Clark:

*"A citizen locally appointed but having authority under the Crown for the protection of life and property, the maintenance of order, the prevention and detection of crime and the prosecution of offenders against the Peace."*

We were issued with warrant cards the fold up type without a photograph of the holder. They looked like they were Kellogg's current free gift and it suddenly dawned on us that we were no longer *"civilians."*

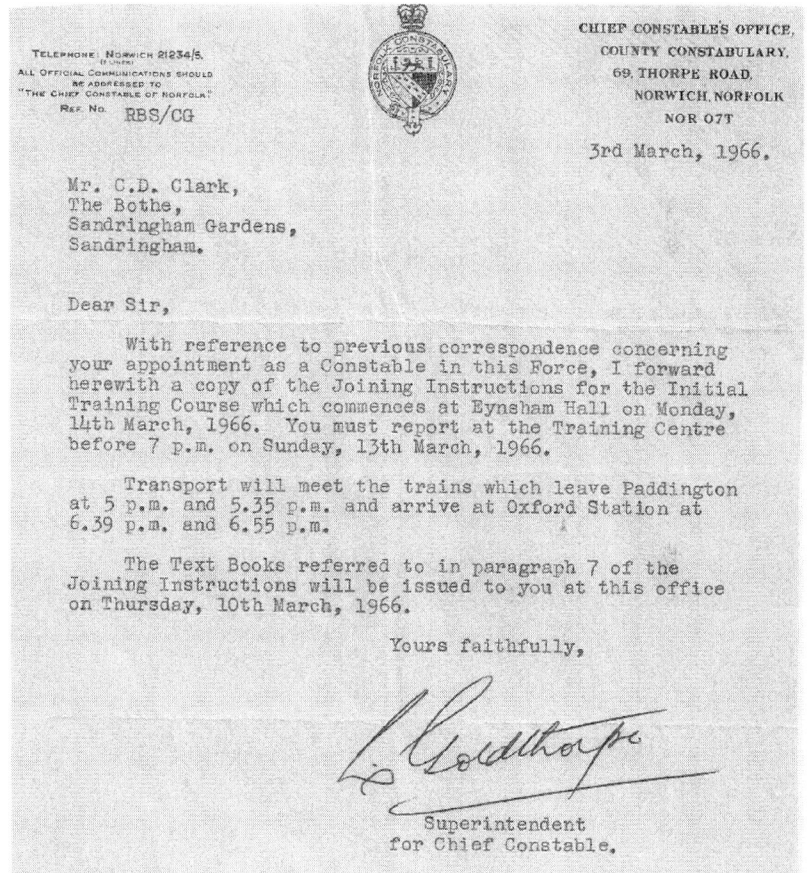

This was the only time in my service that I have been called *"Sir"* by a Superintendent – and he had to retire right after I joined that's a pity we could have got on alright together!

> NO. 5. DISTRICT POLICE TRAINING CENTRE,
> EYNSHAM HALL, NORTHLEIGH, NR. WITNEY, OXFORDSHIRE.
>
> J O I N I N G     I N S T R U C T I O N S
>
> For INITIAL COURSES.
>
> DETAILS OF COURSE   NO. 236.
>
> Date of Commencement:   14th March, 1966.
>
> Date of Completion:   11th June, 1966.
>
> Joining Date:   13th March, 1966.
>
> LOCATION OF TRAINING CENTRE:
> 1. The main entrance to the Centre is situated three miles from Witney, on the Witney to Woodstock Road (A.4095), near the village of Northleigh. It is not near the village of Eynsham, and all direction signs to the latter should be ignored.
>
> The address of the Centre is:-
> No. 5. District Police Training Centre,
> Eynsham Hall,
> Northleigh,
> Nr. Witney,
> Oxfordshire.

On Sunday 13th March I travelled with my new colleagues by car from Kings Lynn to "Zee Eynsham Hall" situated near Witney in Oxfordshire *"Siege Hiel!"* what a place it was a bit like Colditz Castle. We were on Course 236 from 14th March to 11th June the worst 13 weeks of my career.

We instantly realized what we had let ourselves in for, it was just like army barracks. Two ex army guys who had arrived in the hall from elsewhere in the country took one look and decided to leave they obviously didn't want any more bullshit. We were completely knackered from dawn to dusk and our heads were crammed full of student lesson notes.

Our PTI was a Sergeant from Norfolk who had recently been promoted to that rank. He was a right bastard and put us recruits through sheer physical hell in the gym, swimming pool, sports field and cross country running. Ugh! I have never been more fit in my life and never want to be again. In the swimming pool he used shout out "Swimmers line up at the shallow end non -swimmers at the deep end!" he would then go up to the non-swimmers and one by one push them in the deep end he would then flail the water with a long boat hook type window opener shouting out *"Swim you bastards! Swim!"*

When we had self defence he would pick on the ones who wouldn't retaliate and he would put on painful hammer lock and bar and wrist holds until they were screaming with pain one of my Norfolk colleagues could vouch for that. There were two things he told us recruits that he hated Ex Cadets and Norfolk men. One recruit on the course before mine was an ex cadet from Norfolk and he also had the PTI's old Constable Numerals and he was told that he was really in for it. I think that the lad held his own though as he was a fit athletic type and played all sports including football.

One day the PTI caught this lad standing in sports kit and scratching his arse through his shorts the PTI shouted out *"Smell it D!"* The lad didn't turn a hair lifted his hand to his face and sniffed his fingers.

With regard to the cross country running I thought *"If I have got to run five miles to catch a prisoner you've got to be joking"* I would start off running with everyone else in a bunch then let everyone run on in front until they were out of sight I would then hitch a lift and get dropped off about a quarter of a mile from Eynsham Hall gates and run in to the finish. However I always made sure that I was in the middle of the stragglers as I didn't want entering for any interforce competitions!

Years later I got my own back on on this PTI when he was a Superintendent at North Walsham and in the Norfolk force rugby team. The team turned up at Kings Lynn Nick en route to North Walsham after an out of force area match and wanted to use our showers and

Chris Clark

Me third from left middle row

facilities. The Superintendent came to the front counter and rang the bell and asked to be let in. I made out that I didn't recognise him in his muddy strip and demanded to see his warrant card and he had to go back to the team coach to collect it before I would let him and his colleagues in. When he eventually transferred to Kings Lynn in the 1980s as Deputy Divisional Commander he didn't hold it against me. I was installed into "G" Class on Course 236 along with three other Norfolk men and billeted into room 30 dormitory.

It was strange at first sleeping with eleven other men in the same room all snoring and farting, however after a while things were more enjoyable apart from *"apple pie"* beds or waking up in the morning handcuffed to a leg of the bed and realizing your mistake of allowing your arm to fall out and dangle during the night, thanks for that Roy! Course completion dances were held once a month and Roy would volunteer to be a waiter. About midnight he would barge into the dormitory wake us all up with an array of booze sandwiches and cakes that he had *"commandeered."*

Chris Clark

"The Nine Pints Of The Law
Clarence Lawson Wood 1878-1957

The Laughing Policeman

"The Nine Points Of The Law"
Chris Clark 1966

The Deputy Commandant at Eynsham was a Superintendent from Oxford City Police, he was a big man and was like a cross between Winston Churchill and a bull. He had this great bellowing voice which would have been ideal at a holiday camp with a broken tannoy system! He instilled more fear in me at age twenty than my father had done when I was seven.

One funny story I remember about him was when one of the cleaners found a used condom in one of the beds in a dormitory. He called all three courses of officers to assembly and stood on the stage and in a voice which sounded like Churchill growling *"We will fight them on the beaches"* announced to the assembled riffraff the finding. He said *"One of you here has been caught out with an object of ill repute the culprit is a masturbator and to put it in the vernacular a dirty wanker!"*

Well the whole room erupted to unabated laughter but our humour was short lived when he then said *"All weekend leave is cancelled until the man responsible is found"* We then put all of our combined detective skills to the test and identified the culprit without the help of DNA! (First used to catch an offender in 1987) we found out whose bed the thing had been found in. The offender enjoyed having black boot polish applied to his genitals and being dunked in a cold bath before making a formal admission to the Superintendent and our weekend leave re-established. His identity shall remain anonymous other than I can say he was a Norfolk Officer, the shame of it!

The food was mainly crap! Boiled eggs for breakfast twice a week for the whole course and Instructors alike amounting to some 300 eggs were piled into and cooked in a huge copper with a wire basket a bit like an enormous deep fat fryer only with boiling water instead of oil. If you were really lucky you got the eggs from the middle of the heap which were ok otherwise if they came from the top they were undercooked with runny whites and from the bottom of the pile hard boiled. The only food which stands out in my memory of the place were the Elmswell

Suffolk pork sausage rolls which I purchased in the Club of an evening with a pint of Carlsberg. Now I don't know if they were exceptional tasting rolls or if the food we had served to us was that bad anything would taste good! However this *"haut cuisine"* served to us at Eynsham prepared my stomach for a bigger shock when I later went to Kings Lynn in the following year.

Somehow I made the grade and passed out from Eynsham in June and was involved in the Annual Open Day ceremonial marching parade. This was done completely in time rhythm without a spoken word from our Drill Instructor who was from Oxford City Force and a former Army Regimental Sergeant Major.

I received my posting to the Hellesdon Section of "G" Division Norfolk Constabulary, the police station being situated on Reepham Road, Hellesdon. The Divisional Headquarters was at Thorpe very close to Headquarters and it had a Superintendent, a Chief Inspector and two Inspectors; my Section was ran by an Inspector and a Sergeant.

```
GENERAL ORDERS (CO.T'D)      - 2 -         6TH MAY, 1966

TRANSFERS (CO:T'D)

     11th June, 1966

(a) P.C. 54 Burrows to Sprowston,  )
    (84, Cannerby Lane).           )
(b) P.C. 284 Bussey to Sheringham. )
(c) P.C. 409 Clark to Hellesdon.   )   From Training
(d) P.C. 437 Saye to Caister-on-Sea.)      School
(e) P.C. 438 Warnes to King's Lynn )
    (38, Newlands Avenue).         )
(f) P.C. 439 Wilmore to Dersingham.)
```

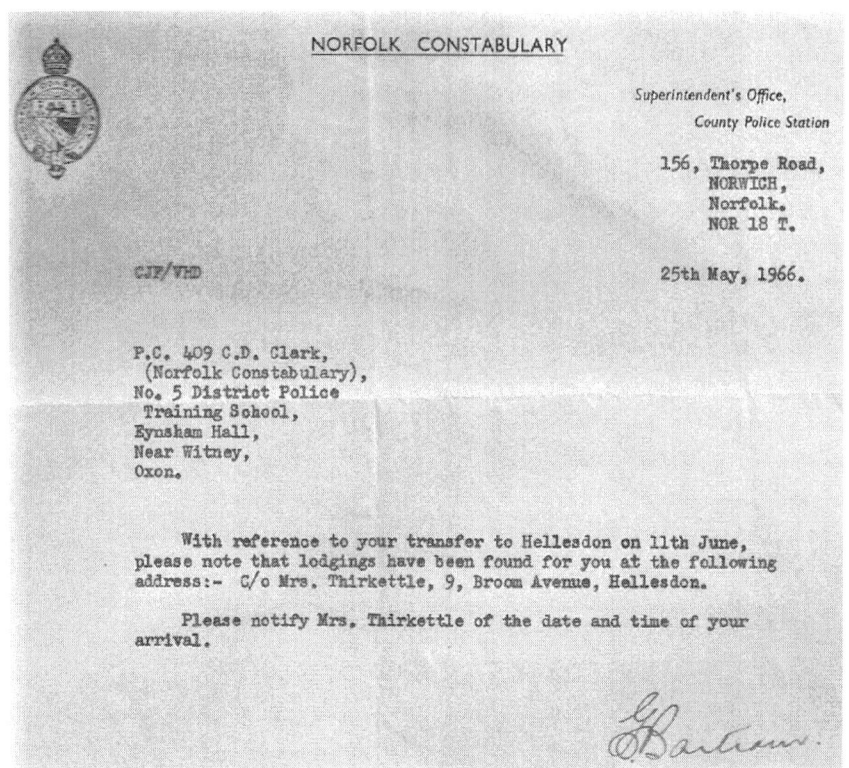

*Letter from my Divisional Superintendent George Bartrum*

Peter Garland was my first Chief Constable and had been in that rank since 1st July 1956 previously he had joined the Metropolitan Police as a Constable in 1934 at Paddington. During World War 2 he went into the RAF and was trained as a Navigator/Bomb Aimer on Bomber Command. My Dad at the same time was a Wireless Operator/Air Gunner with Coastal Command and then on Middle East Command. Mr Garland returned to "The Met" in 1945 and transferred in 1952 to Norfolk on promotion as Assistant Chief Constable and was quickly promoted to Deputy Chief Constable and finally Chief Constable. Peter Garland retired in March 1975 and died in November 2000 age 88years.

*Chief Constable Peter Garland*

1966 saw the introduction of Traffic Wardens at Norwich and Kings Lynn. When I moved to Kings Lynn the following year I found our Wardens a good asset and they were more like the Community Support Officers of today. The Force Establishment was 655 officers including all ranks.

During this year the Norfolk Force was said to be *"waging an uphill battle against a staggering crime increase."* Crimes had risen to 5,547 compared with 4,814 in 1965 with a detection rate of 39 per cent which most Chief Constables would give their right arm for these figures nowadays. In 1966 motor vehicle ownership was becoming more affordable and criminals were more mobile than before.

On my first day at Hellesdon for the first four hours I was driven around the Section by the Sergeant in – you've guessed it – a Hillman Husky! This Section included the villages of Felthorpe, Horsford, Horsham St Faiths, Hellesdon, Drayton and Taverham. On arriving back at Hellesdon *"Nick"* the Sergeant said *"Right Nobby you've got a bike off you go"* which years later the expression changed to *"On yer bike."* Those four hours was the full extent of my tutor constabling I was then alone in the World with a truncheon, handcuffs and whistle as my aides. Personal Radios were essentials that had recently been introduced to Cities like Norwich which was then a separate force and I mean separate and at Towns including Great Yarmouth and Kings Lynn. The only radio communication was from Headquarters out to radio controlled vehicles.

Lamp boot and typewriter allowances supplemented pay and CID Officers in addition received a clothing allowance. I used to work all sorts of shift combinations including split shifts e.g. 8am – 12 noon and then 8pm – 12 midnight. I used to work 8pm – 4am and 10pm – 6am night shifts and the only officer on duty in the Section. My next nearest colleague would be some 5 miles away in another Section. I had no contact with my Station Division or Headquarters. If I needed any help I had to cycle to the nearest telephone kiosk and ring in. You would not have thought that this hardened streetwise copper just six months previously was a shy wimp who was frightened of the dark and couldn't get up early to save his life.

My first run in with the *"local gentry"* was at *"The Boundary Café"* this was situated on the Norwich City ring road and as the name implies divided the County from City. This is where the latter day *"Hell's Angels and Rockers"* would hang out drinking espresso coffee the new American craze and playing records on the juke box. Their favourite pastime was to put a single 45rpm vinyl record on then hell off down Reepham Road on their machines down to The Bull PH roundabout up Middleton's Lane and back to the café via the Cromer/Holt road before the music had finished.

I made an early fatal mistake one evening by parking my cycle at the front of the café to do some property checks at The Boundary Garage and other nearby premises. When I returned to my cycle both tyres were flat and I had the embarrassment of pumping them up whilst the occupants of the café were grinning at me through the windows. I had the last laugh though, the following evening I crept up under cover of darkness and took the valves out of the tyres of their motor cycles and threw them away – the motto of this story is that anything you do to me I will go one better. After this we treated each other with mutual respect and I had no further trouble from them.

I had quite a patch to cycle around including a large industrial estate and RAF Horsham St Faith Camp which is now Norwich Airport. The street lights in Hellesdon went out at the stroke of midnight up to the city boundary, the city lights stayed on until sunrise and I might as well have been on the dark side of the moon. I adopted several survival techniques which would not be in any handbook then or particularly now, one being at the furthest point away from the city before the lights went out I used to cycle along with a glove covering the front lamp so that my impending approach would not be seen by any burglar or other persons out for a criminal intent. I still showed a red light to the rear for any traffic coming up behind. It was at these times that my thoughts went to an old Metropolitan Police Standing Order I had read which said *"If an officer is in trouble summon assistance of colleagues by giving a shrill blast on the whistle."* A fat lot of good that would have been even if the wind was in the right direction it was too far away to be heard by colleagues on duty at the other Sections of Costessey, Sprowston or Thorpe and Norwich City weren't bothered so long as you didn't die in their patch on their side of the boundary!

Talking about dying I nearly did one night with fright, my normal mode of checking the industrial estate on night duty which I had perfected the skill of was to ride up to the door of a premises whilst cycling slowly and lean over and grab hold of the door handle try it give it a push and then without stopping move on to the next premises. Only on this occasion Burton's Cash & Carry staff had been a bit casual – the door to the warehouse flew open inwards, the bike fell over to the left and wedged against the door frame and yours truly went flying headlong with a western roll onto the concrete floor fully convinced that I had been attacked. When I had recovered my senses and damaged pride and realized that I hadn't been set about I laughed out loud with relief.

What a Cop Out! I came across this short article featured in a national newspaper during January 2009. *"A Police force spurned four new pushbikes – declaring officers were not trained to ride them. The £500 cycles were offered to Community Support Officers by York Council. Police Chief's vetoed the idea, saying it was "dangerous to assume that they would not fall off and it's easy to decry health and safety regulations."*

The communications system which operated at that time at Hellesdon and other Section stations was that non emergency calls from the public were received directly by telephone to the individual station, or via Divisional or Force Headquarters or by personal visit to that station. Each of these messages were entered in the Station Occurrence Book and if a particular job required urgent and immediate response the station telephoned Headquarters on a hot line in order for the nearest radio controlled vehicle to respond. For non-urgent or appointment calls the job was passed to the on duty local patrolling officer by way of a telephone call to a pre determined location hourly point at a designated telephone kiosk, where the officer waited for ten minutes before moving on; or to the resident beat officer to his home. It was a disciplinary offence not to make a point without good reason.

Also on occasions a supervisor wishing to make contact with the patrolling officer would make a point at the location he would be at. I remember being at various points whilst on night duty normally at midnight, when the kiosk phone would ring; it would be my Sergeant Bob Cross checking on me from his bedside. He would say *"Everything alright Nobby?"* I would say *"Yes Sergeant"* he would then say *"Well you know where I am If you need me."* That would be the only contact I had for the rest of the night. To this day I wonder what would have happened if I had been in need of urgent assistance. First of all I had to get to a telephone kiosk, in those days there were very few people going about lawfully after pub closing time.

*Hellesdon Police Station 2010*

There were two police houses attached one either side of Hellesdon *"Nick"* at that time the Sergeant and his family occupied the one on the right and a Constable and his family the one on the left. During out of normal hours there was a roster and one of them would have the station outside public phone switched through to them. Whilst out on patrol if you wanted a Criminal Record Office name or stolen vehicle check with New Scotland Yard National Indices then you again had to get a kiosk and phone them whilst your intended quarry was disappearing into the night. It normally took on average five minutes to get through to CRO and probably another ten minutes holding on the line for the result as in those days there was no computerised system; it was all held on card index A-Z surnames and 1-999 for vehicle registration. With stolen vehicles it could take up to a week for new stolen vehicle reports to get onto card index and Central Vehicle Index. So if you received a negative result back from CVI you couldn't actually be sure that the vehicle that you were interested in wasn't stolen.

I know of at least one stolen vehicle checked by a patrol in the Downham Market area which when later found abandoned in another force area had the officer's HORT1 request left in the vehicle; this asking the driver to produce documents at a specified police station within five days, naturally this driver didn't honour this request.

For Vehicle Owner and Taxation enquiries you sent off a brown card to the Local Taxation Office in the area where the vehicle registration plate was issued, this could take up to two days for Norfolk County Council LTO and up to a fortnight for others. When Force HQ moved to Martineau Lane Norwich in 1968, there was a facility for HQ Information Room staff to do an out of hours manual check in LTO which was across the car park from them. The request had to be fairly urgent though. The NCC LTO when Swansea opened became an annexe of Headquarters and was the Force Recruiting Training/Driving School/Force Firearms Departments.

GENERAL ORDERS (CONT'D)    - 4 -    6TH MAY, 1966

CENTRAL VEHICLE INDEX - CRIMINAL RECORD OFFICE

A Central Vehicle Index has been established in Information Room at New Scotland Yard. This Index is intended to provide one accurate and up-to-date source of information available to all Forces.

Details will be included of vehicles which have been reported to Police as:

(i) Lost or stolen
(ii) Seen in suspicious circumstances
(iii) Removed by police
(iv) Seized by finance companies

Particulars of lost or stolen vehicles will be retained up to twelve months.

The C.R.O. index of lost or stolen vehicles, based on registration marks, will now cease to operate but a record of engine and chassis numbers known as "Vehicle Records" will be retained there for up to ten years. Form 150 will continue to be submitted to C.R.O. who will be responsible for the publication of supplement F.

Enquiries on engine and chassis numbers will be made to C.R.O. (Whitehall 1212, extension 37). Between 6 p.m. and 8 a.m., Whitehall 7800.

All other checks on motor vehicles will be made with the Central Vehicle Index in the following manner.

1. URGENT CASES

(a) By public telephone to Whitehall 9501.
(b) Through the private wire system or Whitehall 1212, extension 1052, or by asking for "Central Vehicle Index".

2. NON-URGENT CASES

(c) By teleprinter to Telegraph Office at New Scotland Yard. Messages will be headed "CARCHECK" followed by the name of force and station concerned. The text should include the vehicle registration mark(s) and brief reason for the check, e.g. apparently abandoned, process etc., and the number or name of the officer on the enquiry.

Great care is to be taken to ensure that recoveries of vehicles are reported to Information Room at New Scotland Yard forthwith, giving the registration mark and date reported lost only.

In case of difficulty, enquiries regarding the Central Vehicle Index should be made to the Inspector in charge of Information Room, Whitehall 1212, extension 1039.

(Vide Police Gazette 30.4.65, c.55)

> GENERAL ORDERS (CONT'D)    - 5 -    6TH MAY, 1966
>
> CENTRAL VEHICLE INDEX - CRIMINAL RECORD OFFICE (CONT'D)
>
> NAME AND OTHER SEARCHES
>
> Direct lines have been installed at the Criminal Record Office to improve the service. The exchange number is WHItehall 7800.
>
> In the interests of efficiency searches by telephone should only be made in URGENT cases. Non-urgent searches should be made in writing and where appropriate listed in alphabetical order.
>
> NAME SEARCHES
>
> These can be made at ANY TIME on WHItehall 7800.
>
> SEARCHES IN OTHER INDICES
>
> Between 8 a.m. and 6 p.m. Mondays to Fridays and between 8.30 a.m. and 1 p.m. Saturdays, requests for searches in the following indices will be made through WHItehall 1212 on the extensions shown:-
>
> | | |
> |---|---|
> | Stolen Car Index | 37 |
> | Cheque Index | 500 |
> | Property Index | 711 |
> | Method Index | 626 |
> | Property Index | 712 |
> | Cycle Index | 708 |
> | Vehicle Records | 37 |
> | Officer in Charge Property Index | 1000 |
>
> At other times (including Christmas Day, Good Friday and Bank Holidays) all search requests will be made on WHItehall 7800.
>
> (Vide Police Gazette 15.1.65 and 22.2.66 -

Training was done at Divisional Headquarters in Thorpe by Inspector's Gerry *"Redchester"* Dunn and Bill *"Fink"* Nelson and this was combined with their normal duties. Gerry's nickname came from the fact that he was always meticulous at paperwork and when asked what to do with an enquiry his reply would be *"put it in the register"* but as he was a County

Durham man to us Norfolk boys it sounded like *"Redchester"* Bill's nickname came from the fact that he was a Cockney and he was always saying *"I think"* but came out as *"I Fink."*

A later funny story on Bill was when he was promoted and posted to Force Control Room Chief Inspector was that someone had doctored his locker and he demanded to know why he had to share a locker with Inspector Fink! That reminds me of another occasion when he was in the Force Control Room, in those days the Force Radio was on permanent *"talk through"* so that you could hear both headquarters transmissions and subsequent replies from the patrol crews. On this occasion there was a report of a road traffic accident on the Acle straight en route to Great Yarmouth and In those days of pre-computerisation Headquarters Control Room or Information Room as it was known had a set of Red and Green lights for each radio controlled vehicle in the County; two Green lights meant Available or 10/1, one Red and Green light for Loosely Engaged or 10/4, and two Red lights meant fully Engaged or 10/5.

Anyway *"Fink"* looked at the availability board and saw that the nearest vehicle on two Green lights was Alpha Two and he got on the Force Radio and called *"Alpha Two Alpha Two from VK over"* Alpha Two crew replied *"Go ahead VK over"* Fink said *"Alpha Two attend a RTA on the Acle Straight at Berney Inns over"* Alpha Two replied *"No can do VK"* Fink replied *"This is Chief Inspector Nelson here you will attend this RTA."* Alpha Two came back with *"Hello Sir we are The Broads Motor Launch!"* There was then a deathly hush over the radio. Poor old Bill he was always making *"cock-ups"* in the Information Room and he would have been better as a Divisional Chief Inspector.

Force HQ Information Room had a telex facility connected to each DHQ all transmissions received by DHQ were then passed verbally by telephone to each Section Station. This often laborious time consuming long winded and seemingly irrelevant messages had to be written long hand into the station occurrence book. You could sometimes be on the

45

phone and writing them in for a good half an hour, these then had to be relayed by telephone to each of the beat houses!; we went through a lot of bound foolscap books in a year. A Norfolk saying *"Keep Yew a Troshin' Bor"* springs to mind; it means when something is long winded and labourish and to keep on going or keep at it.

Split shifts as I explained earlier, were common for resident beat officers who were invariably on call for 24 hours a day, on Rest Days they had to phone in and request permission to leave the beat to go shopping in Norwich etc and an entry was made in the occurrence book to that effect; the only time that they were really free was when they were on Annual Leave. If there was a non urgent response job to be covered in their absence then the on duty officer in the Section covered it.

I remember one instance when there was a non-injury RTA received by myself by telephone at Hellesdon on a Sunday late turn, by the time I had ridden the several miles to the village and scene in question, the accident had long since solved itself and the parties involved gone on their way, all I found was a pile of debris, I then cranked the several miles back to Hellesdon thinking that there must be a better system than this.

Life in Hellesdon was fairly uneventful though even stray dogs coming in from the public via the front doors went out of the back door just as quick and the occurrence book being endorsed "escaped from custody". This was before the advent of Council Dog Wardens and the only way of getting them to the stray dogs pound was by police vehicle and the only one was the Sergeant's and he didn't want a soiled car to have to clean; so he frowned on the retention of them.

Life in *"The Met"* was far different on 3 July there was an Anti Vietnam rally in Grosvenor Square near the US Embassy involving 4000 protesters. 200 police officers cordoned the area off and in the melee a police motor cyclist was knocked off his machine and as petrol leaked from it one of the protesters threw a lighted match into it.

On Saturday 30 July big things were happening at the old Wembley Stadium it was the final of The 1966 World Cup 93,000 spectators – including the Queen and Prince Philip filled the stadium and a further 400 million around the world including myself watched it on TV. England along with my hero Bobby Charlton beat West Germany 4 goals to 2 and the whole nation was on top of the World.

## "The Shepherd's Bush Police Murders"
## AKA "The Braybrook Street Massacre"

PC Geoffrey Fox 41       Sgt Christopher Head 30   PC David Wombwell 25

However just two weeks later on Saturday 12th August 1966 the Nation was united again when it mourned the loss of three unarmed police officers. Detective Sgt Christopher Head, Detective Constable David Wombell and Constable Geoffrey Fox (the driver) all attached to Shepherd's Bush Police Station were gunned down in cold blood by Harry Roberts and John Duddy. Some 48 years later as I am reviewing this part of the book Harry Roberts has been released!

A character of those times was the Constable of Old Catton an adjacent

Norwich Beat, he was spotted one day by officers of a patrol car pedalling furiously towards them in the opposite direction with cape flying and they slowed down thinking he needed assistance and as they drew level he shouted out *"Don't go down there boys there's been one hell of an accident"* and continued on his way. His Son some years later later moved into rented accommodation with me when he joined and was posted to my Relief at King'S Lynn.

### "Stiffs and Stench"

A few sudden deaths that I was involved in at Hellesdon shows just how quickly one had to grow up fast in those mainly long forgotten times of nearly 50 years ago.

The first sudden death that I dealt with was of an elderly woman, she lived in a small cottage and had not been seen for a couple of days and she hadn't collected her milk from the front doorstep. I attended and had to make a forced entry and upon climbing some narrow winding stairs found her looking very peaceful dead in her bed but with rigor mortis very apparent.

After dealing with all of the formalities including contacting her local Doctor to certify death I contacted Mr Brown the experienced civilian employed by Norwich Division for collecting bodies and transporting them to the mortuary. When we went to move the lady still covered in her bedding for modesty, Mr Brown got hold of her shoulders and started to lift her and I got hold of her left foot and started frantically searching for her right one under the quilt. Upon not finding anything I had to lift up the covers and then it dawned upon me, the lady had an artificial right leg which was undone and lying beside her! We then had a heck of a job to get her down those narrow winding stairs with me holding onto her left leg and right hip.

On another occasion a man had died peacefully in his armchair in front of an electric fire and wasn't discovered for some six weeks. By this time the heat of the fire had accelerated the rotting process and the first thing that we officers were met with was the huge number of "Bluebottle" flies in the windows of the address. When we broke in the stench was overpowering and when we tried to lift the man into the body box his guts split open and everyone had to get outside and throw-up. Even the note money we took from the house for safe keeping stank Hellesdon Nick out!

If you think that is bad enough try thinking about us dealing with someone who has drowned and not been discovered for some time, the body and head bloat to an enormous size looking like the alien creature Commander Strax the Sontaran in Doctor Who and trying to fish the body out of the water when it resembles boiled ham that has been soaked in cider overnight and falling to pieces, coupled with the smell, is not an enviable task.

### *1967*

A PC was posted to Hellesdon who was later stationed at Kings Lynn and eventually promoted up the ladder. His first full tour at Hellesdon was on a night shift on his own so when I finished my late turn at midnight I stayed on and doubled up with him cycling round "our patch" and unofficially *"tutored"* him. It's strange how life pans out as years later he was to be my shift Inspector and Sub Divisional Chief Inspector at Kings Lynn and supervising me. This happened a lot during my service, training *"still wet behind the ears"* coppers who went on to be high ranking officers. Most however never forgot their beginnings and reminded me when I met them as senior officers how I had helped *"kick them into shape."*

As of the 1st of March I had a pay increase at age twenty one from £835 to £870 per annum (this would rise to £940 at the completion of my probation period on 10th March 1968)

### *"Murder At Outwell"*

On Friday the 10th of March I celebrated having achieved my first year in Norfolk Constabulary, blissfully unaware that across the other side to the West of the County, a murder most foul was taking place in The Fens close to Wisbech and the Isle of Ely. At 10.30pm that night a crime which has been described as one which reached the most hideous proportions was committed at The Woodlands in Outwell, a remote farmhouse.

Three men wearing nylon stocking masks over their faces and wearing balaclava helmets and carrying a shotgun forced their way into a detached farmhouse. They attacked and bound the 59 year old wife of the occupier and stole a safe (which contained 4 shillings) from the house. The 62 year old occupier Mr Auger was later found bound, gagged and battered to death outside the house, excessive violence had been used.

Following a long and intensive investigation by Detective Superintendent Wally Virgo of Scotland Yard and Detective Superintendent Reginald "Reggie" Lester of Norfolk together with a team of detective and uniform officers from Norfolk three Wisbech men were arrested and all appeared at Hertford Assizes on the 27th of June 1967 indicted with Murder, Manslaughter and Burglary. Somehow they were found Not Guilty of Murder but Guilty of Manslaughter. They beat the poor man's head until it was smashed like an eggshell, whilst he lay bound and helpless, one got 15 years and the other two both got 12 years apiece; they should have been hanged for this dreadful pre meditated crime.

I wonder how events might have turned out if Mr Auger had vision of foresight to arm himself with a shotgun on that fateful night and had actually shot these men in self defence who *"he was in fear of his life from"* and turning to the events 32 years later in the days of political correctness, or is that political crap? when a certain near neighbour Farmer called Tony Martin in that isolated district of Fenland Norfolk had not had a shotgun to protect himself; during another fateful night on August the 20th 1999 when confronted with night intruders who had travelled many miles from Nottinghamshire to his home for who knows what, they said to burgle, and put him in fear of his life!

Later Commander Wally Virgo was himself imprisoned to 12 years imprisonment during May 1977 together with five other members of The Met Obscene Publications Squad, including Detective Chief Superintendent Alfred Moody, for having accepted £100,000 a year (now over £640,000) from porn dealers.

On the 28th March until the 7th April I went on a Constables Intermediate Course at Dishforth in North Yorkshire and travelled there with two other officers by car. One name stands out from those who were on that course he was an ex cadet and the boss's *"blue eyed boy"* some years later in 1974 he was convicted of the rape of a *"Tiller Girl"* Dancer of Sunday Night at The Palladium fame whilst she was on a boating holiday close to The Broads where he was the local beat bobby; he had gone on board masked up, gloved and armed with a starting pistol, however at one stage he had taken the gloves off and left his fingerprints on the headboard of the bed. All recruits have their fingerprints taken and that is how he was caught. There had also been a spate of *"peeping tom"* and *"flasher"* crimes committed in the area, by a man wearing a Blue shirt and Black trousers. For the Rape crime he received seven years imprisonment.

Superintendent's Office,
156, Thorpe Road,
NORWICH.

3rd March, 1967.

AE/VHD

P.C. 54 Burrows;
P.C. 117 Mayes;
P.C. 109 Clark. (5/3/67)

### Intermediate Continuation Course No. 37

Arrangements have been made for your attendance at Intermediate Continuation Course No. 37, at No. 2 District Police Training Centre, Detached Wing, Dishforth, Thirsk, Yorks. from Tuesday 28th March, 1967.

Officers travelling by road should report to the Duty Officer at the Training Centre, Dishforth, before 1p.m. on 28th March.

A train leaves Norwich at 6.37a.m., changing at Ely, Peterborough and York, arriving at Thirsk at 12.55p.m. A 'bus will leave Thirsk Railway Station at 1.10p.m. and convey the officers to Dishforth. If you intend travelling by rail, you should telephone the Training Department at Headquarters <u>not later</u> than Tuesday 7th March.

Joining instructions attached hereto.    Please acknowledge receipt.

Also attending the Course:-

P.C. 47 Brooks, P.C. 179 Rout (Attleborough Division);

P.C. 5 Bell, P.C. 65 Daynes (Dereham Division);

P.C. 264 Bussey, P.C. 327 Buttolph (North Walsham Division);

P.C. 270 Ward, P.C. 438 Warnes, P.C. 236 Wilmore (King's Lynn Division).

Chief Inspector
for Superintendent.

Copy to:- Insp. Woolf;
Insp. Buck;
P.S. Nash;
P.S. Denny;
P.S. Cross.

*"A Townie"*

On the 9th April at my own request and for personal reasons, My Mother was ill with anxiety and depression and I needed to be nearer to her, I had an Interview at Headquarters with the Assistant Chief Constable Mr Gordon Taylor; following this I was transferred to Kings Lynn and occupied room 65 in the Single men's Quarters.

NORFOLK CONSTABULARY

Inspector's
Superintendent's Office,
County Police Station

3rd April 1967

P.C. 409 Clarke,
Norwich Division Headquarters,
Thorpe Road,
NORWICH.

Transfer to King's Lynn

Reference your transfer to this Division on 9th April 1967, you will reside in the Singlemen's Quarters and occupy room No. 65.

You have been posted to 'A' Relief and your Patrol Sergeant will be Sergeant Lake.

Report to Chief Inspector Richards at 12 noon on Sunday, 9th April 1967, for instructions. If you require lunch at this Station on that day, please telephone me at this office before 1.00 p.m., on Friday, 7th April 1967, and I will make arrangements with Mrs. Pink, the resident housekeeper.

Your Weekly Rest Days are Monday, 10th and Tuesday, 11th April 1967. Your first tour of duty in uniform will be 2.00 p.m. to 10.00 p.m., on Wednesday, 12th April 1967; parade at 1.50 p.m.

H. E. Nobbs,
Inspector

The present Kings Lynn Police Station took three years to build at a cost of £75.000 and was fully taken into use during June 1954 after the staff moved from its former premises situated within The Town Hall when it had previously been a Borough Force Station.

Divisional Police Headquarters, St. James Street, King's Lynn

My room consisted of a single bed, wardrobe and chest of drawers, I also had a wash hand basin with hot& cold taps there were 8 bedrooms in the quarters when I transferred. This would be increased to 15 when the police station was later extended to the rear.

There was a toilet/shower/bathroom complex, a large lounge, a massive dining room able to seat 30 people comfortably and a washing/ironing room. Seven of us billeted there were probationers attached to the various shifts; Now one was not a lad, he was a bachelor from Great Yarmouth and coming up to retirement, he was a 6'4" anti social cantankerous set in his ways man and didn't fit in with us young men and he let us know it. Most of the time when he was off duty and not down the pub, hogging the TV or newspapers in the lounge or occupying the snooker room playing billiards on his own, he spent locked in his room. On one of the few occasions when I attempted to speak to him was when he was washing his long johns in the large stone sink in the wash room. I said *"Hi Bob are you doing your washing then?"* He replied gruffly *"No I'm cleaning bloody cockles!"*

I had room 65 and a lad who I will refer to as Buzz Lightyear had room 67 opposite mine at the end of the corridor next to the wash/ironing room. Off duty he was always on the go with one girlfriend or other at River Bar or other establishment and burning the candle at both ends. One particular morning I was up for early turn and coming out of my room, when I saw this vision of Buzz through his open door lying on his bed in full uniform like a corpse. He was holding a double repeater brass alarm clock with both hands clutched to his chest which had obviously activated and run down several hours before. I shook him awake and he said *"Shit! I came in for meal break at One am and set the alarm for a quarter to two so I could have a kip."* With that he ran downstairs booked his radio and Panda Car in and went back to bed. When he was on early turn he was normally holed up in some field gateway, how he never got caught I don't know.

Chris Clark

When I was posted to King's Lynn there were three main "Foot Beats" to patrol

One Beat or the Town Beat had to be patrolled 24/7 as it consisted of all of the high value commercial retail shops and banks of the town.

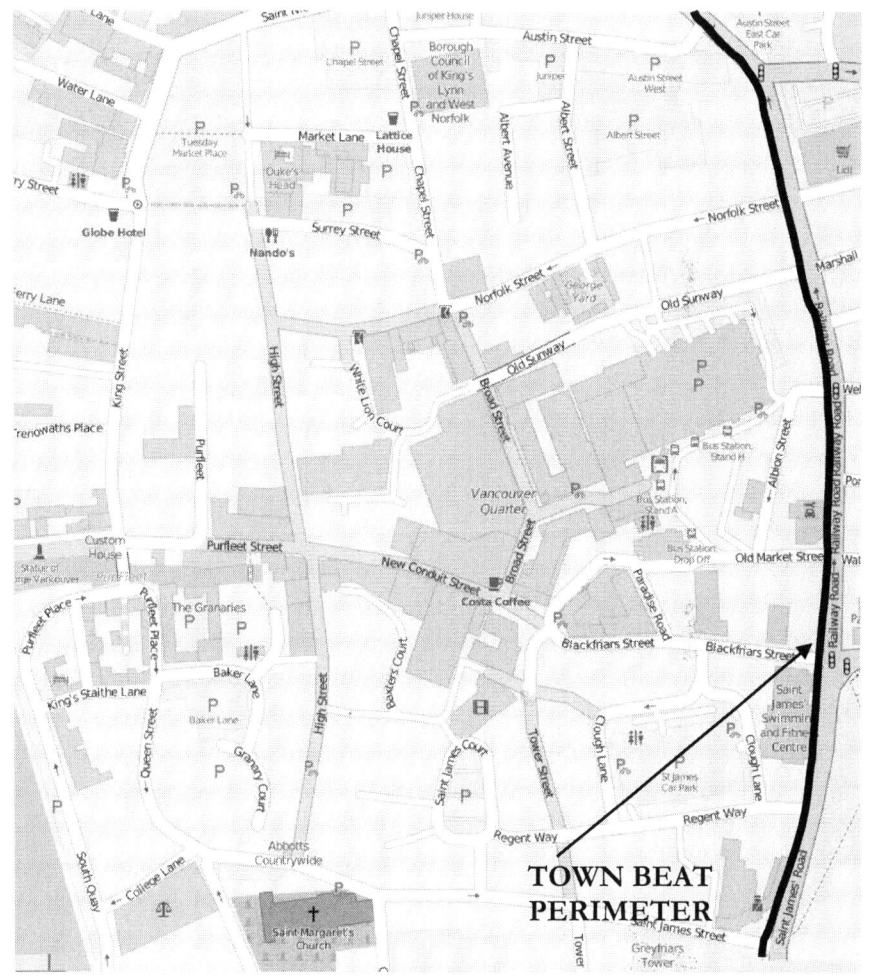

*One Beat*

Chris Clark

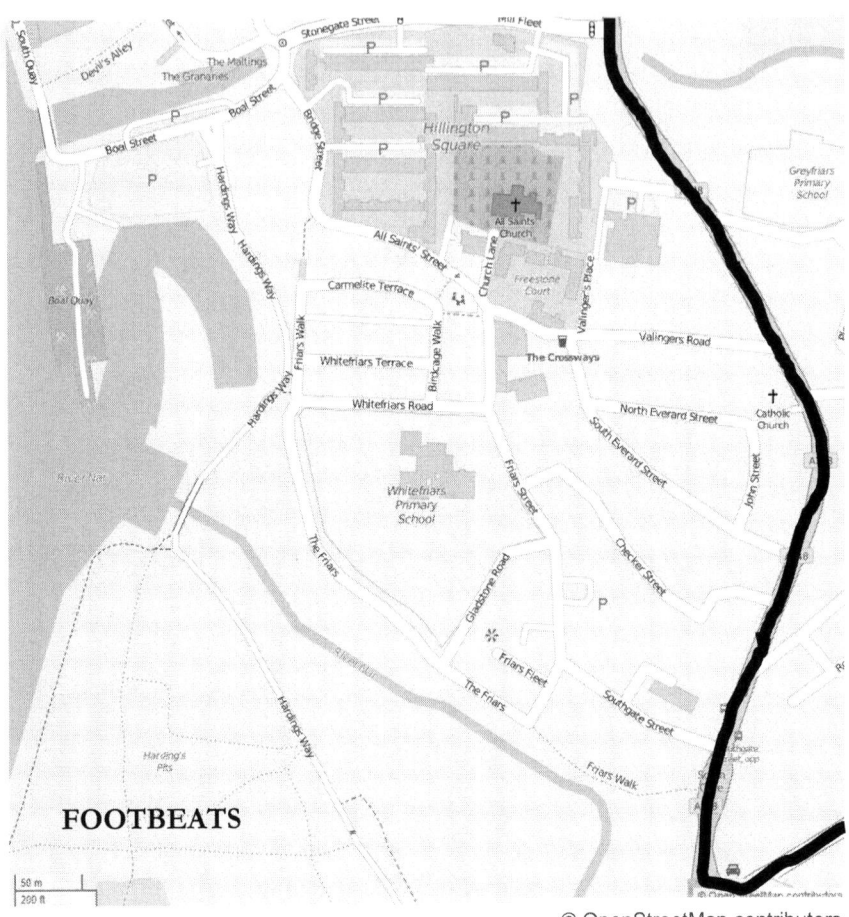

*Two Beat*

The Laughing Policeman

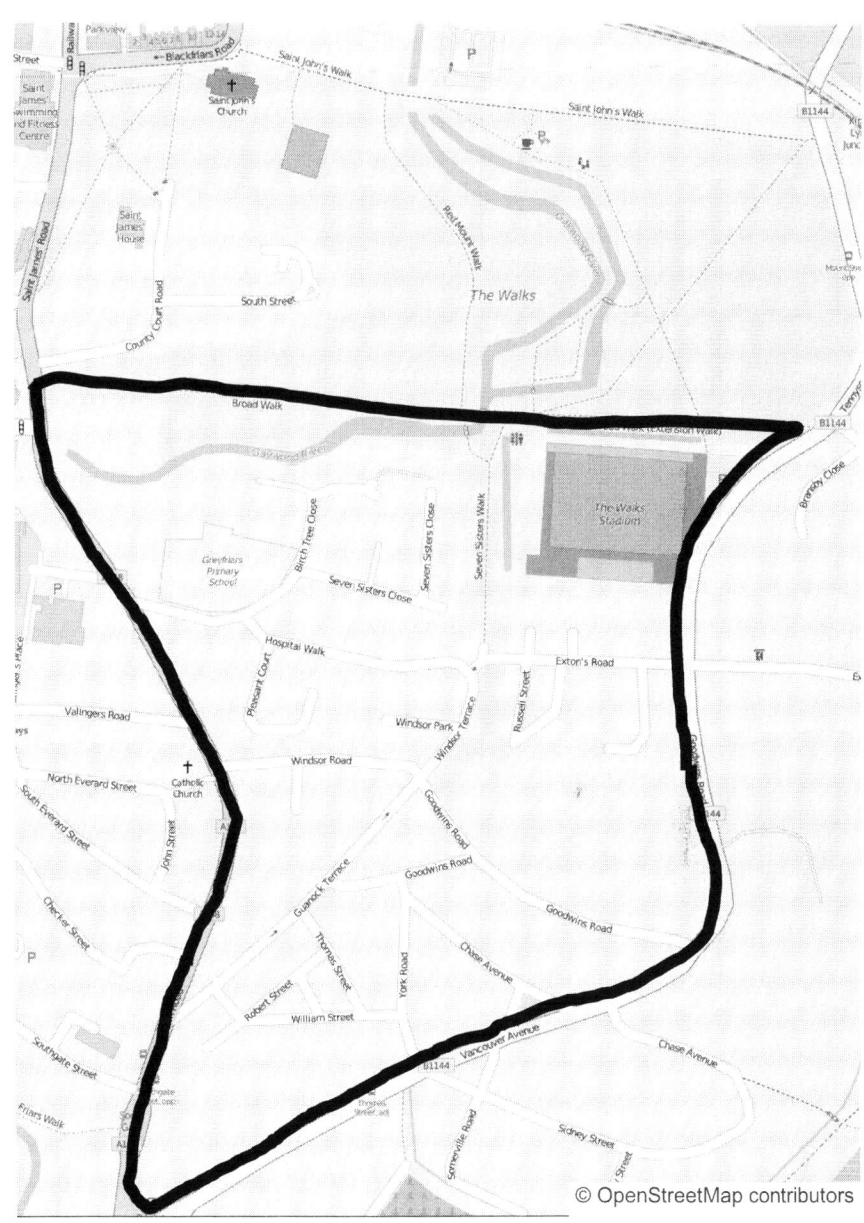

*Three Beat*

*The old Borough Police Station
Saturday Market Place, King's Lynn*

Fred Calvert was Chief Constable of the Borough of Kings Lynn Police from 1945 until the 1st April 1947 when it was amalgamated with Norfolk Constabulary and became a new Division of it and Fred reverted to the rank of Superintendent in charge of it. He was formerly an Inspector at Bradford and was one of sixty five applicants for the

Kings Lynn Chief Constable post and he was appointed on the19th of September 1945, he was 34 years old and one of the youngest Chief Constables in the country. He was famous for being a hero during the awful East Coast Flood of Saturday the 31st of January 1953 (that night my youngest Sister was born in Stanhoe Norfolk and I remember it well) Fred also was the author of "Calvert's Powers of Arrest and Charges" of which there were a number of updated volumes, this was a small pocket size book which was used all over England and Wales as a "policeman's bible".

Fred Calvert takes a look at the sixth edition of his work Powers of Arrest and Charges which established itself as the policeman's Bible.

At Hellesdon I had to type out my own reports for courts, etc, on the station "steam" typewriter; when I transferred to Lynn I was able to put my reports verbally onto dictating machines, these were then typed out by a civilian typist on a modern typewriter and returned for checking and signing, this made life a lot easier.

On Monday 24th April, I had an away day, I commenced duty at 6am and later caught the 1.36pm train from Kings Lynn to Liverpool Street with a mature policewoman Joan the Drone and a female prisoner remanded in custody by Kings Lynn Magistrates Court to Holloway Prison. Joan and I caught the 6.35pm train back and completed duty at 9pm. In those days there was no normal duty paid overtime just time to be taken off in lieu when it suited the shift Sergeant.

As part of my development training I was CID Aide from 26th June to 27th July. At this time there was a separate Policewomen's Department, they dealt with primarily Women and Children cases.

At this time there were no Collator's Intelligence Systems DC Ray Wright kept an A to Z nominal index and numerical 1 to 999 index in a converted Occurrence Book; when I arrived I became Ray's official scribe and kept this book updated with current active criminal names their vehicles.

The outer areas of the town which included Gaywood, North Lynn, Grange Estate, Fairstead Estate, (Overspill from London) South Lynn and Hardwick Industrial Estate were covered by Four and Five Cycle Beat – consisting of one or two officers, depending on shift manpower or shortage of breath!

The Laughing Policeman

Gaywood and Fairstead Estates

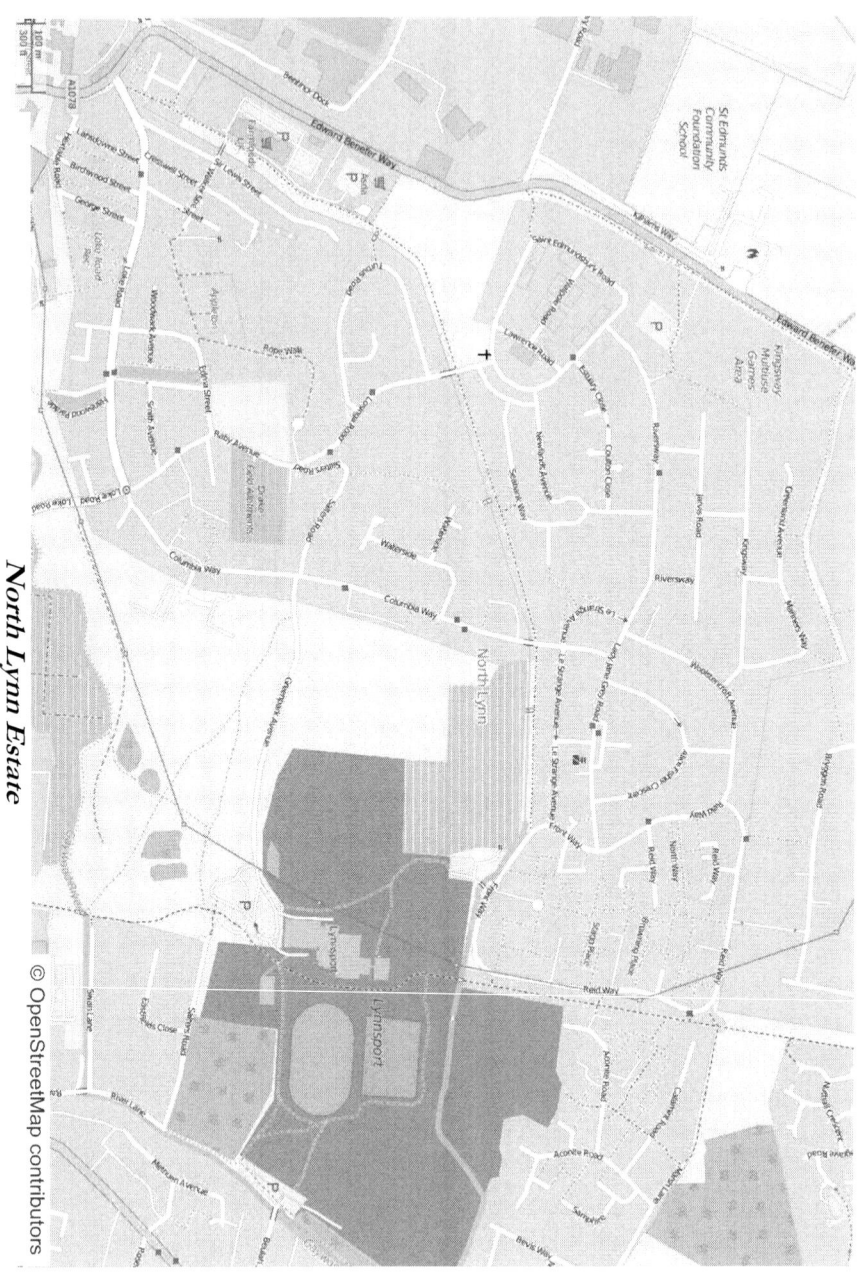

# The Laughing Policeman

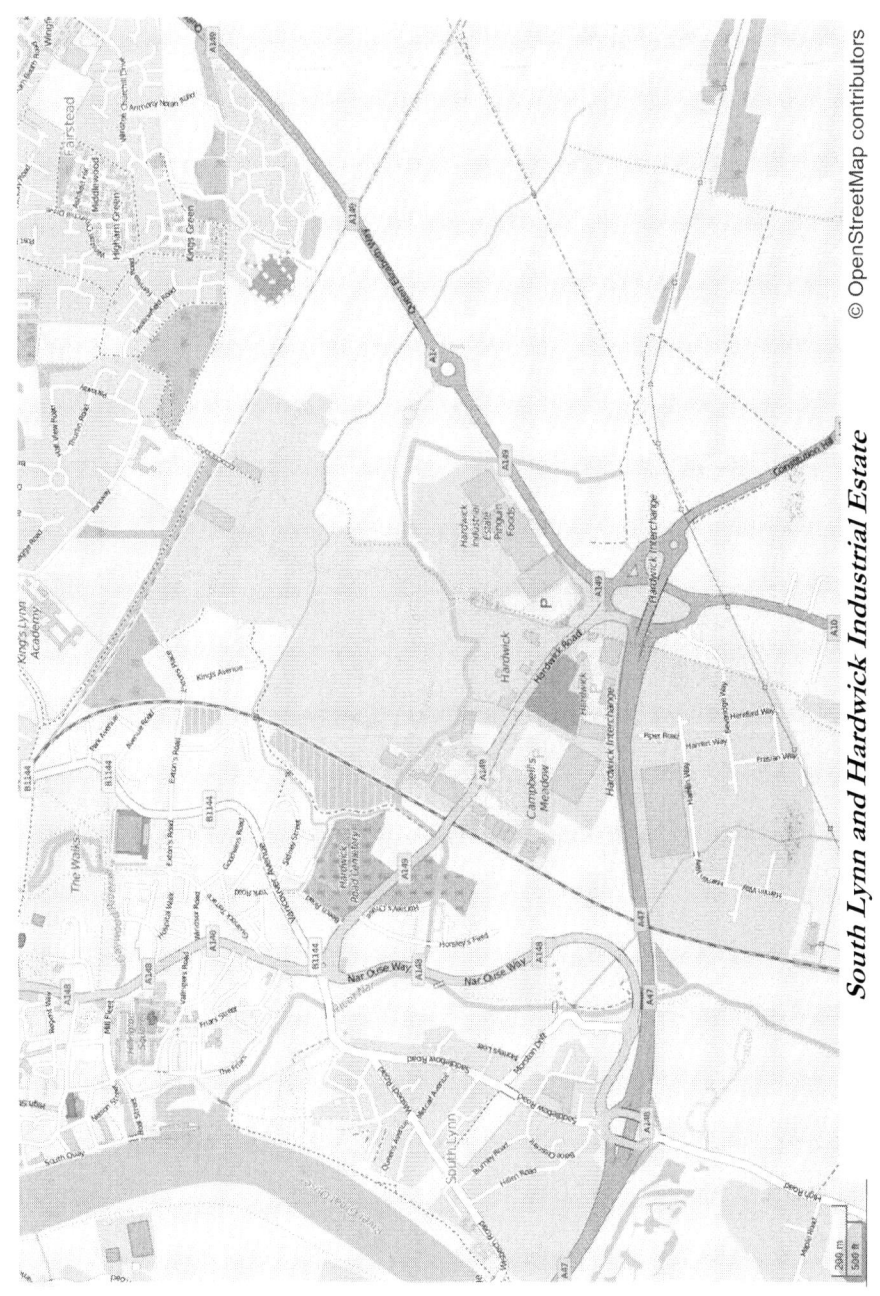

*South Lynn and Hardwick Industrial Estate*

The Woottons South and North Wootton, these were covered by a resident beat officer working from a police house home.

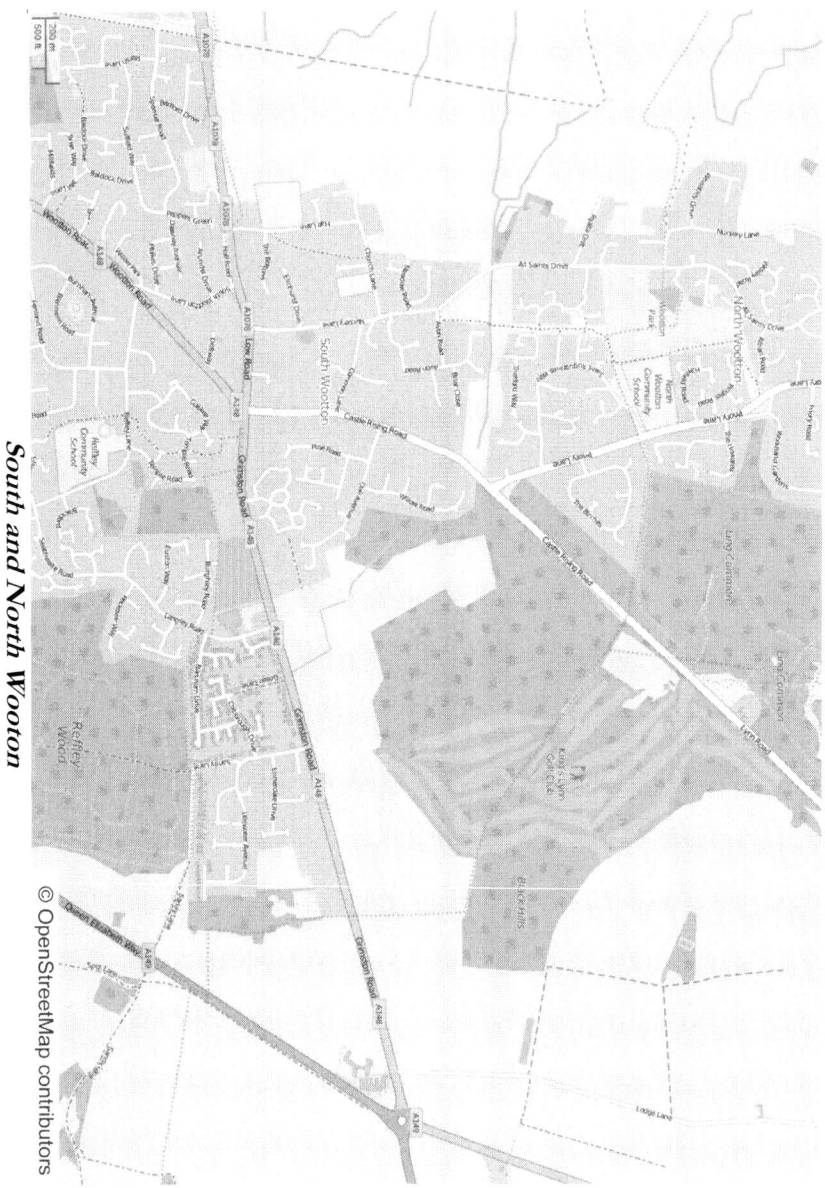

South and North Wootton

Each Parish in West Norfolk had its own resident policeman in a police house, most of these were built in the 1930s under Chief Constable Captain Van Neck's reign, and most of them also had large gardens to maintain. Combined with their duties this was his way of keeping his men from going astray. Each Section a cluster of villages had at that time a home based team of Inspector, Sergeant and Twelve Constables to operate a 24/7 coverage of the area.

This was the picture before centralisation and the closure of beats and each community had a locally accountable force who gave good service. The old adage should have applied *"If it aint broke it doesn't need fixing."*

This is how it should have remained throughout Great Britain, superimposed by specialists i.e. traffic, CID, SOCO, dogs, crime squads, helicopters, intelligence, etc. If The Home Office then had not had short sight and had recruited more police officers and not been hell bent on amalgamations and centralisation, together with vast civilianisation and not closing beats; the public would still have a force second to none whom they knew and trusted in.

*"Jock"* Leys was our found/lost property officer and other station duties. Some years before he had been on traffic patrol and on one particular night duty was in the station playing dominoes with other colleagues, awaiting a call from The Isle of Ely Police at Wisbech for a handover of The Queen's Royal Mail at the Jubilee Café at the county boundary at Walsoken, after the call he continued with his game until it was unfolded and then realizing that he had few too minutes to spare, raced off in the patrol car along the A47. At Terrington St John, there is a sharp left hand bend with a drop to a large ditch known to local police officers as *"Leys Leap"* it is so named because *"Jock"* travelling at speed failed to negotiate it and landed the car with just his pride hurt, belly deep in water. To further exacibate his situation, as he clambered mud bedraggled out of the stinking mire a nearby resident looking out of his window and seeing the uniform and not realizing that Jock was the

cause of his abrupt awakening but had been called to it, exclaimed *"You were quick, its only just happened!"*

Here I remember a couple of stories relating to Ted *"Bogey"* Mason our Traffic Sergeant, the first is concerning someone he was putting through his paces as a pursuit driver. They were out in *"the sticks"* around Watlington and thundering along a country road with left and right hand bends and *"Bogey"* said *"Read the road ahead by the way the telegraph poles go."* This lad did, a bit further along the telegraph poles diverted away from the road and went straight across a field and so did the police car! The second incident *"Bogey"* was driving his patrol car along and the chap following was right close on his tail, Ted eventually tired of this and put the Police/Stop lights on and got out and opened his boot, he then walked up to the other driver and said *"Do you want to get in?"* Gesturing to the boot of the police car. The other driver said *"Pardon Officer?"* Ted said *"If you don't want to get in, get off my arse!"* And then promptly drove away. Ted retired in 1967 and his place was taken by Frank Hall, later to be promoted to Traffic Inspector. Frank was a tall man with a moustache with about size fourteen shoes and a *"dead ringer"* for *"Blakey"* Inspector Blake from the TV and Film series of *"On the Buses"*. He was a bit of a whiner and had a dead pan face. One day one of the lads was parking his police car in the yard and pulled his handbrake up on the ratchets without releasing the button, Frank heard this from his office and called out in a *"Blakey"* type voice *"It's not a musical instrument you know!"* He was such a dour character. A couple of jokes that ran around was that on his day off he was either playing piano in the Wheelwright Arms at West Lynn or kick starting Jumbo Jets at Heathrow Airport.

## THE TOWN HALL

On night duty 10pm to 6am and at weekends, the Town Hall had to be physically checked internally every two hours by the One Beat Officer, there was a large Victorian era key kept on a large wooden fob at "The Nick" for that purpose. The first time that I checked the place I decided not to turn the lights on and bravely walk round the building using my torch where necessary and after climbing the stairs to the first floor and walking through the Magistrates Court I opened the door that gave access to the Magistrates Retiring Room and shone my torch. Immediately my heart skipped a beat and cold sweat broke out as gripped with fear I realized that there was someone there! Was it the ghost of some 18th Century Highwayman who had been kept in the old Gaol House and hung? *"No you daft Pratt! Clark"* I uttered, it was my own reflection caught in the full length mirror of the room, soon relief and laughter was surging through me.

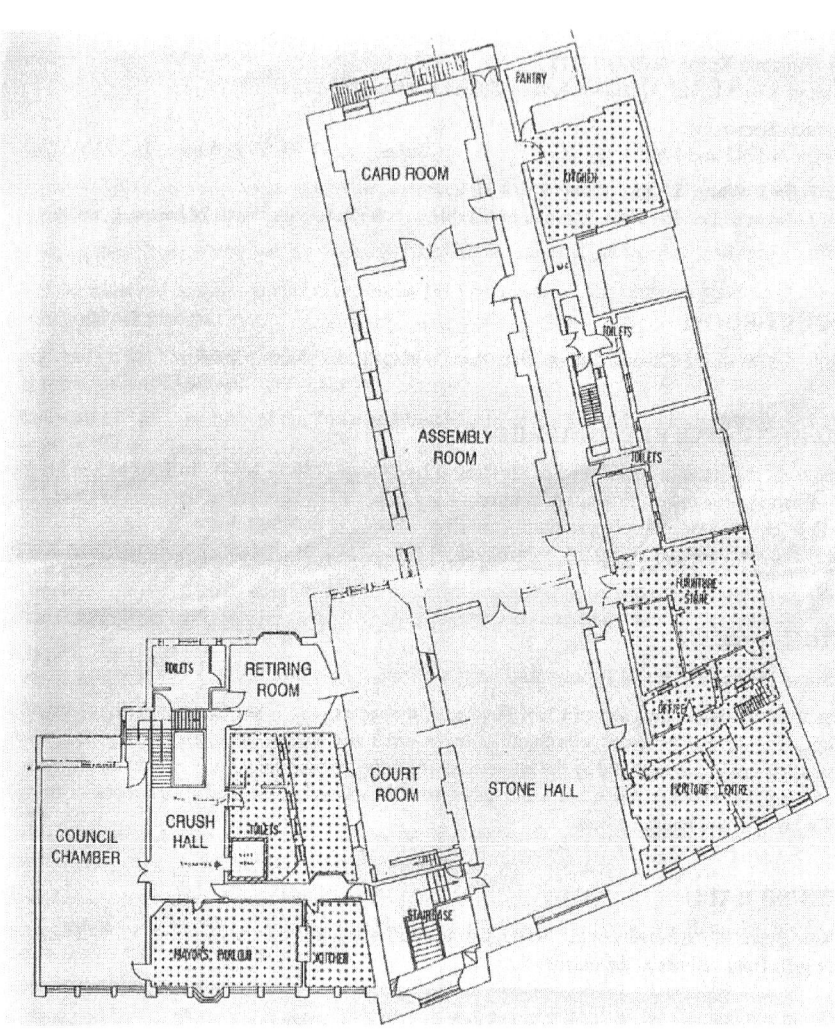

Many a new recruit fell foul of the Town Hall *"Ghosts"*. Some of the Relief would previously secrete themselves in the building after removing the lighting fuses from the box and when the unsuspecting officer was sent in alone with just his torch for comfort to check the building, he was met with all sorts of strange things going on in the darkness; like a piano playing itself, wooden staircases creaking and a light bulb flickering on and off together with distant faint wailing noises.

Also on nights and at weekends, a vulnerable property patrol was conducted on premises like jewellers, butchers, post offices, etc, this started at the Southgate's, went via the town centre and finished in North Lynn; it had to be completed in one and a quarter hours and four times during an eight hour tour – on foot! And we had Sergeants who would hide up and make sure that we did our work. Yours truly used to conveniently locate an abandoned cycle en route and then book it in as found property at the end of the shift, this speeded things up no end and stopped blisters and the need for mustard in washing up bowls; the days before foot-spa's! It is alleged that a certain officer whilst doing this knackering duty was approached by a member of the public, who was informed *"Sorry! I can't stop I'm on VPP! Report it at the police station."* I don't know whether it was the same officer who was always acting the prat, whom on one occasion was asked for directions and replied in an Italian accent *"No speakedy English!"* and on another when asked by a lady where the nearest toilet was, retorted *"It depends how bad you want to go!"* He was always the court jester and on another occasion whilst on his traffic attachment on night duty as observer, booked on duty over the force radio in a thick West Indian accent *"Hello VK from Kilo three over!"* these were the days before we had ethnic background officers. He later moved to Norwich and I met him at Fakenham many years later when he was attached to the Central Crime Unit and he hadn't changed one bit.

On early turn 6am to 2pm if I was on 2 Beat which area covered *"The Nick"* I would have to go in at 8am and get the male prisoners out of their cells to wash and shave ready for their appearance at Court and escort them there for 10am, I would serve them breakfast on a tin plate and mug which was sent down by Mrs Pink from the Single men's kitchen above, via a dumb waiter lift using a rope pulley. An entry which I made in my PB on Friday 21st April, 1967 reads *"8.30am Gave prisoners Breakfast consisted of 2 fried eggs, bacon, fried bread, bread and butter and sauce, mug of tea"* Now that paints a nice image doesn't it? The truth is it was crap, the eggs were either slimy or as hard as bullets, the bacon just shown to the frying pan for a few seconds or dried up like a pair of braces. That reminds me of an old *"Laurel & Hardy"* film clip where *"Stanley"* didn't have any bacon so cut up and fried *"Ollie's"* braces and served them to him.

The fried bread and the bottom of the plate was swimming in enough oil to run a lamp. More often than not the breakfasts would go back up the lift the way they came down untouched, they prisoners complained about the state to us and were then sympathetic when told that is what we got as well. I also sat in on prisoner's visits where their wives, girlfriends or friends would bring in cigarettes and other treats for them, listening to their conversations I learnt a lot about each individual, what made him tick and some really good info on what he had been up to *"off the record."*

Mrs Pink would not have her own cookery show like Delia Smith, she is the only person I know who could start off with perfectly good food and ruin it. I remember one occasion when coming in for meal break one late turn 2pm to 10pm, at around 6pm and went to the gas heated food warmer compartment, which she either set at maximum and was like a miniature crematorium, or low so the food was cold as well as inedible. There was my evening meal consisting of a jacket potato cooked with hard baked soil attached, a corn on the cob which still had some leaves and tassels attached and dried up congealed baked beans. I promptly put my plate onto a tray and marched down the corridor to where Colin Parker's office was he was Chief Inspector Administration and supposedly in charge of the running of Single men's Quarters and supervision of the catering & cleaning staff. I said to Colin *"This is what we have to eat and what we have been complaining about, would you eat it?"* Colin picked up my fork from the tray and gingerly turned the potato and sweet corn over at arms length and didn't say anything; I repeated the question and he said *"Well No."*

Anyhow things didn't get any better and this led to my decision to get out of Single men's as soon as possible. Most of the time we were paying for food that we couldn't eat and then going out buying takeaway like Chinese or fish & chips. On Tuesdays "Pinkie's" day off, we were ok though as we had Edie (Edith) one of our cleaners, from Castle Rising cooking for us and she knew how to prepare and cook delicious meals and she was like an Aunt and spoilt us lads.

The best fish & Chips were from Clough Lane where the St James Kings Lynn Swimming Pool now stands and talking about Chinese food reminds me of a restaurant in the town centre owned by a Chinese couple, they were friends and I used to be a regular paying customer there. I was invited by them into the rear of the premises when I was on night duty after the last customer had left around 12.30am and they would serve me a lovely meal during my unofficial mealbreak. Police Regulations stated *"meal breaks to be taken between the third and fifth hour."*

Anyway you always get greedy coppers who spoil a good thing, once some of the other Relief's cottoned on to this *"freebie"* as they saw it they were all lining up to get in. I thanked the couple for their previous hospitality and told them not to do it for anyone as it was costing them and they were too polite to refuse the others. Some years later I was involved with them in a kidnap case involving their children.

This *"mumping"* is what one ex Met policeman would later call it, I suppose a London reference to *"scrumping"* reminds me of other occasions when greed has prevailed and it concerned a certain Relief.

Campbell's Soup factory on Hardwick Industrial Estate had staff sales of slightly dented cans of their products and the police were allowed to go down on certain dates and times to purchase these at a substantial knockdown discount of the normal retail price. All was well until a Director of the Firm found cases of his products being sold in a seconds shop in the town at just under the firm's retail price! That killed the goose that lay the golden egg, the same occurred at Dornay Foods (Master Foods) where one of our Constables left and went to work with as a security officer and he supplied us with staff discounts. The best (worst) I think is a dear who owned a Gaywood Dairy Shop, he left a key above the door to the store and told us *"Lads if you need milk for the police station on nights don't buy it, help yourself to a pint."* Well this same shift went down when they were on nights and took a whole crate and shared them out to take home! It's little wonder that they got the dross put on that relief and some turned out as criminals, more on this later.

We also had a bent copper on our Relief who I will refer to as BC this bloke was all swagger and dressed in expensive suits with shot silk lining and had all the hallmarks of being affluent, on a *"coppers"* pay then, you've got to be joking, most jobs in civvies street paid better. Anyhow unbeknown to us then, he was going into a paper shop near *"The Nick"* and bouncing cheques on him for substantial amounts.

BC then organised this *"knockout"* Snooker Tournament for all of Kings Lynn Police to participate in and everyone chipped in a £1 note to cover the occasion and winners prize. Those latterday members of The *"Nick"* are still awaiting the return of their money, but that's not all.
One day on late turn at shift briefing I said to Frank *"Rigger"* Leech who was *"Acting Jack"* whilst the Sergeant was on leave, *"Sarge, I need to go and nick P for some vehicle offences."* At the time I was a non driver and P was a second hand car dealer and regularly sold unroadworthy and undocumented vehicles to villains. *"Rigger"* looked around the motley assembled crew and said *"Who can drive Clarkie out to Terrington?"* BC raises his hand and says *"I can Sarge"* *"Rigger"* being a shrewd old boy says

*"Have you got a force driving permit?"* Whereupon BC" replied *"Yes."* So we then drove off to my assignment and I booked P and on our return *"Rigger"* called us in and said to BC *"You silly bastard! I have checked and you haven't got a force permit and what's more you've only got a provisional licence, that means you had no force insurance cover and no licence to drive the car; what the hell are you playing at, if this gets out we are all in the shit!"* BC mumbles *"Well they are always on my case so I thought that I would piss them about."* At this stage *"Rigger"* had to have the utmost composure to stop thumping and knocking him out.

I have saved the best until last I mentioned earlier that *"Jock"* Leys was our found/lost property man and when he was off-duty the property cupboard, situated in an annexe off the Front Office/Control Room was left unlocked for 24 hour access; this area later became the Telex Room when we had one. Found property started to go missing on a regular basis, i.e. purses or wallets with no loser's ID inside containing cash and unbeknown to me the CID had BC as their suspect and were keeping tabs on him.

On this particular Sunday 2pm to 10pm shift I was on duty in the front office/control together with the aforementioned Constable BC who was 9am to 5pm. He always hung his *"civvie"* jacket on a peg inside the door of the property cupboard and at the end of his shift went to collect his jacket and guess what! His wallet had been *"stolen"* from the inside pocket. Apart from yours truly as far as I was aware no other person had been in the room, imagine the dilemma that I was in, I hadn't taken it but who else was there? Anyway it was obviously a ploy on BC's part to deflect any suspicion on him over the missing found property and he duly reported it stolen to CID and I had to make a statement to the CID denying any knowledge of its disappearance.

Amongst the items BC reported that were contained in the *"stolen"* wallet were two numbered tickets for a forthcoming Police Dance at the Dukes Head Hotel, which he had purchased from *"Rigger.* Come the night of the Do along sauntered BC with his girlfriend of the moment and showed his tickets to the doorman. Woh Behold! The same two reported stolen along with his wallet and the CID pounced on him like a cat on a mouse and very soon BC was tendering his resignation which was duly accepted and it was good night from him and good riddance from me.

We had a Divisional Dog Handler in the shape of PC 230 Derrick Pimlott who had as his able companion the first of his three dogs *"Rex."* Derrick and I became firm friends until his retirement when he moved to Spain. There he had a heart attack and died about two years into retirement. Derrick and I are involved in several passages later in the book.

***Derrick with Rex***

Personal Radios were a new innovation at Kings Lynn taken into use during 1966 and they were still in their infancy when I transferred there, they were a bulky "Stornophone" make with a long car like aerial which had to be fully pulled out before use, these tended to get snapped off easily, either by accident or whilst tussling with some yob and then they were tendered useless and unable to transmit. A colleague Terry Sturman, whom I later served with on "B" Relief modelled this one for the local press in The Walks.

APPENDIX 'A' TO GENERAL ORDERS NO. 21/66 DATED 27TH MAY, 1966

POLICE COMMUNICATIONS

PERSONAL OR POCKET WIRELESS SETS

1. Personal or pocket wireless sets have been the subject of experiment for some years and it is anticipated that in the foreseeable future they will be taken into general use by all Forces. In the meantime a number of Forces have been issued with a limited number of sets on an experimental basis; the King's Lynn Sub-Division has been issued with eight such sets.

Equipment

2. The basic equipment is as follows:-

   (a) A base station located in the main Police Station or other centre as required.

   (b) A number of wireless transmitter/receiver sets for issue to beat patrol and supervising officers.

   (c) A remote control, if required, for use by static supervising officer.

   (d) A battery charger.

3. A variety of sets are in production including G.E.C. (Lancon) Campbell-Bruce, Cossor, Pye, and Stornophone. King's Lynn has been issued with Stornophone sets.

4. All equipment is on hire to Police Authorities and is subject to maintenance and supervision by Home Office Wireless Engineers. The apparatus is valuable and will of course be handled with care; the most vulnerable item is probably the telescopic aerial.

Control

5. Personal wireless sets, like walkie talkies, have a limited range and are therefore subject to very local control; normally they will be under the direct control and supervision of the Duty Sergeant. If required for any special purpose, viz. crime, traffic, etc., they will be under the control of the Officer in Charge or his delegated subordinate.

6. When a Duty Sergeant or other officer details a network of personal wireless equipped officers for duty he will allocate a specific wireless set, all of which have been numbered, to individual Officers at the same time as he details the beat or particular duty to be performed. The Supervising Officer will enter the set number allocated under the name and number column of the Duty Register. The Supervising Sergeant will also be responsible for the return of the set at the termination of a tour of duty.

\- 2 -

8. In the event of a set failing to operate no attempt will be made to effect a repair. Faults must be reported to the Duty Sergeant who is responsible for informing the Traffic Superintendent, Headquarters, through Divisional Office. Headquarters will make the necessary arrangements with the Home Office Depot at Cheveley or the Regional Wireless' Representative at Norwich.

## Operational Use

9. The object of the personal wireless set is to provide the beat constable with a means of communication with his main station supervising officer and to provide the latter with a ready means of deploying and contacting his team of patrol constables. The use of the set does in effect produce an efficient team of patrol officers with a Sergeant in command. It is essential that priority of issue be to patrolling beat constables and the sets should not be diverted for other purposes except in emergencies or for special enquiries.

10. The main base station will be at the Sub Divisional or Section Headquarters and the Supervising Inspector or Sergeant will always be in possession of a pocket radio set when performing outside supervisory duties.

## Conference Points and Supervisory Visits

11. There will be no necessity for beat patrol officers to be required to make Conference Points on occasions when they are in possession of personal wireless sets, unless supervising officers consider this necessary because of any particular crime or traffic condition. Supervising Officers will however keep in touch both by wireless and by personal visit to constables under their command Time and location checks should be made regularly at intervals of not less than one hour. Constables should make wireless contact with their Divisional Headquarters at the same interval unless they have already been contacted or are in difficulties or require advice or assistance.

12. The personal wireless set does not provide supervision in lieu of personal visits. It is operational equipment for deploying personnel, receiving situation reports and giving orders. Visits are personal matters between Supervising Officers and individual Beat Constables; they are of considerable value, especially to the young Constable, and should be made as frequently as possible.

Prior to the advent of personal radios and which were still occasionally in use was a telephone kiosk point system every fifteen minutes by kiosks on Tuesday Market Place, Saturday Market Place , Broad Street, Norfolk Street and Railway Road. These were supplemented by Police Boxes operated from the Police Station and they had a blue light which was activated when the phone rang, to draw the officer's attention in order for him to answer it and be dispatched to an incident. These boxes were situated at:

1 Southgate's Roundabout – which I some time later, after it became redundant, acquired for the South Lynn Play Scheme Association as a "Dr Who Tardis".

2 Highgate/Littleport Street

3 Estuary Close/St Edmundsbury Road

4 Wootton Road/Roseberry Avenue – when this became redundant it was purchased from the force by the adjacent property and incorporated into that garden as a children's play house.

In each police box there was a message pad and occurrence book and the officer had to make an entry in the book on each occasion he visited.

# The Laughing Policeman

## POLICE BOXES AND POSTS

In many forces a police telephone box or post is erected on or near each beat and patrol. The telephone is connected by direct line with headquarters or divisional or sub-divisional stations, where further connection can be made. Constables should use these telephone facilities on all matters relating to police duty, quite apart from "ringing-in."

Boxes and posts are locked, and a standard pattern key is issued to each officer. If a key is lost or if the key or lock is defective, the fact should be reported.

At the top of the box or post there is an emergency signal light, controlled from the station, for use in calling the patrolling inspector or men on duty. Any officer seeing this signal must answer it promptly.

Any defect in the telephone should be reported to the station quickly so that the station officer may notify the Post Office Engineer. The officer discovering the defect should remain in the vicinity until relieved or the defect is repaired.

The facilities afforded by the box system may be summarized as follows:

*For the Police*
 (a) To send or receive information or to obtain advice or assistance from the station.
 (b) To report to the station at prescribed intervals.
 (c) To prepare reports of occurrences.

*For the Public*
 (a) To enable them to obtain prompt police assistance for any proper purpose.
 (b) To make enquiry or obtain advice on any matter within the range of police duty.

Members of the public should be encouraged to use the telephone on any matter which affects police.

A first-aid outfit is supplied to each box and post. Officers using any of the contents are to notify the station for the purpose of replacement. A fire extinguisher is also supplied, and its use must also be reported.

A box diary is provided for the purpose of recording messages received or sent. Entries should be timed and initialled by the officer concerned. Recent entries in the diary should be read by all visiting officers. The first officer visiting after 6 a.m. should inspect the box and its contents, and record the result in the diary.

The boxes and posts are illuminated during darkness, but waste must be avoided. When leaving, officers should lock the door or flap and see that the telephone instrument is properly replaced.

Boxes are cleaned periodically by an appointed cleaner. Officers using them are expected to keep them tidy and properly ventilated.

There was also a red light system, one attached to St Margaret's Church at Saturday Market Place one above Burtons Menswear in High Street and one at the gasworks on Wisbech Road at South Lynn Nar Bridge all of which could be activated from the police station to alert patrolling officers who would then ring in or be rung from a public call box situated close to these locations.

Kings Lynn was a complete contrast to Hellesdon, I had colleagues and was part of a team and on every shift I worked there was always a fresh and varied challenge. I really enjoyed this and threw myself into this new and exciting method of policing. I hadn't been there long when I was involved with burglars.

On Tuesday 2nd May I paraded for night shift and at the briefing we were told that reliable information had been received that two active burglars were planning a job to go off tonight either a jewellers or cigarette store and to report any sightings of them. At 1035pm an officer received a report that they were in Broad Street and at 1045pm found an attempted break-in and the would be intruders had flown. At 1150pm I checked a row of derelict terraced houses in East Street behind Norfolk Street which were awaiting demolition. It was known that the two aforementioned slept rough in there on occasions, however on this occasion they weren't there.

Then on Saturday 6th May again on night shift, at 3.45am there was alarm activation at the *"Blue & Gold"* Kings Lynn Football Supporters Club and on arrival by colleagues it was found broken into and a quantity of cigarettes spirits and cash from the gaming machines had been stolen. I kept observation from some pens in the Cattle Market (Now Kings Lynn Bus Station and Sainsbury's Car Park) which was a route from the burglary to East Street and at around 4.30am I saw two figures running across the Cattle Market towards Norfolk Street both laden and one carrying a large teapot. I circulated this over my personal radio and the shift approached and encircled East Street and upon arrival there found that the culprits had barricaded themselves in.

We called for the night duty CID officer who was Detective Sergeant "Ronnie" Brown a canny experienced man. When he got there he shouted up to the bedroom window of number three *"Come on you two get down here, the games up!"* One of the two said *"Mr Brown we're not letting you in unless you've got a warrant."* Now a Superintendent's Warrant ready signed by *"Fred"* and with the time/date/venue left blank was kept in the *"Nick"* for such occasions but *"Ronnie"* wasn't going to mess about with these two. He whispered to me *"Nobby have a look in my car and find a couple of sheets of written paper"* this I did and duly found some and gave them to him. He then rolled them up and called out to the two inside *"Right you two, here's the warrant, stop messing about and let us in or I'll get my lads to kick the door in."* With that the two opened the door and they were nicked, inside we found the proceeds from the *"Blue & Gold"* Club break and the teapot I had seen one of them carrying earlier. It was full of cash from the gaming machines and till; all in all a good result.

On Saturday 13th of May I was on late turn 3 Beat, this area covered the Southern part of the town down to The Southgate's and at 8.30pm I was called to the south gates gents toilets which was down a flight of steps about eight feet below the footpath a dark dank stinking hole of a place this was a notorious hangout for *"queer"* goings on, males importuning for male sex, acts of gross indecency giving each other hand shandies, blow jobs or the full Monty! But any member of the public wanting to use the facilities had to run the gauntlet of these perverts who drilled holes between the cubicles and deliberately smeared the toilet seats with excrement or semen Yugh! It was eventually closed down.

A thirteen year old lad from South Lynn was using the toilets for the correct purpose and had been propositioned by this 39 year old bloke from Sutton Bridge and an off duty Special Constable had intervened, both the victim and perpetrator were there. I took details from the boy and then spoke to the man M and cautioned him and said *"What is alleged is that W came down to the toilets and that you were inside one of the toilets and peeping through the door whilst he was having a pee and that you then grabbed hold of him and said "Will you come in the toilet with me?"* He refused and ran off"

M said *"That's a pack of lies. I didn't touch the lad at all."* The family didn't want to take the matter further so I went back to *"The Nick"* and rang Lincolnshire Police who said that he didn't have any convictions but that his Brother had several for Indecent Exposure so obviously just a normal family from cauliflower land!

On Saturday 17th June I was on early turn and had my meal break at 9.20am and at 10am I was called to a male collapse in St James Street outside the Mecca Bingo Hall. The man was found to be dead and a doctor was called to certify that, he had died of coronary thrombosis (heart attack) and I went with him in the big van to the mortuary and then completed the sudden death forms, which had to have four copies made.

There weren't any pedestrianised streets in Kings Lynn at this time and large delivery Lorries drove along High Street, Norfolk Street, New Conduit Street and Broad Street and parked vehicles caused severe congestion during the day.

An aerial view of King's Lynn just before the destruction of several streets for the shopping precinct of the 1960's and below is High Street during a winter's evening.

*High Street a December evening how I remember it in 1967*

## *"Rigger and Digger"*

This reminds me of the time on an early turn Tuesday when I was being driven down the High Street from Tuesday Market Place (TMP) by *"Rigger"* who was Acting Sergeant in yes you've guessed it a Hillman Husky! It was a lovely hot sunny day and we had the windows of the vehicle down and the High Street resembled an ant's nest with people walking everywhere a bit like a large football crowd. As we drove slowly just past Burtons the Tailor heading for Saturday Market Place (SMP) we spotted this middle aged very well endowed woman who was obviously in a hurry to catch a bus or similar running along the footpath towards us, I think water melons being swung in a net springs to mind. Well *"Rigger"* without turning a hair leant out of the drivers side window and yelled at the top of his voice *"Don't run like that missus, you'll turn your milk sour!"* The poor lady stopped dead in her tracks and went beetroot red; meanwhile I slid down in my seat as far as I could and tried to hide behind the dashboard.

A few other stories involving Frank *"Rigger"* Leech and his co partner in "crime" John *"Digger"* Graves who was at St Germans when I went to Lynn, but who some years before had been on the beat with *"Rigger."*

Way back in the early 1950s when both *"Rigger"* and *"Digger"* were stationed at the Borough Police Station in the Town Hall they had a Sergeant who was a bit of a bastard to them, so they decided to play a prank on him. On night shift this Sergeant would bring in some fresh eggs to compliment an early breakfast and on this occasion both reprebates went down to the South Lynn Wood, Sadd & Moore Egg Depot and selected some rotten eggs left out for disposal. They returned to the police station and swapped the Sergeant's good eggs for the rotten ones, which he duly broke into a frying pan with the result that the kitchen literally stank of bad egg gas.

One night just before completing duty they found a large branch which had fallen from a tree and dragged it down the High Street to the junction with New Conduit Street at Burtons Corner by the original tailor's Fosters Menswear where they stuck it in a manhole after lifting off the cover and they waited for the first unsuspecting victim. Shortly after a high top David Greig grocery lorry came along and the unsuspecting driver thinking it was a new feature of street furniture that the council had put up, pulled over to the right in order to get by and in doing so the top of the lorry got stuck under the overhanging parapet of Scott's China Shop. They slunk away chuckling and booked off duty, leaving the early turn High Street man to find the *"incident."* I don't however think that this was the reason that Scott's on the opposite junction sold up and the premises pulled down and rebuilt as Boots the Chemist.

The Laughing Policeman

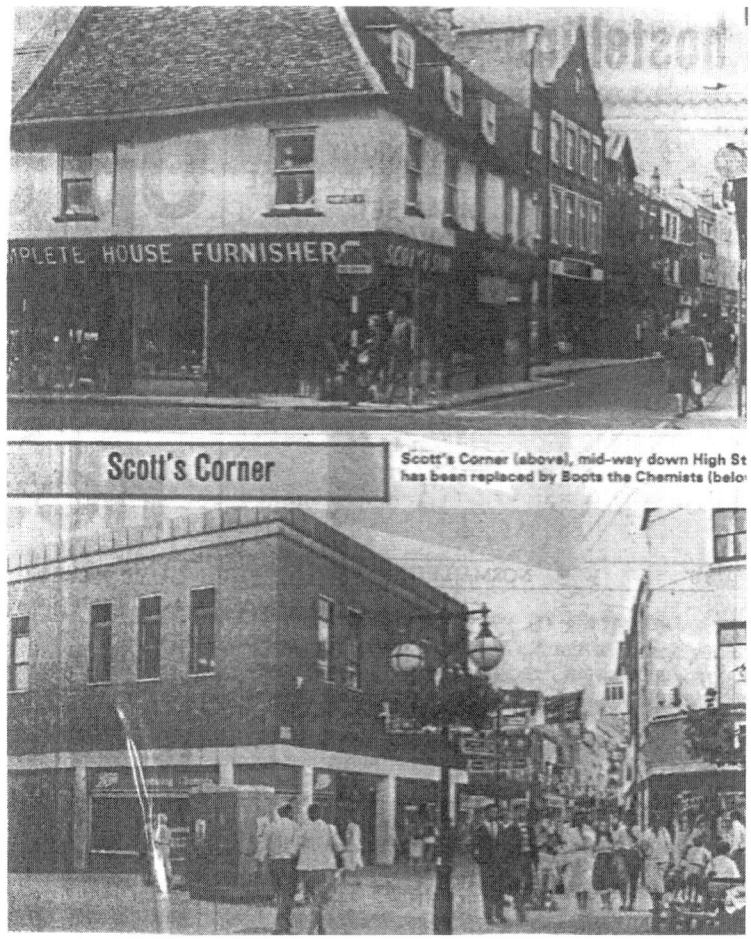

Scott's Corner (above), mid-way down High St has been replaced by Boots the Chemists (below)

On another occasion the two reprobates were again on night duty and carrying out a property check on the flat roof Marks & Spencer shop on the corner of High Street and Norfolk Street when they spotted their Inspector Bill *"Fink"* Nelson, who was stationed at Kings Lynn before he went to Norwich Division at Thorpe where I later saw him as a probationer. As he walked past below en route to the Tuesday Market Place the TMP they both pulled out their appendages and dutifully began to pee onto the unsuspecting Inspector! He was heard to exclaim to himself *"I fink it's raining!"*

The next story I cite is of *"Rigger"* on his own. There was a man living in a flat above one of the shops in High Street who was having problems getting up for early shift work and he asked Frank if he could help. Frank devised this system of getting the chap when he went to bed of tying a long piece of string to his big toe, lower it out of the sash window of his bedroom and leave it to dangle about six feet from street level to stop yobs grabbing it. Frank would then come along at the prearranged time the following morning reach up and pull on the string and wake him. Apparently this ingenious system worked!

All sudden deaths where a post mortem was required, including fatal road traffic accidents, suicides etc were collected by us police officers from the street, house or other location in the general purpose big van call sign Kilo 3 and taken to the Town Hall Mortuary. There we had to strip the body of clothing, identify it by tying a brown cardboard hand written label to the big toe and place it into the next available empty sliding container like a large filing cabinet and store their clothes and any other property including valuables in property bags; to await the attention of the mortician.

I was involved in quite a few of these sudden deaths with *"Rigger"* and when he was undressing the bodies he would to talk to them like they were still alive *"Lift your arms up there my beauty and let's get these off you"* he would say. I suppose it was his way of dealing with the surreal circumstances. We had a particularly sad one to deal with, this young engaged couple had left the road in their soft top Austin Healy Sprite sports car at *"Faulkner's Tunnel"* at West Walton and it had gone upside down in a deep muddy water filled ditch and drowned. We drove out there in the van and collected them and took them back to Kings Lynn Mortuary where we laid them out on seperate slabs to clean them up by hosing them down. They were still warm and lying side by side the scene was very poignant *"together for ever."*

CARRYING SHEETS FOR MOVING BODIES    GENERAL ORDERS 11/2/66

Two prototype carrying sheets have been obtained and they are kept at Norwich Divisional Headquarters and King's Lynn Police Station respectively.

The carrying sheet is likely to be especially useful in moving bodies in confined surroundings, e.g. carrying a corpse down a narrow winding staircase, or moving a corpse which is in an advanced state of decomposition etc. It is made of washable material, with a pocket at one end to take the feet of the corpse, and an attached cover which is secured by merely pressing together the two parts of the cover; there are carrying handles along each side of the sheet. When not in use, the sheet is carried in a lightweight waterproof bag. It is waterproof and if it becomes soiled it can be washed easily.

Officers should bear in mind the possibility of using one of these sheets if a body has to be moved in difficult surroundings, if it is badly decomposed or injured, or if members of the public are present, e.g. on a crowded beach.

Any requests for the loan of one of the sheets should be made direct to the appropriate Division.

A couple more stories about Frank Leech which I witnessed when he was on Front Office Duty: Frank was heavily involved as a Trainer at The Friars Boxing Club in Globe Street near The Harbour Master's Office and trained some good local prospects; one of who would have turned professional if he hadn't got into *"speed"* amphetamines and then into crime.

On one occasion a teenager had been brought into the *"Nick"* high on drugs or alcohol and was playing up in the Charge Room. Frank who was on Front Office duty heard the commotion and on recognising the lad came in to try and calm the situation. This lad then told Frank *"You can fuck off you slimy leech."* Wrong thing to do with Frank whose craggy friendly and normally happy face suddenly darkened and he changed into *"The Hulk"* grabbed this lad in a headlock and started to throttle him saying in a quiet menacing voice *"What did you call me?"* Anyway we managed to extract Frank from this lad who had suddenly realized the error of his ways and became profusely apologetic.

On another occasion Frank and I were on Front Office/Control duty together when this chap in his early twenties came in and said *"Watch yer Leech'y come on then"* and started sparring on the other side of the counter. Frank who was game for a laugh started doing the same on our side and growled *"Why don't you fuck off!"* He then let fly with his right fist and caught this guy right in the face his *"Mivvy"* to use Frank's expression and the resulting impact knocked him back about three feet and his left eye suddenly needed raw steak or frozen peas or both but no chips! This guy then shook his head and just walked out of the foyer we never did find out what he came in for. Frank had not actually meant to make contact with fist to head but to parry and stop just short. He was shitting himself for the next two days waiting for a complaint of assault but it never was forthcoming!

A song that Frank was always singing when we weren't busy in the Front Office was from the A.A. Milne song *"When We Were Very Young"* from *"Winnie the Pooh"*:

First verse *"They're changing the guard at Buckingham Palace, Christopher Robin went down with Alice, Alice is marrying one of the guards, a soldier's life is very hard, says Alice."*

Verse two *"They're changing the guard at Buckingham Palace, Christopher Robin went down with Alice. We saw a guard in a sentry box, one of the sergeants looks after their socks, says Alice."*

With four more verses to go Frank would sing the lot with the bottoms of his uniform trousers tucked into his regulation long Norwich City football socks whilst at the same time marching up and down doing a Max Wall impression (he was a stand up comedian of the 60s and 70s). That reminds me of another Front Office story that I was involved in:

When I was in the last year at Dersingham Secondary Modern we had a pupil in my class called BS who was a bit of a simpleton who one day in art lesson got his willy out and started painting it with green paint when our art teacher Mrs Bell saw him she called out "What on earth are you doing S?" He replied *"I'm painting my willy like a snake Miss!"* She then picked up a black board rubber and hit him with it. So with that in mind about ten years later when I was on Front Office duty and the foyer was full of people with different enquiries in walked this guy now aged about 25 to report his racing cycle stolen. I immediately recognised him albeit having not seen him since we left school and called out *"You're BS from Harpley you got your Willy out in art lesson at school!"*

The noisy atmosphere of the waiting room suddenly quietened until you could hear a pin drop B went bright red and walked out and he never came back to report his bike stolen.

Another clown we had was our soon to retire Inspector Henry "Nobby" Nobbs a really nice man who had been a Constable during the 1953 Flood who on retirement went as security officer to some vegetable canning factories at West Lynn. One evening he raided the Found

Property cupboard and located a wig and a black trilby hat under everyone's noses then furtively stole back to his office and reversed his white shirt so that the collar was to the front donned the wig and hat together with his black civvies jacket and crept out of the side entrance/exit. He then walked round to the front of the police station and went into the waiting room and rang the bell. The poor unsuspecting me who answered it thought he was a vicar and didn't recognise my own Inspector so much for my observation and identification skills!

There were a lot of *"characters"* in the job then a few who spring to mind are:

(i) Sgt Ray Spinks was called *"Winky Spinky"* by the lads as he had this affliction and was constantly blinking.

(ii) Bill Beverley at East Winch who stuttered and came out with different meaning words a couple of examples are when asked by a motorist *"Why did you stop me officer?"* Bill's reply was *"Cause cause cause the point is we're the bloody police!"* As well as referring to Clarence Hazelwood from Middleton later to be our Collator as *"A bloody Collaborator"*

(iii) PC87 John *"Jack"* Troup giving evidence at Grimston MC from the Witness Box *"Your worships the undergrowth was overgrown with the overgrowth!"* On another occasion he stopped reading from his pocket book and when asked by the defence why, replied *"Because I can't see, can you put some bloody lights on!"*

Jack was blind as a bat and roared around West Norfolk from Hunstanton to Downham Market on a Norton motor cycle booking everything and everyone. He was a straight down the line no nonsense copper and is famous in Norfolk Police History for unseating HM The Queen and her Grandson Viscount Lindley when he was a lad whilst they were out riding near the Norwich Gates at Sandringham. Jack had parked his patrol motorcycle on its stand as the Royal party approached and saluted HM & HRH and both horses shied up onto their back legs and both The Queen and the little Viscount fell off. Jack went to their assistance and in the meantime the radio on his machine blared out and the horses took fright and ran off; Her Majesty was not pleased! And blurted out *"You! You! Spaceman!"* and Jack was *"Detained at her Majesty's Displeasure"* and later admonished by Fred Calvert.

JACK TROUP

Jack wrote a book after retirement called *"The life that Jack lived"* it covers all of his life including being a Barnado's Boy, his WW2 Army career and his career as a policeman after the war until his retirement in 1974. I served with Jack in the Front Office at Lynn at various times from 1968 until he retired and got close to him, he was like an Uncle to the lads.

**Retirement day, 1974**

Jack Troup with Wife Valerie and Son Stephen shaking hands with Chief Superintendent Fred Calvert.

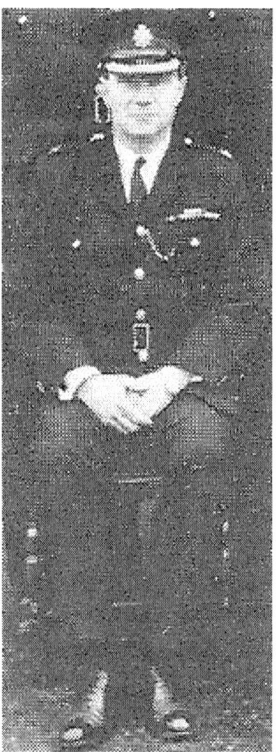

***Chief Superintendent Fred Calvert 1967***

On Wednesday 24th May whilst on early turn, at 1.50pm I was called to the Kings Lynn Labour Club in Chapel Street where they had found a *"body"* it was a four feet high cardboard replica of a Wild West cowboy. Enquiries were made in the area and it was discovered that the cowboy had been removed by high spirited revellers from the Maids Head Hotel on the nearby Tuesday Market Place the night before, during a Country & Western Show.

On Friday 2nd June, HM the Queen's 14th Coronation Anniversary I was on night duty and at 1130pm was called to a fight in Wellesley Street between American Servicemen from Lakenheath and local yobs I broke this up and the parties went on their way with no complaints. In the middle 1950s during the *"Teddy Boy"* era there were always fights at weekends between them and the Yanks from Sculthorpe.

Just round the corner from where I had just been was a fish & chip shop on Railway Road the owner was from a well known organised crime family from West Norfolk and a *"fence."* At weekends after the pubs had turned out all the riff raff congregated outside this place and there could be up to 200 drunken people milling around. Invariably there would be a fight going on in the centre of it and yours truly would have to wade in and sort it out on my own. On one particular occasion there was a nasty fight going on between some South Lynn criminals and some Irish road layers. As I went in the one of the South Lynn lot a hard guy in the crowd said *"Fuck off copper or you will be next!"* it was quite an ugly scene and then a voice from the gathered crowd who I recognised said to the hard man *"Leave him alone or you'll have us to deal with."* I showed fear nor favour to anyone but I built up a lot of respect from criminals in how I dealt with them, fairly and honestly and on this occasion it paid off big time. Some years later the same man helped me out in a similar way and he was one of those involved in it, but stopped his mates from doing me even though I arrested him for GBH with intent and getting him banged up, thanks Dave you were a star.

On another occasion the four Irish Brothers who are now established local businessmen, really nice men but a handful when drink set in were having a meal in *"The Phoenix"* a Chinese Restaurant in Tower Street, this was opened in 1966 and has long since closed. I received a call to go there as they were refusing to pay the bill and were getting heated. On arrival I went into the premises which was packed full of local riff raff and approached their table. The cause of their gripe was that the food was crap which I had to agree with, but it was cheaper than the China Garden in New Conduit Street and that's what attracted so many of their clientele. They agreed to pay a reasonable amount of the bill but to save face asked if I would leave before them which I did, fully expecting a bottle to the back of the head or something similar. But they all filed out behind me each shaking my hand and thanking me for the way I had dealt with it. This was no mean feat because normally if there was no-one to fight, they would fight amongst themselves; I suggested and recommended the China Garden next time.

Police sport was looked on favourably and we had teams participating in football, rugby, cricket, bowls hockey and ten pin bowling on USAF bases at Lakenheath & Mildenhall and at RAF Marham. I took part in football and cricket for Kings Lynn Division as well as cricket and competed against other Sunday league teams, including the Downham and Sandringham Police Divisions, I also learnt the rudiments of grass bowls under the tuition of former PC Henry Pitcher our civilian police driver; this game was played as though it were a religion.

In 1967 The Larceny Act was still in force (to be repealed the following year by The Theft Act 1968) and The Road Safety Act 1967 which included the breathalyser was on its way in, prior to this act suspected drunk drivers were subjected to a sobriety test.

Sgt John Rosier (Ex Met) and Inspector Gerry Dunn (Ex Durham), the latter having moved to Lynn from Norwich Division, were the probationer training officers and we had one day a month on new legislation. With John it was very much a practical demonstration on the administration of law, one day whilst teaching and discussing offences committed by licensed betting shops, he took all twelve of us probationers to Priory Lane off Church/Stonegate Street and booked the proprietor for not having his licensee board displayed. His favourite expression when asked for advice on a particular legal question was *"Fang Em!"* He also had an unusual habit. During the small hours when he was night Shift Sergeant cover at Kings Lynn, he would drop metal tea trays from the first floor balcony into the public waiting area; these landed with a resounding crash startling everyone in earshot. He hated cracked crockery and his method of disposal if he found any in the canteen was to throw them over his shoulder onto the tiled floor.

One of the funniest memories I have of John is when Fred Calvert, who was heavily into Amateur Dramatics had a Tuba delivered during his absence, which was left outside his locked office on the first floor corridor. John picked this up and was seen marching up and down *"The Nick"* blowing *"Oompa! Oompa!"* On the infernal instrument.

On other occasions when he wanted to go and see *"the guvnor"* John would knock on Fred's door and Fred would sing out *"Come In!"* John would sing back *"I'm Coming!"* Fred however was a sport always with a twinkle in his eye and a really good *"guvnor"* the sort who left you to get on with the job and backed you up if the wheel came off, which it invariably did on occasions. He was a rare breed the like we were seldom to see again. Fred had a brilliant criminal law mind, if you had a prisoner in at night that you wanted to hold for CID but weren't sure of your grounds, the Front Office/Control could ring him say at 3am he would answer the phone within two rings from being fast asleep, quickly listen to the circumstances then tell you the Act, Section and page in Stone's Justice Manual to hold or charge on.

On another occasion Frank Leech received an old fashioned wash board over the front counter as found property, as he was in the middle of an impromptu skiffle version of *"Cumberland Gap"* with his uniform trousers pulled above his knees and wearing his civvie flat cap; the front office door to the corridor opened and a coin was thrown in and Fred's voice boomed out *"Move into the next street, Leech!"* Frank could have written his own book on his exploits and it would good reading, but he was also a good *"old fashioned"* copper and has helped many a wet behind the ears probationer including myself aspire to greater things. Frank it was really good to have known you as My Friend as well as colleague and sorry that you have departed us but God needed a Court Jester. There was a PC who was stationed at Walpole St Andrew close to the borders with The Isle of Ely (Now Cambridgeshire) and Lincolnshire Police. He was an ex guardsman and 6'6" tall and with a muscular build and he was posted thre as there was a large influx of "Pikeys" in The

Fens during the fruit picking season and they were always brawling outside the local pub. Well this particular night as they spilled out in their usual fashion, they caught the sight of N the new policeman on duty and holding a pick axe handle and with both hands banging it on the road to test its strength! That was enough and N never had any more problems with them.

My first sight of him was when I was in the rear yard of Kings Lynn police station one morning, I saw this Police Mini Van with shit (mud) up to the gunwales parked by the petrol pump. In the rear I could see two gun dogs, a shotgun, rifle and an array of wildfowler gear and then the figure of N striding down the back steps with the petrol book and key in his large hand he was in full uniform complete with cap and hair that went way past his collar and he was wearing waders! Many years later I saw him at Swaffham Police Station when he was The Force Rural Surveillance Officer or "CROPS" man (like DC John Fordham the "Met" under cover officer stabbed to death by Kenneth Noye) N showed me his gear and it was just like an "SAS" survival pack, he had a full army camouflage outfit and a white snow camouflage outfit and amongst all of the other items he had a large hunting knife and a stun gun; now that has described the man who Fred Calvert took on.

The only time that Fred was lost for words was with N. In those days before the Crown Prosecution Service (CPS) Fred was the Prosecutor at Kings Lynn and he was going through a file of N's of a man who he had arrested for being drunk. N stated in his report in the conclusion of his evidence the words *"In my opinion the man was drunk."* Now the only person who can give opinion in court is an Expert Witness and the definition states *"An expert is a witness, who by virtue of education, training, skill, or experience, is believed to have knowledge in a particular subject beyond that of the average person, sufficient that others may officially and legally rely upon the witness's specialized, scientific, technical or other, opinion about an evidence or fact issue within the scope of their experience."*

Fred sent N report back endorsed in red ink. "PC M *"How can you say, in your opinion when you are not an expert on the matter?"* N's reply *"Sir having been a guardsman, a heavy drinker with experience of street life and having a conviction for drunkenness myself I claim to have some knowledge of the subject."* The file was submitted and the man convicted and Fred was a wiser man.

During this year The Metropolitan Police Headquarters moved from Scotland Yard, Victoria Embankment where it had been since the Victorian era and the famous telephone number Whitehall 1212 to New Scotland Yard, 10 Broadway, London SW1, which I was to visit on several occasions from 1988 to 1991.

On Wednesday 19th July (My Grandmother's 80th birthday) I went to Headquarters for my fifteen month Interview with the ACC Mr Gordon Taylor. And he endorsed the occasion by inserting his signature in my pocket book.

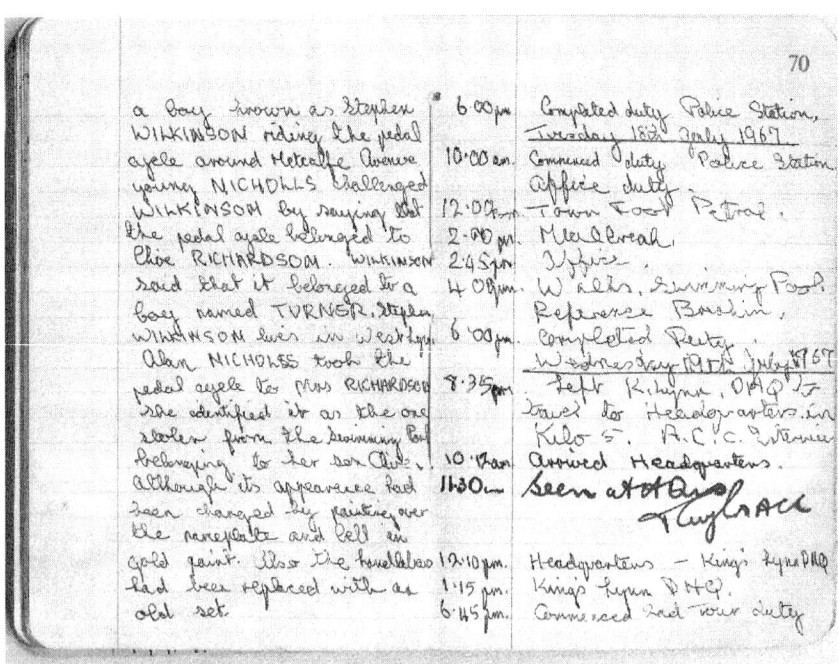

This was the last time that I visited the old Headquarters at 69 Thorpe Road, Norwich.

I also have a rarity from that era a point and signature from a Chief Inspector, "Taffy" Richards. He was always out and about on the beat and dealing with everything just the same as if he was an ordinary copper.

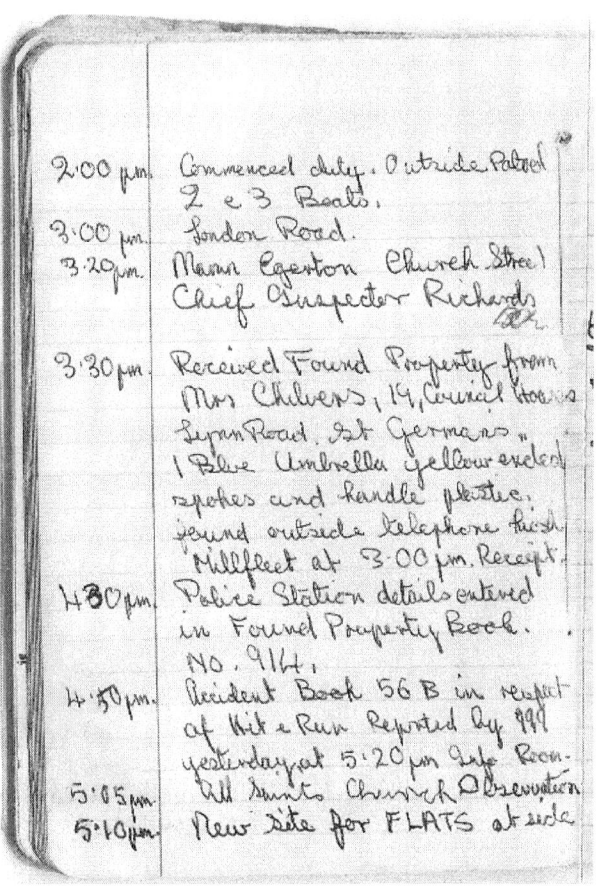

On August Bank Holiday Monday 28th August which was an allocated rest day I worked a late shift and was entitled to eight hours overtime and to claim eight hours paid overtime.

On Wednesday 30th August I went to Bagge Road and took a complaint from a Mother of two boys age five and eleven years that they together with a friend had been playing in woods near St Faith's Church when a man came up to the five year old and pulled down his trousers and played with the boys willy. The description was aged 20 – 25 years 5'6" to 7" slim build with large protruding teeth and large ears close to head, a long face with pointed chin and black scruffy hair. Details were obtained and the description circulated. At that time we did not have a collator's system of intelligence gathering otherwise this offence could have been put into the indecency index and later put to my man. However I found out that a local man had been remanded to Norwich Prison for indecency offences and he lived in Raleigh Road not a stones throw away from my case.

On Saturday 9th September I left DHQ to travel to Norwich Prison to interview this nearly 18 year old named AB who fitted the description given by the boys. At 10am I found that he was in the area at the material time, he said that he remembered the boys playing, but denied that anything had occurred. I said to him *"On the 31st of August this year at Kings Lynn you did indecently assault MS aged 5 years in Cemetery Drive Gaywood. You are not obliged to say anything, but anything you do say will be put into writing and may be given in evidence"* AB replied *"I didn't indecently assault him, I didn't even put a finger on him."* I then said *"I am satisfied that the evidence I have is sufficient to report you for Court appearance."* After a further caution AB replied *"I didn't even touch the boy."* I returned to Kings Lynn and completed a Process Report and completed duty at 4pm.

I was then on annual leave until I had my Final Continuation Course at RAF Debden in Essex from Monday 25th September to Friday 6th October, at this time it was home to the RAF Police Dog Section and it was nice to see them being put through their paces.

On Monday 9th October John Rosier gave us probationer's a demonstration on the now infamous "Alco test" breath testing device, prior to us using it out on the street and during the first half of the month I was back on a pedal cycle whizzing around the Gaywood and

South Wootton areas.

From Monday 16th October until Sunday 12th November I had my Traffic Attachment. I dealt with the normal traffic document stuff but I was a crime man and in the main it wasn't my scene. It wasn't all traffic though, on the first day I went as escort to a youth who had been remanded by Kings Lynn MC to Bramerton Remand Home near Norwich and en route back stopped at the old Headquarters.

Photograph Force fleet type of vehicles at Headquarters 69 Thorpe Road Norwich

Beat Motor Cycle, Traffic Patrol Motor Cycle, Beat Van, Section Officer's Car, Traffic Patrol Car and Divisional Van, all radio-equipped, 1967

## Traffic Department

### MOTOR PATROL PERSONNEL

Authorised Establishment — 1 Sergeant   62 Constables

Actual Strength
(18th August, 1967) — 1 Sergeant   52 Constables

#### DEREHAM DIVISION

Authorised:   8 Constables
Actual:
P.C. 138 Hawkes  )
P.C. 93 Williams ) Dereham
P.C. 99 Jones    )

P.C. 369 Irwin  )
P.C. 91 Cason   ) Fakenham
P.C. 89 Coker   )

P.C. 7 Myhill (m/cyclist) Dereham

#### DOWNHAM DIVISION

Authorised:   8 Constables
Actual:
P.C. 139 Bunting  )
P.C. 405 Bokenham ) Downham Market
P.C. 216 Crussell )

P.C. 373 Allinson )
P.C. 196 Rose     ) Swaffham

The undermentioned Beat Officer is authorised to drive Patrol Cars when required to do so for relief purposes:—

P.C. ___ Shepherd at Swaffham

#### ATTLEBOROUGH DIVISION

Authorised:   10 Constables
Actual:
P.C. 198 Brown  )
P.C. 362 Horley ) Attleborough
P.C. 410 Tickle )

P.C. 131 Davies    )
P.C. 181 Gross     ) Wymondham
P.C. 453 Tiddenham )

P.C. 160 Green   )
P.C. 187 Whitaker) Harleston

#### NORTH WALSHAM DIVISION

Authorised:   10 Constables
Actual:
P.C. 265 Moore   )
P.C. 193 Collins ) North Walsham
P.C. 3 Allen     )

P.C. 108 Powell )
P.C. 106 Kent   ) Stalham
P.C. 405 Wells  )

P.C. 57 Brown    )
P.C. 150 Burgess ) Holt

- 2 -

**NORWICH DIVISION**

Authorised: 11 Constables
Actual:
P.C. 84 Taylor )
P.C. 357 Riches ) Norwich
P.C. 191 Merchant )

P.C. 329 Dowle ) Acle
P.C. 112 Elflett )

P.C. 115 Hadlett )
P.C. 363 Gadby ) Loddon
P.C. 304 Jacob )

P.C. 76 Smith ) W/Cyclists - Norwich
P.C. 306 Bailey )

The undermentioned Beat Officer is authorised to drive Motor Cars when required to do so for relief purposes.

P.C. 297 Dean - Acle

**BANNINGHAM DIVISION**

Authorised: 7 Constables
Actual:
P.C. 100 Platten )
P.C. 291 Hardinant ) Bersingham
P.C. 8 Clarke )

P.C. 345 Askew )
P.C. 35 Saunders ) Docking
P.C. 143 Gibson )

P.C. 297 Higson (W/Cyclist) Hunstanton

**KING'S LYNN DIVISION**

Authorised: 1 Sergeant; 7 Constables
Actual:
Sergeant Mason
P.C. 208 Waters
P.C. 103 Brookes
P.C. 81 Green
P.C. 344 Stone
P.C. 419 Jordan

P.C. 417 Davenant (W/Cyclist)

Then the next day I was on a 4pm to 12mn duty and at 11.10pm we were sent by HQ Information Room to a *"Bleep Mat"* sounding at the premises of Frederick K Pidgeon, London Road, King's Lynn. On arrival we found my "A" Relief colleagues had already arrived and made two arrests for burglary; these we conveyed to Kings Lynn Nick. A bleep mat was a rubber mat with wires which led to a battery powered radio device which could be hidden under a carpet or rug of premises that were regularly being broken into or there was good intelligence that it was to be broken into somewhere in the force area. When trodden on it activated and emitted a series of bleeps like Morse code which went out as a radio signal on the force radio frequency. The HQIR staff then checked from the series of bleeps which premises it was coming from.

Whilst on night shift at 2.50am on 19th October I went to Wisbech Police Station and from there escorted HM the Queens Royal Mail van, firstly to Kings Lynn GPO and then to Sandringham House, arriving at 5.45am .

Thinking about it now and upon looking back, the Queen and Prince Phillip must have been getting ready to celebrate their 20th Wedding Anniversary on 20th November, as it was unusual for them to visit at that time and Sandringham was one of the few places where they could *"let their hair down."* The Queen would normally go around in a coat, wellies and headscarf and walk through the woods on her own with her dogs or even down to Dersingham. Prince Philip would dress like a gamekeeper and would either go down to Wolferton Marshes or would practise his horse and carriage skills that he became famous for.

They had married at Westminster Abbey on the 20th of November, 1947 she HRH Princess Elizabeth and he Lieutenant Phillip Mountbatten the Son of Prince Andrew of Greece, after which he was bestowed with the title of HRH Prince Phillip. Earlier in that year from February to May Princess Elizabeth had accompanied her Father, His Majesty King George V1 and her Mother, Her Majesty Queen Elizabeth on their

Royal Tour of South Africa, Rhodesia and other countries since re-named and during the tour she celebrated her 21st Birthday.

My Father, Flight Lieutenant Thomas Buchanan Clark as previously mentioned was a Signaller/Wireless Operator on *"The King's Flight"* which had just reformed after World War 11 and was on that tour with The Royal Family as well as others during his service. Following George V1's death the unit was re-named *"The Queen's Flight."*

Author's note: HM the Queen and HRH the Duke of Edinburgh celebrated their Blue Sapphire 65 year's anniversary on 20/11/2012 and at the time of writing due their Platinum anniversary in 18 months time on 20/11/2017.

On Wednesday 25th October from 10am to 1pm I was at our monthly probation class during which at 10:30am there was a visit from Her Majesty's Inspector of Constabulary. Then at 4pm I went on a late shift until midnight in the patrol car and today I decided to do a *"Traffic Blitz"* on some of the local "Mr Bigs" active elements who were getting away with crime. At 4.15pm on London Road I saw a green Bedford van being driven by a man who I recognised as B from his photo on our *"Criminal of the Week"* poster, there was no tax disc displayed on the vehicle. At 4.30pm I went to an address in St Edmundsbury Road and parked outside unattended was the same vehicle. I knocked on the door of the house and B's Wife answered it and I said *"Is B in?"* She replied *"Yes he's here"* he came to the door and for the first time met B, he was the main receiver of stolen property in West Norfolk together with his family and had built up a small empire of organised crime. They were also involved with gangs from Wisbech, Peterborough and further afield in the Region. We were destined to be involved with each other for the next 15 years mainly in a village outside Lynn.

At this time whilst he was living in North Lynn he was getting away with buying up vehicles and not registering them so that when they were involved in crime and abandoned there was no come back on him. So any sighting placing him or others with a particular vehicle could prove invaluable in the future, I decided to be a long term thorn in his side.

He said *"What the f...ing hell do you want?"* I said *"Hello B can I see you outside for a minute"* and then near to the vehicle I said *"Have you got a current vehicles excise licence for this?"* He replied *"No I haven't got any f...ing tax"* He then said *"F..k off, I'm not going to have any of it"* and with that he went back into the house and slammed the door.

Back in the 1950s he had been running a brothel from the back of a van parked on Tuesday Market Place near the Maids Head pub when he was busted he got off at Magistrates over a law technicality which led to Appeal and Counter Appeal and it became a bench mark *"Stated Case."*

We then went on our way around this family and their associates, all in all we uncovered quite a few document offences which would later sting their pockets after appearing at Court and they became more respectful and behaved themselves in the main when I was about. I caught up with B again on Friday 27th October when at 7pm he was driving the same van along London Road, I stopped him and I said to him *"You will be reported for not having a vehicles excise licence on the two occasions on the 25th of October and again this evening."* After caution he replied *"All right fair enough."* he elected to produce his other documents at Kings Lynn.

At 7.25pm on Friday 3rd November whilst on 4 -12pm shift I attended the scene of an RTA at Jubilee Bank, Clenchwarton (in those days it was part of the A17 road before the bypass was built) I discovered that there had been a 3 vehicle shunt and a Black Mk 1 Ford Zephyr had driven off. A quarter of an hour earlier a colleague had tried to stop it on Hardwick Road, but it sped off. Enquiries were made to trace the car and driver and on Tuesday 7th November at Kings Lynn "Nick" I interviewed a man from Fakenham who was a disqualified driver who I then reported for failing to stop for a police officer, driving whilst disqualified 2 occasions, driving without due care and attention and failing to stop after an RTA. I was to later deal with him for many more offences and had Tom Humphrey our vehicle examiner inspect his car which was in a dangerous condition it had 11" play on the steering wheel. As he didn't stop driving he appeared at court on the 10th of November and was disqualified for a further 6 years.

He having failed his traffic career turned to crime; at 5.15pm on Wednesday 22nd November I was in Kings Lynn Cattle Market keeping observation for a shoplifter who had stolen a pair of designer sunglasses from an opticians and at 6.30pm he turned up near a Mini containing two other suspects all three were nicked and the property recovered. On Friday 24th November I went as prisoner escort to HMP Norwich at that time we had Bert Farrell as our new civilian driver. I also did duties with Arthur *'Sammy'* Crookes who was 6'6" and built like an outside toilet, he had been a Spitfire pilot in World War 11; they must have used a shoe horn to get him in and out of the tiny cockpit!

During this year I was regularly on patrol with a PC who was later to transfer with me onto "B" Relief. He was married and lived in a police house and he painted the ceiling of one of his rooms Black, like the night sky complete with Moon and Stars. He was later to be involved in criminal activities after he moved to another Section.

It was during this time that I started having trouble with some of the local yobs who were also active criminals because they were associating with two of my sisters. On Tuesday 28th November I was back on the cycle beat on late turn when at around 10pm I saw a Green Ford Thames Van parked at the Millfleet and as I approached on foot I saw that it contained some of the elements referred to previously. One of the occupants shouted out *"Watch out look who's coming, it's that cunt Clark!"* I stopped near the van and said to him *"Stop swearing."* Another who had been sitting in the rear of the van, got out and stood with his 6'3" frame intimidating in front of me blocking my path and leaned forward and said *"Shut your mouth and fuck off you big cunt!"* I said to them both *"Who's *going to make me?"* the first one said *"We will get you when you are in civvies, not when you're hiding behind that uniform"* the other said *"Your days are numbered, you'll have to go home sometime and when you do I'll knock your legs from under you so that you won't be able to ride a bike."* I then spoke to the driver who was amenable and he told the others to shut up, they took no notice and the tall one pushed me and knocked my bike over. I then forcibly arrested him as he was struggling and still swearing, he was later charged with obstruction under Highways Act 1959 and using obscene and indecent language contrary to Kings Lynn Borough Byelaws and bailed to Kings Lynn Magistrates' Court KLMC for the 1st of December.           .

At KLMC on that date I reported the other one for using obscene and indecent language, the Magistrates adjourned the case for a fortnight pending enquiries. They were both eventually convicted and although I still had dealings with them for crime, no further hostilities were levelled at me.

During night shift if the type of people just mentioned were out and about and up to no good eyeing up places to burgle, the mere sight of policemen going around *"on the ball"* was enough to deter them and they would leave it until a certain Relief were on nicknamed *"Who Cares Who Wins"* and have a spree. We gave them this title after bastardising the SAS Motto *"Who Dares Wins."*

I would do my foot patrol after parading and be out sharp by 10.10pm and leave no door handle unturned or window checked until I had done the complete lockup property on my beat. There was hardly a week that went by without me finding one that the staff had forgotten to lock up, I would go in to say a tobacconists I had found unlocked and phone the key holder from there and out they would come red faced and apologetic; it's a good job that I didn't have a bad character otherwise I could have cleared the store out..

Some misdemeanours which I got up to on nights after property check and the town had gone to sleep:

(a) Was to unscrew one of the orange plastic flashing Belisha beacons from the "Zebra Crossing" in Church Street and the shift would assemble around 3am and we would play football on the Saturday Market Place.
(b) When Norway sent over the large Christmas tree to the town and it was put up on SMP, it was decked with different coloured 40 watt light safety bulbs; we would unscrew some of the lower ones and post them through letterboxes.
(c) There was an International Stores in High Street just up from Wenn's Hotel and the staff would pack Kellogg's' Cornflake boxes up against the large plate glass window, I learnt (through boredom) that if you shook the glass for a while it set up a motion which knocked the cornflakes down onto the floor. They didn't learn though as the next night they would be re-stacked in the window.

During December we were issued with new Force Warrant Cards ready for next year's amalgamation, these had the bearer's photograph for the first time. I completed a late turn on Christmas Eve and celebrated my 22nd birthday on the 25th.

On Saturday 30th December I was again on early turn and on 4 beat cycle patrol in South Lynn, when at 6.30am I found a break at South Lynn Community Centre, I requested CID and SOCO as the point of entry was the same when it was last broken into. On that occasion the offender had excreted on the floor and then trod in it leaving a perfect impression of his trainer soles and he was convicted of the burglary on that evidence; you could say that he dropped himself in the shit!

As the year closed we were looking forward to major changes with force amalgamation, the closure of beats and the introduction of Unit Beat Policing, together with new radio communications and a Collator with a local intelligence system.

End of an era Chief Constable Peter Garland and senior officers of the Force taken outside the old Headquarters at 69 Thorpe Road in November 1967. Fred Calvert is the first left on the front row.

## Chapter Three

## "From Heartbeat to Z Cars 1968 – 1973"

### 1968

During 1966 the Home Secretary Roy Jenkins announced large scale amalgamation of Police Forces throughout England and Wales, amongst his proposals was the amalgamation of Norfolk Constabulary with Norwich City Police and Great Yarmouth Borough Police. This was scheduled to take place on the 1st April, 1967 but postponed until the 1st of January 1968 to coincide with the opening of the long planned new County Headquarters at Martineau Lane, Norwich, however it was further delayed until the 1st of April, 1968 with Peter Garland becoming Chief Constable on the 24th of February of the new amalgamated Force; so for Norfolk Constabulary read *"Norfolk Joint Police."* The new Force Badge was made up to include the top half of The Rampant Lion the original Norfolk Constabulary crest and the tail of a Great Yarmouth Bloater and The Norwich City Gates. I don't know what idiot designed that one! We were stuck with this new force name Joint and badge design for a further five years *"Carve Up"* springs to mind!

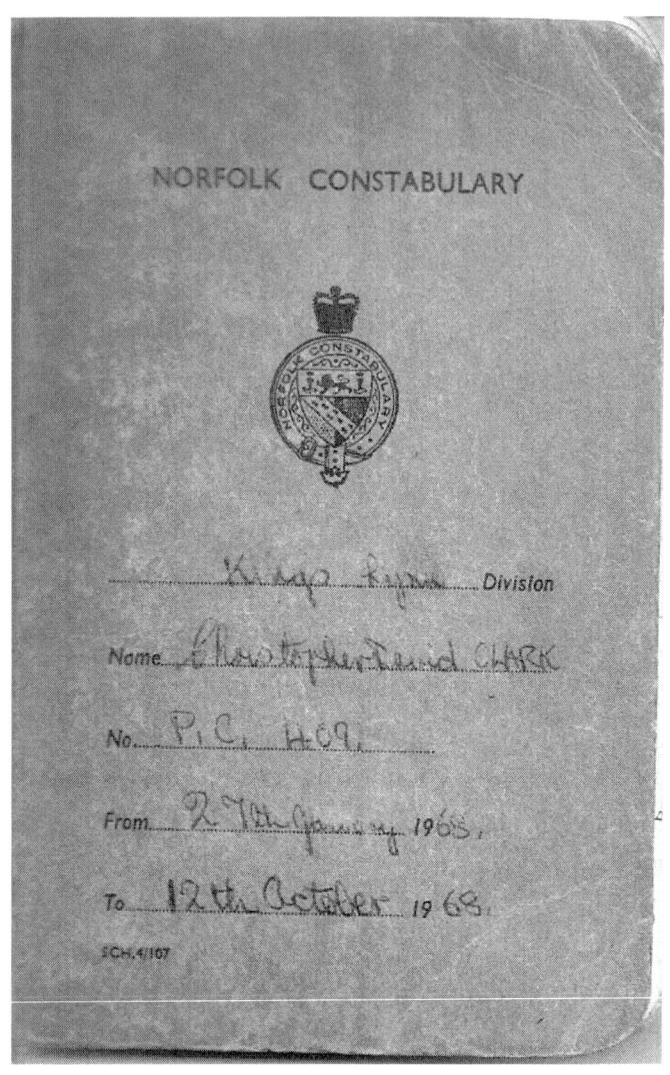

*My last Norfolk Constabulary issue Pocket Book*

*Norfolk Joint Police 1968-1974*

Chris Clark

*Our new Headquarters at Martineau Lane*

# Norfolk Joint Police Force Establishment

# Jan1968

APPENDIX TO GENERAL ORDER NO. 1/68 DATED 1ST JANUARY, 1968

## NOMINAL ROLL
### NORFOLK JOINT POLICE

|  |  |
|---|---|
| Chief Constable | F. P. C. Garland Esq. |
| Deputy Chief Constable | C. G. Taylor Esq. |
| Chief Superintendents | G. W. Bartram |
| | F. Calvert, M.B.E. |
| | A. George |
| | H. P. Haverson |
| | * R. Lester |
| | J. Muldoon |
| | C. G. Reynolds |
| | F. D. Slack |
| | H. Spencer |
| Superintendents Class I | D. W. Beamis |
| | F. Lilley |
| | H. J. New |
| | S. G. Shaw |
| Superintendent Class II | S. Burton |
| Chief Inspectors | * N. Ball |
| | D. J. Benns |
| | P. L. Finbow |
| | R. W. Goodings |
| | W. C. L. Richards |
| | J. Southgate |
| Temporary Chief Inspectors | * J. H. E. Blake |
| | A. J. Bocking |
| | H. J. Green |
| | A. B. Hardy |
| | T. A. J. Hatchett |
| | A. J. Jermy |
| | * C. P. Nourse |
| | D. W. B. Pardon |
| | H. F. G. Reynolds |
| | T. Smith |
| | A. Turner |
| | J. Wright |
| Inspectors | W. Aherne |
| | M. B. Ayres |
| | * L. J. Bennett |
| | T. Braithwaite |
| | * R. H. Brighton |
| | G. Brown |
| | R. G. C. Browne |
| | A. Buck |
| | R. M. Butty |
| | A. W. Chisholm |
| | H. J. Churchyard |
| | R. Cordy |
| | G. Dunn |
| | * H. Elliott |
| | * W. C. Fleming |
| | H. Garrett |
| | L. E. Heavens |
| | C. Mileham |
| | W. Nelson |
| | * G. Neville |
| | H. E. Nobbs |
| | W. Painter |
| | C. Parker |

Inspectors (Cont'd)

Addison, W. G.
Allen, F.
Ashworth, G. R.
Atkins, P. M. G.
Baker, H. T. F.
Barnes, J. P.
Bartram, C. A.
* Bass, R.
Bell, P. K.
Bellamy, M. F.
Blake, M. J.
Brook, D. H. R.
* Brown, R. W.
Bull, K.
Bunn, C.
Bunn, D. R.
Bussey, E. J.
Calthorpe, J.
* Caspall, H. F.
Cass, J. S.
Catchpole, A. J.
Chenery, J. M.
Clutterham, R.
Cockerill, J. J.
Cockerill, J. D.
Cook, F. J.
Cox, A. D.
Cross, R.
Curry, A. C.
Danny, B. S.
Dixon, M. V.
Downes, J. G.
Dye, D. J.
Dye, G. E.
* Dye J. E.
Eagle, J.
Edmunds, A. J.
Engledow, D. J.
Farman, J. P.
Fleming, P. S.
Francis, P. S.
Freeman, A. E.
Furlonger, S.

J. Riches
R. Scothern
V. E. Shirley
H. A. Shurety
R. Spalding
A. J. Stevenson
J. B. Strange
R. Taylor
G. W. Ward
D. Warren
L. N. B. Woolf

Woman Inspector — C. E. Petty

### SERGEANTS

Garton, R. J.
Green, C.
Grist, K. A.
Hall, F. H. C.
Hardy, J.
Harris, L.
Harrison, D. T.
Haydon, R. J.
Heard, R. C. E.
Herrington, A. A.
Hipperson, R. G. E.
Howes, H. W.
Hubbard, B. W.
Husam, N. E.
Hunt, J. A.
Jolly, F. C.
* Jones, T. D.
July, G. P.
Knapp, A.
Kybird, B. C. W.
Luke, B. J.
Lanham, A. W.
Lester, J.
Lewis, F. C.
Lines, R. J.
* Looke, A. J.
Mansfield, J. R.
Markham B.
Marriot, W. R.
Marshall, D. B.
Martin, D. H.
* McLennan, J. C.
Miles, E. L.
Monument, A. G.
* Moore, K. P.
* Morgan, S. E. D.
Morson, M.
* Mutimer, J. W.

Nash, P.

Orriss, J.

- 1 -
- 2 -

124 Dingle, D. H.
125 Spanton, H. E.
126 Waters, E. S. J.
127 Clarke, P.
*128 Matsell, J. A. W.
129 Duthie, A. E.
130 Day, R. P.
131 Davies, D. P.
*132 Wright, R. C.
133 Hutchinson, M. D.
134 Rix, M. V.
135 Dye, W. E.
136 Seaman, B. C.
137 Horn, R. S.
138 Hawkes, H. L.
139 Bunting, W. R.
140 Hewitt, E. G.
141 Codling, N. J.
142 Smith, N. A.
143 Gibson, T. D.
144 Gould, C. L.
145 Tyrrall P. F.
*146 Lakey, A. J.
*147 Farnham, M. J.
148 Smith, J. J.
149 Gilmore, R. H. J.
150 Curson, J. M.
151 Taylor, A.
152 Holmes, C. A.
153 Reay, A.
154 Graves, A.
155 Martell, G. R.
156 Bayfield, C. G.
157 Hales, P. K.
158 Harcourt, J. A.
159 Smith, P. F.
160 Green, R. E. L.
161 Edwards, A. J.
162 Harris, P. A.
163 Worby, E. P.
164 Riches, F. J.
165 Willis, M. C.
166 Langley, R. W.
167 Bates, P. D. J. P.
168 Jermy, R. F.
169 Painter, J. F. W.
170 Sheldrake, K. G.
171 ███ P. P.
172 Page, J.
*173 Valleley, P.
174 Eastaugh, T. H. A.
175 Hammond, E. C.
176 Dellow, L. M.
177 Flint, W.
178 Marshall, G. C.
179 Rout, P.
180 Airs, R. E.
181 Gross, J. D.
182 Crookes, A. S.
183 Barrs, L. C.
184
185 King, B. J.
186 Parke, B. R.
187 Whitaker, C. M.
188 Platten, R. B.
*189 Napthan, G. W. A.
190 Yaxley, I. W.
191 Merchant, G. R.
192 Elwin, C. J.
193 Collins, D. C.

194 Harvey, H. F.
195 Marsters, C. W.
196 Rose, R.
197 Pendall, R. L.
198 Brown, L. G.
199 Bullen, J. W.
200 Webb, A. N.
201 Law, T. D.
202 Lamb, P. C.
203 Alexander, M. G.
204 Atkins, R. P.
205 Lovewell, T. R.
206 Garman, S. D.
*207 Wallace, G. A. B.
208 Waters, D. G. B.
209 Craske, R. K.
210 Elliott D. J.
*211 Self, J. C.
212 Brooking, G. J.
*213 Booking, F. T.
214 Thompson, M.
215 Nash, A. J.
216 Crussell, D. J.
217 Bruce, R. J.
218 Bray, J. W. B.
219 Wood, C. B.
220 Bracey, A. E.
221 MacDonald, J. H.
222 Nunn, R. J.
223 Mayes, R. W.
*224 Boothby, D. E.
225 Daniel, R. T.
226 Gromett, M. F.
227 Walls, C. A. M.
228 Roberts, A. W.
*229 Colman, R. A. J.
230 Pimlott, D.
231 Pegden, R. V.
232 Cooke, J. R.
233 Elliff, B. E.
234 Pearce, T. L.
235 Dawes, J. T.
236 Hall, C. J.
237 Dingle, W. G.
238 Smithdale, D. L.
239 Baker, J. E.
*240 Coady, P. M.
241 Webster, A. W.
242 Nimmo, C. F.
243 Hood, R. S.
244 Bennett C. R.
245 Bird, A. S.
246 Golding, H. D.
247 Garwood, M. R.
248 Johnson, D. P.
*249 Hobart, G. H. M.
250 Warnes, B. J.
251 Auckland, D. J.
252 Dye, B. L.
253 Taylor, R.
254 Bailey, B. J.
255 Scott, J. A.
256 Wiseman, G.
257 Dean, W. T.
258 Dennison, R. J.
259 Wyatt, D. N.
260 Glister, T. G.
261 Bane, R. T.
262 Sibley, W. A.
263 Woodhouse, S. G.
264 Harper, A.

265 Moore, B. J.
266 Hooper, D.
267 Dunton, K.
268 Thompson, F. F.
269 New, G. H.
270 Ward, V. C.
271 Catling, G.
272 Thompson, J. F.
273 Syer, A. R.
274 Brown, C. J.
275 Edwards, P. S. W.
276 Cooper, H. C.
277 Lummis D. S.
278 Beeston, R.
*279 Spurgeon, A. T.
280 King, R. A. B.
281 Roberts, A. G. P.
282 Morris B. A.
283 Newby, S. R.
284 Barrett, G. A. P.
285 Wild, M. C.
286 Garwood, T. C.
287 Higson, P. C.
288 Kerrison, B. G.
289 Johnson, B. G.
290 Hardiment, B. R.
291 Sturman, T. C.
292 Scott, P. M.
293 Perry, G. G.
294 Lacey, S. G.
295 Beart, C. W.
296 Stockwin, A. D.
297 Stevens, W. G.
298 Cordy, A. F.
299 Allan, D. A.
300 Mundford, R. H.
*301 Richardson, B. W.
302 Bearman, T. V.
303 Smith, E. G.
304 Elliott, R. V.
305 Symonds, G. H.
306 Bailey, J. R.
307 Rowley, J. D.
308 Moore, N. C.
309 Burgess, H. W. G.
310 Feller, P. S.
311 Dye, G.
312 High, M. W.
313 Greenacre, B. T.
314 Harrold, C. A.
315 Johnstone, D. E. A.
316 Hobart, D. P.
317 Burrell, B. M.
318 Blaza, T. G.
319 Bunton, H.
320 Mackley, N. A.
*321 Humphrey, T. H.
322 Merrikin, E. G.
323 Hewer, A. B.
324 Finbow, T. P.
325 Otty, K. A.
326 Guymer, L. J.
327 Buttolph, R. J.
328 Jonkinson, G. G.
329 Dowle, P. O.
330 Nourse, J. C.

331 Church, D. F.
332 Ramsey, C. J.
333 Lines, G. D.
334 Halls, A. W.
335 Hazelwood, C. D.
336 Leys, J. G. F.
337 McGee A. L.
338 Norwood, P. A.
339 Dent, J. R.
340 Jarvis, D. A.
341 Hooke, G. N.
342 Chiddick, D. H.
343 Beck, A. J.
344 Stone, J. E.
345 Asker, M. J. E.
346 Barnes, D. W.
*347 Cole, M. E.
*348 Walker, B. G.
349 Lawson, D.
350 Hewitt, L. D.
351 Neave, L. H.
352 Thetford, S. D.
353 Goodrum, W. C.
354 Turner, J. S. J.
355 Johnson, R. D.
356 Emblem, N. C. J.
357 Riches, T. E.
358 Gibbs, D. L.
359 Speakman, J. T.
*360 Hansell, J. T.
361 Barley, G. W.
362 Morley, E. F.
363 Cadby, D. T.
364 Jacob, A. P.
365 Elmer, G. A.
366 Lee, M. V.
367 Manship, K. J.
368 Goodrum, M. S.
369 Irwin, M. J. E.
370 Charlton, P. F.
371 Sutherland, M. C.
372 Chapman, G. W.
373 Allinson, G.
374 Moore, C. R.
375 Wrigglesworth, A.
376 Norton, B. C.
*377 Gilbert, N. A.
378 Ralph, J. O.
379 Davey, K. W.
380 Davey, K. C.
381 Bayes, H. L.
382 Danvers, B. E.
383 Thompson, D. J.
384 Jarvis, J. I.
385 Humphrey, R. J.
386 Farrow, W. J.
387 Moore, D. G.
388 Howell, R. B.
389 McCarter, B. L.
390 Hall, K. J.
391 Partridge, D. L.
392 Twiss, P. J.
393 Harrison, I. J.
394 Shooter, G.
395 Griffin, P. A.
396 Osborne, B. L.
397 Fox, C. J.
398 Mercer, J. M.

- 7 -

399 Barker, N.
400 Bannister, A. V.
401 Steward, A. W.
402 Youngs, M. I.
403 Nicholls, B.
404 Page, C.
405 Bokenham, E. A.
406 Wells, R. A.
407 Hubbard, D. R. A.
408 Finlayson, D. D.
409 Clark, C. D.
410 Tickle, K.
411 Halliday, K.
412 Buckle, G. C.
413 Coupland, H. R.
414 Pointer, R. S.
415 Jordan, I. G.
416 Stone, S.
417 Thompson, A. T.
*418 Pinches, R. C.
419 Addison, R. W. P.
420 Bond, S. F.
421 Hayman, N. R.
*422 Sandall, R. E.
423 Hughes, D. J.
424 Young, B. J.
425 Taylor, A. L.
426 Diaper, D. J.
427 Garner, C. C.
428 Marshall, R. G.
429 Spurgeon, D. R.
430 Sumser, B. A.
431 Ward, J. R.
432 Waters, M. J.
433 Blower, N. P.
*434 Ogden, B.
435 Johnson, C. A.
436 Tratt, D. A.
437 Thompson, P. J.
438 Warnes, B. W.
439 Wilmore, P. C.
440 Keeley, P. J.
441 Wheeler, P. J.
442 White, P. A.
443 Bone, A. J.
444 Beveridge, J. D.
445 Sissen, R. J.
446 Stuart, D. L.
447 Stevens, D. G.
448 Wolham, R. F.
449 Wilkinson, D. L.
450 Dewing, A. J.
451 Doy M. J.
452 Bernard, E.
453 Tuddenham, A. A.
454 Mitcham, R. W.
455 Smalley, R. J.
456 Conroy, L. A.
457 Bean, D. G.
*458 Humphruy, J. C.
459 Whitbread, G. M. N.
460 Adkins, B.
461 Goldsmith, P. A.
462 Robey, A. E.
463 Laker, I. R. R.
464 Tinder, M. F.
465 Jackson, P. J.
466 Mallett, G. A.
467 Clingo, M. J.
468 Gooderson, R. N. T.
469 Calton, H. J.
470 Rice, J. L.

471 Edgeway, B. R.
472 Phipp, S. J. D.
473 Ford, T.
474 Thrower, J. R.
475 Minns, B. A.
476 Hollis, R. D.
477 Smith, B.
478 Jobson, C. F.
479 Edwards, B. R.
480 Dean, R. S.
481 Howard, R. A.
482 Johnson, I. R.
483 Lynch, R. J.
484 Swatman, K.
485 Collin D. A.
486 Wade, B. J.
487 Mann, E. G.
488 Thurston, T. J.
489 Townsend, J. C.
490 Parsons, I. J.
491 Potter, R. M.
492 Durham I. R.
493 Hilling, A. J.
494 Barton-Smith D. J.
495 Hopkin, D. G.
496 Emerson, P. L.
497 Buller, P. R.
498 Witard, J. C.
499 Fox, R. J.
500 Buckingham, I.
501 Jones, M. F.
502 Bartram, P. T.
503 Savage, J. D.
504 Legood, M. A.
505 Oxley, R. J.
506 Gooch, H. B. P.
507 Robinson, A.
508 Taylor, I. G.
509 Hackett, H. W.
510 Oakley, A. F.
511 Driver, D. F.
512 Harrington, J. S.
513 Roberts, J. C.
514 Blackburn, A. J.
515 Seaman, D. F.
516 Hoyle, F.
517 Burton, K. R.
518 Gooding, F. A. J.
519 Nelson, J. E.
520 Taylor, L. D. A.
521 Jennis, L. J.
522 Paterson, J. A.
523 Burton, T. F.
*524 Halifax, J.
525 Godge, N. H.
526 Balls, N. V.
527 Allen D. J.
528 Ling, C. E.
529 Audley, C. F.
530 Bishop, K. A.
531 O'Malley, J.
532 Calder, J. J.
533 Smith, A. J.
534 Spencer, C. M.
*535 Burrage, R.
536 Gray, A. G.
537 McBride, D. V.
538 Dickerson, E. A.
539 Warner, I. D.
540 Powley, R. A.
541 Drewry, W. A.
542 Heard, M. A.

- 8 -

543 MacLean, M. F.
544 Donovan, P.
545 Craske, A. J.
546 Peake, G. A.
547 Taylor, R. C.
548 Harvey, J. M.
549 Johnson, D. P.
550 Gibbs, J. W.
551 Edmunds, A. G.
552 Bishop, C. A.
553 Banner, K. W.
554 Edwards
555 Bullock, D. A.
556 Wiseman, C.
*557 Smith, I. C.
558 Crisp, R. J.
559 Goodman, J.
560 Robinson, B. J.
561 Sweeles, B. S. A.
562 ....
563 Wilkinson, A.
564 Edwards, R.
*565 Lines, M. D.
566 Allard, G. R.
567 Clubon, J. C.
568 Fairweather, A. H.
569 Colman, J. E.
570 Pillar, J. A.
571 Wells, N. P.
572 Middleton, N. J.
573 Nicholson, A. D.
574 Mileham, B. A.
575 Clarke, D. J.
576 Houghton, K. E.
577 Griffin, A. A.
578 Rawling, B.
579 Fenn, B. L.
580 Houghton, L. S.
581 Hewitt, E. G. W.
582 Higgs, S. F.
583 Wilson, R.
584 Millican, J. B.
*585 Sharman, N.
*586 Lissamore, L. J.
587 Medle, G. T. W.
588 Thurling, D. B.
589 Starling, P. G.
590 Attwood, R.
591 Bayfield, M. T.
592 Clark, R. J.
593 Abrey, T. G.
594 Whittaker, A. M.
595 Goffin, M. T.
596 Hart, J. G.
597 Canwell, P. M.
598 George, F.
599 Hurrch, R. C.
600 Walton, T.
601 George, R. N.
*602 Allen, G. F.
603 Read, J. W.
*604 Kirby, D. G.
605 McDonnell B. R. J.
606 Day, R. W.
607 Cubitt, H. A.
*608 Graham, K.
609 Plume, D.
610 Smith, A. A.
611 Steer, D.

612 Hume, V. G.
613 Groombridge, J. W. G.
614 Crowe, K. A.
615 Brown, J. G. A.
616 Joyce, K. E.
617 Garnham, N. F. G.
618 Skipper, E. C.
619 Granvanell, F. J.
620 Bell, M. E.
621 Allard, D. R.
622 Taylor, A. G.
623 Decks, I. R.
624 Nunn, S. G.
625 Woodhouse, V. F. E.
626 Kent, W. D.
627 Mitcham, G. G.
628 Wilson, S. J.
629 Burgess, P. A.
630 Spelman, E. C.
631 Crisp, R. J. H.
632 Walker, P. J.
633 Paul, J.
634 Rouse, B. L.
635 Wilson, S. R.
*636 Wiseman, M. B. M.
637 Sabberton, F. W.
638 Woodhouse, D. G.
639 Roberts, B. J.
640 Limmer, S. E.
641 Turner, A. J.
642 Joyner, R. J.
643 Elliot, P.
*644 Mancini, T. P.
645 Aukett, R. L.
646 Bartram, A. G.
647 ....
648 Brooks, R. J.
649 Kidgell, I. C.
650 Grapes, J. R.
651 McLaren, R. C. O.
652 Aldous, I. J.
653 Brand, J. W.
654 Little, W. E.
655 Dennis, K. R. A.
656 Reed, R. J.
657 Blyth, A. F.
658 Tyrrell, R. G.
659 Todder, T. E.
660 Oliver, J. E.
661 Butler, J. W.
662 Jessop, C.
663 Ford, B. G.
664 Dritcher, W. F.
*665 Mileham, E. J.
666 Reeve, D. S.
667 Huggins, A. C.
668 Leech, A. S.
*669 Wiggins, P. A.
670 Pearce, L.
671 Barrett, P.
672 Steward, E. J.
673 Postance, G. P.
674 ....
675 Fleming, R.
676 Hall, B. L. W.
*677 Hunt, D. G.
678 Huckle, L. F.
679 Greenwood, D. E.
680 Rowlands, D.
681 Hygrave, P. B.
682 ....

*683 Wright, N. S. C.
684 Thompson, K. R.
685 Russell, V. G.
686 MacRae, I. D.
687 Moore, T. R.
688 Porter, R. C.
689 Hooper, D. A.
690 Cant, D. F. J.
691 Seager, D. A.
692 Barnes, M. E.
693 Chatten, B. S.
694 Norton, R. W.
695 Allander, G. W.
696 O'Brien, W. D.
697 Green, J. W.
698 Lines, H. C.
699 King, P. J.
700 Tooke, P. C.
701 Savage, D. J.
702 Makins, P. M.
703 Everest, P. R.
704 Copeman, A. F.
705 Lightwing, D. P.
706 Thompson, H.
707 Lingwood, R. M.
708 Cook, R. R.
709 Kelly, C. W.
710 Goadwell, L. G.
711 Linstead, J. M.
712 Sharpe, N. J.
713 Bush, N. G. W.
714 Pickstone, A.
715 Wells, B. J.
716 Mallett, B. J.
717 O'Carroll, D. B.
718 Guymer, S. C.
*719 Leggett, M. T.
*720 Wilkinson R. C.

754 Mantle, O. A.
755 Cushion, P. A.
756 Pointin, B. F.
*757 Harding, L.
758 Mason, C. J.
759 Hare, S. N.
*760 Reid, G.
761 Jacklin, D.
*762 Daynes, G. A.
763 Clifford, C. T. H.
764 Henry, M. G.
765 Griffiths, D. J.
766 Johnson, N. I.
767 Perkins, J. C.
768 Brown, P.
769 Croyston, G. G.
770 Billingham, P. L.
771 James, F. R. J.
*772 Gilham, J. H.
773 Smith, A. B.
*774 Caner, T. E.
775 Butler, R. J. H.
776 Tooley, M. T.
777 Hanson, D.
778 Robinson, D. R.
779 Williams, D. T.
780 O'Brien, D. M.
781 Holman, J. F.
782 Hales, V. A.
783 Maxwell, P. M.
784 Williams, J. C.
785
786 Armes, R. T.
787 Loveday, A. B.
788 Pattison, D. C.
*789 Ross, D. G.
*790 London, G. E.
791 Maxim, T. A.

721 Burton-Pye, H. W. E.
722 Rowett, B. C.
723 Bacon, L. J.
724 Pask, J. D.
725 Dowe, H. J.
726 Abbs, A. F.
727 Leggett, D. C.
*728 Brown, A.
*729 Jermany, V. R.
730 Marten, C. H.
731 Abley, L.
732 Gillespie, F. J.
733 Bishop, D. L.
734 Haste, G. D.
*735 Allen, D. J.
736 McAuley, J. B.
737 Goodenough, N. J.
738 Cox, A. S.
*739 Bull, K. J.
740 Hazelton, B. L.
741 Chinn, D. W.
742 Grinner, J. H.
743 Wilson, D. R. A.
744 Tovey, R. N.
*745 Metcalf, B.
746 Poulter, A. F.
*747 Harman, H. G.
748
749 Oakley, A. F.
750 Hill, R. A.
751
752 Butcher, B. D.
753 Mortram, R. J.

792 Fulton, J.
793 Jones, D. R.
794 Frost-Smith, G. A.
795 Sheppard, T. V. J.
796 Hodge, T.
797 Standing, P. E.
798 Young, P. W.
799 Goodson, M. G.
800 Roberts, R. J.
801 George, T. R.
802 Wilkinson, C. G.
803 Anderson, A. P.
804 Roe, R. K. E.
805 Bloomfield, J. S.
806 Harper, D. J.
807 Fletcher, I. S.
808 Jones, M. J.
*809 Stone, D.
810 Johnson, C. D.
811 Mann, C. E.

\* — C.I.D.

## CONSTABLES

### WOMEN

1 Claxton, J. E.
2 Williamson, D.
3 Parnell, J.
4 Soanes, C. J.
5 Scott, P. A.
6 Walker, W. S.
7 Turner, P. J.
8 Taylor, M.
9 Brown, L. G.
10 Nixon, P. A.
11 Thompson, K. M.
*12 O'Brien, C. J.

13 Brown, P. A.
14 White, W. D.
15 Ellis, B. A.
16 Forster, A. J.
17 Watkins, A.
18 Davey, D. M.
19 Downs, C. F.
20 Baker, B. I.
21 Cullington, D. A.
*22 George, S. M.
23 Barker, P.
24 Carter, J.
25 Bloxham, S.

\* — C.I.D.

NORFOLK JOINT POLICE

No. 1/68

Chief Constable's Office,
Headquarters,
NORWICH.

1st January, 1968.

GENERAL ORDER

UNIFORM AND INSIGNIA

Difficulties have arisen in the Home Office over receiving official approval of the Force helmet and cap badges submitted by the Royal College of Heralds, which will hold up for some time the manufacture of these items. This in turn means that the new headwear for the Force cannot yet be taken into use.

Sergeants of the former Norwich City and Great Yarmouth Forces will remove their numerals and Sergeants of the former Norfolk Constabulary the crown at present worn above their chevrons, forthwith.

## KING'S LYNN 'F' DIVISION

### Chief Superintendent Calvert In Charge

| SUB-DIVISION | SECTION | BEATS | REMARKS |
|---|---|---|---|
| King's Lynn | - | - | Provision has been made for Unit Beat Policing in this area which comprises the Borough of King's Lynn and the Beat area of South Wootton which is to be absorbed into the sub-division. |
| Sandringham | Sandringham | (2) Grimston, Castleacre, Great Massingham, Gayton, Middleton | Includes beat areas of Castle Rising, East Winch and Hillington which will be absorbed in due course. |
| | Hunstanton | Heacham (2), Snettisham | Includes beat area of Ringstead – to be absorbed in due course. |
| | Docking | Burnham Market (2), Brancaster, South Creake | Includes beat area of Bircham – to be absorbed in due course. |
| Downham Market | Downham Market | Walsoken, Emneth, ......, Hogenhall, Southery, Upwell (2), Outwell, Fincham, Shouldham (2), Tottenhill, West Winch. | Includes the beat area of Nordelph which will be absorbed in due course. |
| | Terrington | Terrington St. Clement (2), Terrington St. John, West Lynn (2), Clenchwarton, Walpole St. Peter, Walpole St. Germans. | |

On Monday 1st January 1968 I worked the bank holiday on early turn but had the first 3 hours time off and came on at 9am until 2pm, I must have seen the new year in but can't remember that! I haven't mentioned how the shift patterns worked then. We worked a week of nights on A Relief, starting at 10pm on a Monday we then did 7 nights finishing at 6am the following Monday, which was a rest day which we slept into, we then had Tuesday rest day and went on duty Wednesday for a week of late turn finishing the following Tuesday at 10pm and having Wednesday and Thursday rest day. Then we would start early turn on the Friday and finish the following Thursday at 2pm having Friday Saturday and Sunday as rest days. This was based on completing 21 shifts in every 28 days with 7 off. B Relief followed A, C Relief followed B Relief and D followed C Relief.

Anyway getting back to the 1st of January, at 1.15pm I went down Horsley's Chase to B's piggeries and saw one of his sons he said that B had been down there half an hour earlier. I saw that there were two tyres burning near to his sties but at that time thought they were from a vehicle theft and informed CID. It is only much later with hindsight during 1981 that I realized that he was lighting fires all those years previously to burn off identifiable wrappers etc from all the break-ins that his team were taking to him and then hiding them before disposal through their network. It took a further fifteen years to cotton onto B the wily old bastard! And get a result. In the meantime his family *"Empire"* grew and they were connected with most of the organised crime which was occurring in the region.

On Thursday 11th January I was on early turn and after we had a Superintendent's Parade starting at 2.30pm where you were invited to attend. It consisted of the parade room being used as seated accommodation and there would be representatives from CID, Traffic and the Town Policing as well as SOCO, Dog Handler, Process, Admin & Training. All would then have an input into discussion on varying subjects, crime trends, active criminals and targets, prolific disqualified drivers, etc. At this one B became *"Criminal of the Week."*

I remember attending one where it got into a bit of a *"bun fight"* between DC Pete Valleley and Don Waters and Jim Stone from Traffic there was no love lost between those two specialist departments. I suppose that's the price you pay for having *"Hybrids."*

During the early part of this year, due to the number of GPO public telephone kiosks being broken into, the Red ones bearing The Crown before BT took over, a number of strategically placed normally isolated ones throughout the Lynn area were fitted with a cash container alarm, this terminated in an alarm box in the Front Office at Kings Lynn. On Sunday the 11th of February, I was on patrol in Kilo 21 with PC 446 Derek Stuart when at 1.23am Monday 12th we were called by HQIR to attend the A47 road at Pullover Road where the kiosk attack alarm was showing at Kings Lynn Police Station.

As we approached the kiosk we saw a car parked outside with its sidelights on facing towards Kings Lynn, it was a Blue Vauxhall Viva and there were two men inside the kiosk, I opened the door and said *"What are you doing?"*, the taller of the two said coolly, *"I'm trying to get through to Nottingham do you know what the code is?"* He then put the receiver down and relifted it and dialled some numbers, put it down and said *"I can't get through, do you know the number for enquiries?"* I said *"What are your names and where do you live?"* The taller one said *"DG from Nottingham"* the small one said *"CR I'm from Nottingham as well"* They told me that they had been to Wisbech and were on their way to Gap Farm Caravan Site at South Wootton and you had to have a CRO number to live there.

Shortly after *"Rigger"* with Sgt Brian Lake in the supervision car and Bob Langley in a traffic patrol car arrived. I then said to the two men, *"I have reasonable suspicion that you have attempted to break into the cash container in this kiosk and you are both under arrest."* R said *"It's nothing to do with us, we were only making a telephone call."* I then asked for proof of their identities and R said *"I've got my driving licence and papers in the car, I'll get them"*. He got inside and sat on the passenger seat and seemed to be looking in the glove compartment and as I couldn't see very clearly what he was doing I went round to that side of the car and he got out and produced a red purse from the inside pocket of his jacket, inside was a slip of paper which said CR and an address in Nottingham. *"Rigger"* then opened the glove compartment where R had been fiddling and found a stainless steel 12" long screwdriver. Derek and I took one prisoner R to Lynn with us and Bob Langley the other who was found to be ISF of Nottingham and not DG.

We called out GPO Engineers to check the kiosk and telephoned Scotland Yard CRO we found F had convictions for housebreaking, shop breaking, ware housebreaking, larceny and RTA offences and R convictions for GBH, ABH, shop breaking, warehouse breaking, office breaking, shop breaking, larceny and RTA offences. We had got to them before they had forced the cash container off and they were done for attempted larceny.

At rush hour the roads at Gaywood Clock, previously mentioned were clogged with traffic in the days before traffic lights and on Wednesday 14th February on 5 beat cycle patrol, from at 5.15pm until 6pm, I was tasked with traffic control.

On the 12th of February, Unit Beat Policing commenced in the new post amalgamation Norwich Division, this was followed over the next two months at Kings Lynn, Dereham, Thetford and Great Yarmouth. This was a new concept in modern policing and incorporated town foot beat patrol areas, former cycle areas were replaced by *"Panda Car."* Norfolk had chosen the Hillman Imp in Blue and White livery, which had a top illuminated unit incorporating a large POLICE/STOP sign with a Blue flashing light, but no *"two tone"* horns, other Forces had different makes of small saloons, The new *"Mid Anglia"* Constabulary, which incorporated the former Cambridgeshire Force with Huntingdonshire, Isle Of Ely and Cambridge City, had Ford Anglia Panda Car's. This force reverted to its present Cambridgeshire Constabulary in 1974 like Norfolk Constabulary did.

The Laughing Policeman

PC Ian MacRae of Norwich on the first day of Panda Patrol 1968

131

On the 1st of April 1968 it was King's Lynn run

The Chief Constable of Norfolk, Mr F. P. C. Garland, at King's Lynn police station today for the inauguration of panda cars in the division. Next to him is the Mayor, Mr F. R. Barton.

Seeing the photograph of the Panda Cars lined up reminds me of one occasion when on a Sunday late turn I crept out into the back yard of the police station whilst one of our unsuspecting drivers was in for mealbreak with two pieces of black paper cut to size and sellotaped them diagonally and upwards from the letter "L" of the "POLICE" marking on the sides of the Hillman Imp and made it an "N" and it spelt "PONCE". He drove around with it for the second half of his tour without realising it. On other occasions I would greet one of the station officers and pat him on the shoulder whilst affixing a sheet of sellotaped paper with *"Kick Me"* on his back and see how long before someone told him.

## Panda cars in action at Lynn

PANDA patrols took to the road at King's Lynn today. They were already in being in Norwich and Yarmouth, and Major S. J. Pope, vice-chairman of the Norfolk Joint Police Authority, said that as soon as the financial situation, which was the limiting factor, was easier, the intention was to extend Panda patrols in the joint force.

Major Pope was one of the visitors to the King's Lynn Divisional Headquarters to see the inauguration of the Panda patrols at Lynn.

Today, too, saw the inauguration of the new beat scheme at Lynn in which constables living in five areas of the town will have direct responsibility for the areas in which they live in the same way as the village policeman.

### OWN DETECTIVE

A Panda car will be allotted to each two area beats, providing a 24-hour patrol, and each car will also have its own detective.

Today, before the first two Panda cars went out on patrol, the drivers and detectives concerned with the Pandas, and the area police constables, were inspected at divisional headquarters.

The Chief Constable of the Norfolk force, Mr. F. P. C. Garland, accompanied by the Mayor of Lynn, Mr. F. Barton, Major Pope, Mr. F. J. Jackson, vice-chairman of the Norfolk County Council, Mr. D. F. Burlingham, chairman of the borough magistrates, Chief Supt. F. Calvert (head of the Lynn Division), Supt. S. Burton (in charge of the Sandringham sub-division), Chief Inspector W. E. Richards, and Det. Inspector C. F. Nourse, spoke to each of the men.

### EXPERIMENT

Afterwards the Chief Constable's party went into the divisional headquarters to see various aspects of police work at the divisional headquarters, including the experimental "visual briefing system" which Lynn claim to be the first to be introduced in the police. Instead of the conventional parades for passing information, it is put on display panels.

They also saw the new filing system which has been introduced and in which everything which comes to the notice of each officer on the force and which may have some future value, is collected and permanently filed.

133

The defined system of Unit Beat Policing at Kings Lynn was:

| | |
|---|---|
| Area Residential/Neighbourhood Officer Unit/Area/Panda Car Officer | Area Constable Unit Constable |
| Collator's/Intelligence Office | Collator |
| Constable Radio Controller Constable | Control Room |
| Walking Patrol Officer | Town Foot Beat |

In Kings Lynn there were two Units, Unit One from the Millfleet South and Unit Two from the Millfleet North, the CID were split into the two Unit areas and the Panda Car also superimposed the foot beats area, as a backup for fast response jobs.

The Laughing Policeman

The Parade Room became The Visual Briefing Room and we had a Collator's Office adjacent to the Front Office/Control Room, the Collator's system held an A to Z surname card index system of criminals and suspects and a numerical card index of the vehicles used, as well as all new local stolen vehicles. There were also sub indices on specialised offences like Indecency, Antique Theft, etc. The Collator maintained these indices, also a number of boards in The VBR he was responsible for keeping updated: Active Criminals, Stolen/Suspected

Vehicles, Wanted/Missing Persons. He was also responsible for publishing a regular Pink coloured "Collator's Bulletin" with matters of interest on. In the VBR there was also a black bound Void Houses book for each foot beat and each Panda Area containing cards for private addresses away on holiday. In those days a member of the public was encouraged to report their house empty date from/until and a card was kept on it until their date of return and each shift checked the property whilst on patrol, so not only did we physically check business premises we also did private addresses in those days as part of our normal routine.

PC Ivan Jordan was our first Collator and I was his Deputy (He was followed by PC Clarence Hazelwood and again I was his Deputy) The Collator's System had been devised Nationwide as it was realized that there was no central source of Crime Intelligence in Divisions and that when Officers moved or retired, the information they had gleaned about criminals and their activities was lost to the local Force area.

We also had the first of a new generation of small personal radios – be it in two separate units, a receiver which clipped to the jacket lapel and had an on/off wheel which incorporated a volume control and a transmitter carried in the pocket with a small aerial, which was pressure released when the transmitter button was pressed. Both of these units known as the "Pye Pocketfone" had batteries which were charged up in units in the Station Sergeant's Office.

The Laughing Policeman

Chris Clark

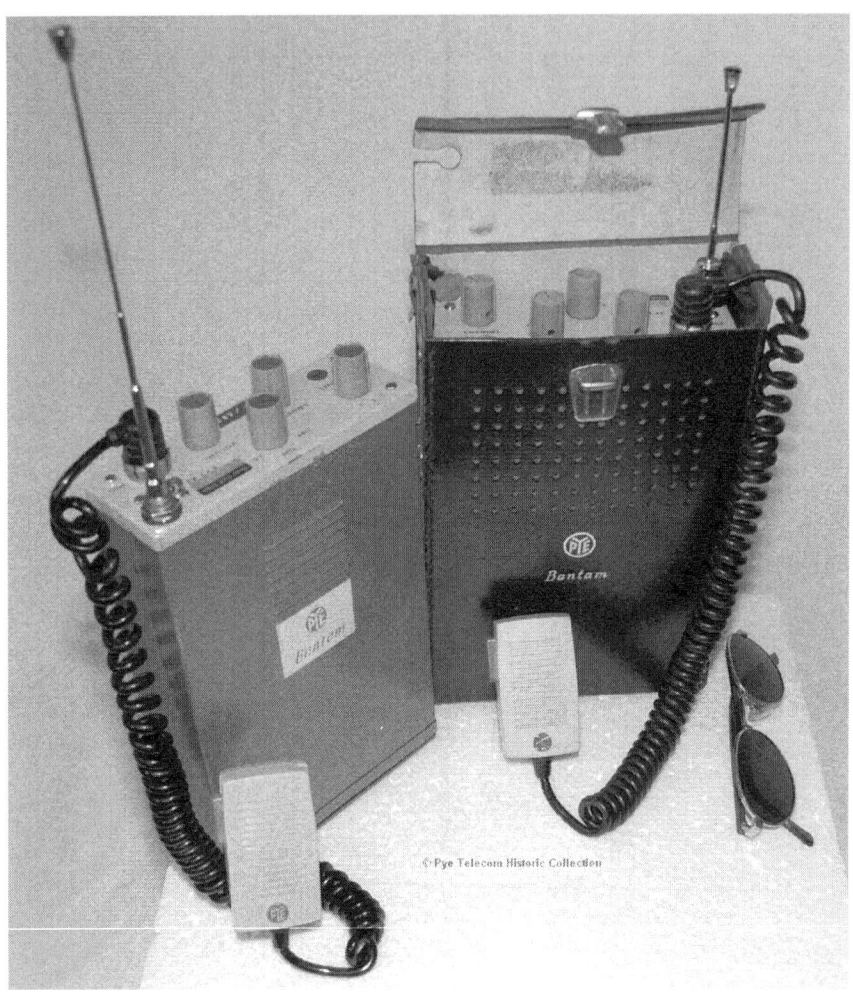

*Pye Bantam shoulder carried AM and FM, VHF mobile solid state*

*For use as a Control in the field*

Officers continued to wear their whistle, but it was only for decoration. We now had Hiatt's handcuffs, although they were datemark stamped 1960, these were the slim line, ratchet type which could be used with one hand.

However we continued to use the traditional lead lined wooden carved truncheon with leather strap.

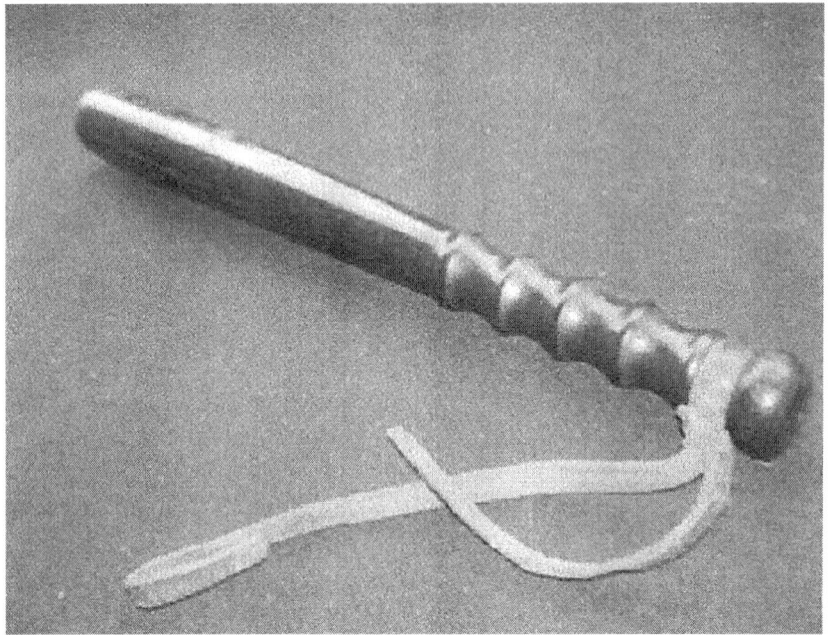

On Saturday 24th February I was on late turn on 4 and 5 pedal cycle beat and at 8.40pm was called to Scott & Son's China Shop in High Street corner of Purfleet Street, Intruders on premises! I arrived at 845pm after cycling furiously from North Lynn and climbed over the rear fence into the courtyard, whilst other officers were at the front and side of the building. I found the point of entry a rear door glass panel had been taken out, but *"the birds had flown"*, I circulated over my personal radio that one had worn gloves and may have traces of putty on them. The immediate area was searched by Derek Pimlott & Rex, other uniform officers and CID to no avail on this occasion.

## *"B" Relief*

On Saturday the 24th April I transferred from "A" Relief onto "B" Relief where I was to remain for the next nine years, *"man and boy."* All the Relief's apart from one had a strong partisan sense of shift pride and guarded their successes jealously. There were good officers turned out from that other Relief but it was mainly due to their own character and initiative and not getting embroiled in that shift's culture.

My Sergeant on "B" was Brian Taylor he was from the old school and a stickler for discipline and he would spend most of his patrol time trying to catch his shift officers out doing some misdemeanour or other and thus keeping them on their toes.

On nights when on foot beat after doing all of my property check twice, once before midnight and the other from 1am to 3am instead of going into the station for meal break, as it was far too late to eat sandwiches I used to go to one of the various car sale showrooms dotted near the town centre like Mann Eggertons or Murkitt Brothers.

There I would find a car on the forecourt that was unlocked and get in it and listen to Radio Luxembourg for a while before resuming patrol and re-checking property for a third time. One particular night around 3am I found one such vehicle, a Jaguar on the forecourt of Murkitt Brothers in North Street at the junction with John Kennedy Road (this road was built in the mid 1960s and named after The President JFK who was assassinated in 1963). No sooner had I got in when I heard the distinctive sound of Brian's police vehicle pull up. My ears then, unlike now, were fully tuned to every little sound emitted at night and able to identify them, so saving time running around needlessly. A burglary in progress has a distinct sound from say, someone opening the sluice gates at The Dock Head; now I would not hear anything until someone touched me on the shoulder!

He then got out and checked the garage doors and windows, he then started checking the vehicles on the forecourt and started coming closer and towards the one I was laying on the back seat in! I just managed to press the button door lock down on the driver's door before he tried the handle, luckily he didn't use his torch. Whew! What a relief when I heard him drive away, but cheeky as always I put his name in my pocket book for that time and location and left a space for him to sign it. When I approached him later he said *"I didn't see you there"* I said *"Well Sarge I was there and I saw you!"* He gave me a funny look knowing I had got one over him and he signed my book. Brian was always playing cat and mouse with the Relief and some of my colleagues at that time were Terry Sturman, who was lead man, Roy from Training School times, Pete also at Eynsham when I was there, Chris, Dick, Derek, and Dave (Cadet). Brian was always catching out our *"three musketeers"* of the shift Roy, Chris and Dick (you could call them Tom Dick or Harry) on some escapade or other; like all three on Early Turn having breakfast with the porter in the Globe Hotel at the TMP (Tuesday Market Place) junction with King Street; when they should have been on separate adjacent beats.

# The Laughing Policeman

A PC on our shift who had the nickname *"Blossom"* I suppose because he was a freshman on probationer was struggling to make the grade he was too nice to be a copper and he just didn't have any court cases. Brian Taylor asked me to take him out and get some process as he was unlikely otherwise to complete his probation period. So during the spring and summer I did and on one particular late turn we were patrolling London Road together when I spotted a car parked within the zig zag lines of the *"zebra"* pedestrian crossing at the junction with Windsor Road the driver was obviously in White's newsagents. I thought *"What could be simpler, this is an absolute offence with no defence and that will be a process for him."*

We waited for the driver's return and made sure that the PC reported him correctly, checked the vehicle excise licence and issued him with an HORT1 for production of his licence insurance and test certificate and away we went. Anyhow the driver saw Ben Pearson a clever criminal defence lawyer, who went on to be a judge and paid him a handsome fee to look in Stones' Justice Manual and other legal reference books and they pleaded not guilty; because the approach to the crossing only had eleven pairs of studs instead of twelve pairs.

Never mind that he shouldn't park within the limits of a pedestrian crossing obscuring a pedestrian waiting to cross; and he got off! After that the lad just gave up and he didn't make it to the end of probation. Sorry *"Blossom"* you just weren't cut out to be a copper, you were too nice a human being.

Our allocated shift Inspector (which was a new post) was taken by Lewis Heavens, *"A Diddyman"* transferee from Essex, so called because Essex dropped their recruiting height to 5'8" when others were still 5'10" minimum height and after Ken Dodd's small TV characters. Lewis had been a Chemist in Civvie Street and after his retirement became a Lawyer. He also became Editor of Fred Calvert's Police Powers of Arrest and Charges booklet and Author of it, the most recent publication February 2006.

Our Front Office Controllers were Frank Leech "A" Jack Dye "B" Billy Beart "C" and Jack Troup "D". Poor old Billy who was a good beat officer until it closed should never have been a controller. When someone rang the front counter bell one day he slid open the counter door and said *"King's Lynn Police!"* like he was answering the telephone.

In the Front Office our town UHF radio was beside the VHF force radio on a desk as illustrated below.

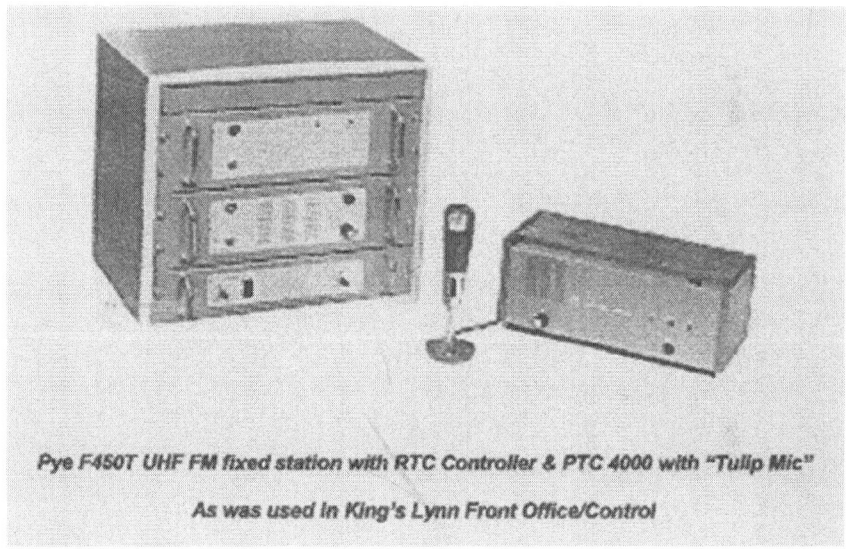

Pye F450T UHF FM fixed station with RTC Controller & PTC 4000 with "Tulip Mic"
As was used in King's Lynn Front Office/Control

One day I couldn't resist the temptation to wind Billy up and I called up on my personal radio *"VK to Foxtrot over"* and Billy answered on the force one *"Go ahead VK Foxtrot over"* and was politely informed *"We are not calling you over."* Can you imagine if they had put Billy and *"Fink"* Nelson referred to earlier in Control together? A bit like the *"Keystone Cops."*

145

**A still from Keystone Cops**

During the year Peter Farman and Brian Taylor were promoted and together with Dave Pearson and Lewis Heavens became the four shift Inspectors. Gerry Dunn was promoted to Chief Inspector; he was a pain in the bum! He used to take a personal radio home and listen in on the late turn or night shift like we couldn't do the job without him. So we had to be very careful with radio procedure and what information we passed out over the air. Didn't he have anything better to do? PC Peter Griffin from Downham Market became our Shift Sergeant, whilst a PC at Downham he had tackled and arrested a man brandishing a smoking double barrel shotgun who had just shot from close range at a Bride & her Groom in their wedding car; he was nominated for a George Medal but awarded a Mention in Despatches.

Police Headquarters Martineau Lane, adjacent to County Hall, Norwich, with 64 rooms on a wing of the Norfolk County Council was taken into use at 3pm on Sunday the 25th of February 1968. When it was originally planned it was designed to replace the original Norfolk Constabulary HQ at Thorpe and not have to accommodate an expanded three into one Force; therefore it was already inadequate for the new Norfolk Joint Police HQ and some departments were housed in redundant police stations and houses scattered around Norwich.

On Monday of 4th March I worked an early turn and went to the brand new Force Headquarters where at 9:45am I had an Interview with the Assistant Chief Constable Mr Gordon Taylor. Then on Thursday the 14th March having finished a half night shift at 2am, at 9am I went to headquarters with Gerry Dunn where at 12noon I saw The Chief Constable Peter Garland and he confirmed my appointment. I was no longer a Probationer. I got back at Lynn at 2.45pm and then went on at 10pm to do a full night duty.

It was amazing how quickly two years had passed since I joined. That night I did Front Office relief from 2am, probably my reward for working earlier in the day and not being a *"proby."* At 3.20am the kiosk alarm in the station activated for the telephone kiosk situated in De Grey Road and at 3.35am a PC brought to the station a known villain whom he had arrested for attempted larceny from the kiosk.

Whilst on foot beat I was passing on loads of info to the Collator on local villains and their vehicles via form C47 and encouraged other officers to do the same; the initial empty filing trays started to quickly expand.

Our Kings Lynn Division call sign had changed from Kilo to Foxtrot and there were now five Divisions instead of ten. We had incorporated the former Sandringham and Downham Divisions as two Sub Divisions of the new Kings Lynn Division.

On Monday the 20th of May we had a visit from Her Majesty's Chief Inspector of Constabulary Sir Eric Johnstone, I saw him along with other officers at 7.10pm that evening. Obviously during the preceding week the station had been subjected to serious bullshit by the bosses, the cleaners had worked overtime and CID desks which were normally completely cluttered with files had been cleared of paperwork. Even Frank Leech's uniform which normally resembled Ventrass's off *"Heartbeat"* was devoid of crumbs and cigarette ash and he actually looked smart and with creases in the right places, Gwen his Wife must have been up half the night with the iron!

Talking of clean uniforms reminds me that around this time a great deal of demolition was taking place in and around the town centre, one large site which had been flattened and awaiting rebuilding was where Hillington Square flats now occupies. On nights I would check this site as there was a large amount of then valuable metal lying around, copper, brass and steel, which this copper had to make sure none would have the brass neck to steal!

Anyway this particular night my thoughts must have been elsewhere as I suddenly found myself hurtling into the abyss and went arse over elbow into a deep piling hole! When I collected my senses I clambered back out and found that I was covered from helmet to boots in dry cement dust! I had to return to the station to completely change. The ensuing jeers which greeted me from my colleagues gave me the inspiration to become *"The Joker"* on the shift.

The Laughing Policeman

The Millfleet (above) was undergoing major changes in the 1960s and is now (below) dominated by the flats complex.

The first probationer who was subject to my dark and sick sense of humour was a PC nicknamed *"Mutley"* he was so named because he had this hoarse laugh which sounded like the Dick Dastardly Dog character in *"The Wacky Races" "Mutley do something."* One night shortly after we had a new Sergeant who was completely different to Brian Taylor and just like one of the lads we set the scene. The scenario: A Captain of a Russian ship berthed at Alexander Dock had phoned to say that his Mate (second in command) had gone berserk on board with a gun and was terrifying the crew.

The Solution: The Sgt who was an Authorised Firearms Officer was carrying his revolver (unloaded) and wearing the belt and holster and for further effect Fred Calvert's *"Sam Brown"* uniform belt. I briefed the shift (they were informed it was a hoax before *"Mutley"* came in) that they were to storm the ship via the gangplank and *"Mutley"* would go into the cabin and distract the man and if he tried to shoot *"Mutley"* then the Sgt would drop him, but Mutley to keep clear of the Sgt's aim! Poor *"Mutley"* when he heard this he went white as a sheet and his arsehole went from half crown to sixpence (for you post decimal people fifty pence to five pence) we then had to tell him it was a windup before going to the docks as he looked ready to faint.

After this windup there was no stopping me and I went from success to success and was responsible for a large number of probationer's having to change their underpants.

Now you've heard of a *"cat burglar"* a burglar who is especially skilled at stealthy or undetected entry of premises well we had one living in North Lynn an *"Overspill"* from London he would select only posh leafy suburb detached type houses set in large gardens where one of the doors or large windows had been left unlocked. Once inside he would stealthily go through the premises taking care not to disturb anything or leave anything out of place and would only take cash or jewellery and leave the premises by the way he had entered. He had a pet cat who he would take on the job with him and if disturbed by the householder he would make out that he was looking for his cat then call it and it would appear; how ingenious is that?

## Assault and Cattery

Talking about cats I remember one night duty checking the rear of properties in the town centre which in those days had unlit dark alleys and yards and I didn't use my torch unless absolutely necessary so as not to *"show out"* to villains. As I went up this particular yard I was suddenly and violently struck on the left hand side of my head and shoulder and felt blood trickling down from a wound on my face. Still reeling and dazed from the attack I shone my torch around and there was this cat that had previously been stalking mice in a confined space who had suddenly been confronted by a monster with a pointed head and it had launched itself at me in order to escape; I am not sure who was the most scared of the two.

## Devil's Alley

Between the South Quay and Nelson Street is a narrow historic right of way cobbled alley formerly Miller's Alley now called *"Devil's Alley."* Legend has it that sometime after the 1880s it is said that a ship arrived at King's Lynn one day carrying the Devil who slipped ashore in pursuit of new souls to claim. A Priest cornered him in the alley driving him back to the ship with holy water and prayer.

Well for this Devil it was employed for a different scenario and the following photograph clearly shows a ceiling oak lintel support at the Nelson Street end slightly lower than the minimum height for a constable plus his helmet.

On nights when I had a new recruit to show around on nights I would get us patrolling on the South Quay near to the alley and suddenly say *"There's someone running away from us up that alley!"* and off I would go up the darkness of Devil's Alley towards Nelson Street with the *"rookie"* in hot pursuit. Just before the end I would duck and emerge into Nelson Street unscathed and then laugh as my prey's helmet hit the oak beam and fell off clattering onto the cobbles with only his pride injured. I only used this trick on the *"short-arses"* and didn't get the taller ones who I left for other devilish deeds like the Town Hall *"ghost."*

On Monday the 27th of May I was a 9am to 6.15pm duty and at 1145am went on prisoner escort duty to HMP Norwich together with Brian (Cadet) and Bert Farrell Civvie driver with two prolific burglars mentioned earlier, they had been remanded by KLMC for appearance at Quarter Sessions. We dropped them off at 1.45pm and then went to HQ Stores and were on the way back to Kings Lynn going along the A.47 road, when we heard a call of intruders at Narborough Hall, the home of Andrew Fountaine. I left the van and dropped off at the scene and helped Pete Parsley the local beat officer and Derrick Pimlott with *"Rex"* search the grounds. I found a case opener and footprints in a flower bed by the point of entry but the intruder had made good his escape.

On Tuesday the 28th of May I saw the cat burglar mentioned earlier together with another known burglar working in a Pet and Grooming Shop in Tower Street, Kings Lynn obviously showing him the tricks of the trade and training up another feline or canine *"apprentice."*
Talking of overspill the Greater London Council as they were then had a desperate shortage of housing in various parts of The Capital so they paid some of the Home Counties to accommodate a large percentage, Norfolk included; so Abbey Farm at Thetford, Seabank Estate at North Lynn and Fairstead Estate at Gaywood suddenly sprang up and a lot of Londoners moved into quiet sleepy Norfolk.

Now some were nice people and salt of the earth but there was also a lot of hardened *"Crap"* who the GLC got rid of to clear their books of trouble elements. We finished up with armed robbers and the like who still had connections down *"The Smoke"* and carried out crime in the capital and came back and lay undetected in our midst, it also made the three estates a bit of a no go area as these people tended to band together and intimidate or recruit other local people who were housed there.

You might think it really mean of me to nick someone for being drunk in charge of a pedal cycle; well that's exactly what I did during the afternoon of Monday the 22nd of July. At 1.40pm I was on London Road and I saw this old boy staggering with a cycle and weaving about between heavy traffic, as I got to him he stank of drink and I got him off the road onto the footpath, a number of times I asked him where he lived and after the eighth time he said *"What do you want to know that for?"* I said "To get you home safely" He said *"I'm not drunk, I'm not going anywhere with you"* and with that he took off again into the traffic. By this time I was pissed off with him, but didn't want him run over or cause an accident and it was over a mile to his destination, I thought the simplest thing to do was arrest him. When I told him he was under arrest he said *"I'm not drunk I can get home alright, I suppose you want a medal for this, it has made your day, You prove I'm drunk"* I called for the van and took him and the bike to *"The Nick"* where he was put through the refused charge book and taken home.

NORFOLK JOINT POLICE

**CONFIDENTIAL**
For Police use only.
Telephone: Norwich 21234/7.

32/68

Police Headquarters,
Martineau Lane,
Norwich,
NOR 07T.

25th July, 1968.

GENERAL ORDERS

1. UNIFORM AND INSIGNIA

With effect from 1st August, 1968, the new helmets, cap and shoulder badges which are being distributed to all ranks will be taken into general wear.

The scale of issue of the new helmet must of necessity be restricted to one per uniformed Sergeant and Constable. This will be worn for tours of duty between 6 a.m. and 10 p.m. with the second best helmet being worn between 10 p.m. and 6 a.m. This situation will continue until it is possible to supply a further new helmet.

Discarded helmets and all badges of the former Forces will be surrendered to Divisional offices for transmission to Headquarters.

Chris Clark

*A feature in the local paper of the 2nd of August 1968*

## New police helmets at Lynn

P.C. R. DAYNES (wearing the old-style helmet) adjusts P.C. L. Betts' new helmet, which was adopted by all policemen in Norfolk as from yesterday.

The new helmet is of the same design as that worn previously by the former Norwich City Police, but with a new badge which has the inscription "Norfolk Joint Police".

Previously policemen of the Norwich, Yarmouth and County forces had worn helmets of differing design. The new, standardised version has been brought in by the new joint police force to cover the whole of the county
(JC 1521)

From the 7th of August until the 17th of August I did Front Office/Control Duty. As previously mentioned the major change in the method of policing which occurred this year both nationally and throughout Norfolk and Kings Lynn Division was the introduction of Unit Beat Policing which was based on the use of small motor cars, thus enabling one officer to cover a larger area than had been previously possible. This move was a major factor in the gradual demise of The Village Policeman and centralisation, however inevitable it was then, it led to great regret from both serving officers and the public, which lasts to this day and very much a pawn thrown around by politicians. It was on a par with Dr Beeching axing the major part of railway lines in 1963.

From September to December I had various spells of duty in the Front Office/Control, at this time it was a very large empty space which housed a tiny switchboard room with what looked like a glorified knitting machine. This had leads with plugs which had to be inserted in the right holes to connect a caller to an extension, or for an extension to make an outside call, everything had to go via the operator; even internal calls from one department to another. It was one up from two empty baked bean tins and a piece of string! Olive Edwards was our civilian telephonist and she would wear headphones, she worked Monday to Friday 8am to 4pm and Saturday mornings. When she wasn't there on her day off or at meal break we had to work this monstrosity and would invariably pull the wrong plug out and cut people off halfway through a conversation or put a caller through to the wrong department or even more funny, connect two internal departments together who didn't want a contact in the first place. As a consequence a lot of internal *"eyeball"* flaps would flash up and down angrily. It was a bit like Frank Spencer trying to play *"The Mighty Wurlitzer"* Organ! When the wheel came off there was only one thing to do pull out all of the leads and start again. I had firstly experienced this type of switchboard during weekend duty at Eynsham Hall Training School but was still none the wiser of its rudimentary functions; Fred's extension *"eyeball"* was coloured red and he would say in his operatic voice *"Who's that, you've cut me off!"* Often we would say we were one of the Cadets and blame him, sorry Dave and Brian. Also he would ring down and blast off about six calls he wanted to make to various people, then you would additionally have to look them up in the directory then ring each and put them through to him; what a ball ache!

*An example of a plug in switchboard*

There was a wooden kiosk in the corner of the front office where you went in to issue flood warning messages, it was quite a bit like going in the contestant's box on Hughie Green's game show *"Double Your Money"* to answer the $64.000 dollar question. Kings Lynn is a Port and having the large river Ouse was very alert to the fact of the flood warning season, as the events of 1953 were still fresh in everyone's memory; but luckily we got away with it season after season until 1978 more on this in my following book.

On nights I would have to type the Daily Information and Instruction Sheets *"The DI's"* with a special keyboard typewriter that would imprint onto duplication skins ready for turning off by the Collator on the Gestetner Machine who would circulate it to departments along with his Bulletin. I used to get the metal filing drawers containing the Collator's Records from his office and keep them by the base control radio for any sightings/checks of persons or vehicles seen by the lads out on the street, thus providing them with a quick response to their request.

---

NORFOLK JOINT POLICE

CONFIDENTIAL
For Police use only.
Telephone: Norwich 21234/7.

Police Headquarters,
Martineau Lane,
Norwich,
NOR 07T.

14th November, 1968.

GENERAL ORDERS

BADGES OF RANK - CHIEF SUPERINTENDENTS AND SUPERINTENDENTS

Agreement has been reached between the Local Authority Associations, the Association of Chief Police Officers, the Police Superintendents Association of England and Wales and the Police Federation that there should be a distinction in the badges of rank worn by the various classes of Superintendent in England and Wales. The Home Office has accordingly instructed that the revised range of badges, as shown below, will be introduced as from the 1st January, 1969.

Chief Superintendent — Crown and 2 Stars
Superintendent Class I — Crown and 1 Star
Superintendent Class II — Crown

A similar distinction was introduced in Scotland on the 15th July this year.

(Home Office Circular No. 245/68 refers).

Chris Clark

### *"Sign Of The Zodiac"*

Sometime during this time I had just completed a night shift at 06:00am in the Front Office and a PC who had just come on early turn was single crew in one of the Black Ford Zephyr 6 Mk 4 Zodiac's which were nicknamed by the traffic branch as the *"Dagenham Dustbins"*, due to their premature metal corrosion. At around 06:30am he was called to attend an RTA (Road Traffic Accident) on the A47 at Necton, situated between Swaffham and Dereham, some 20 miles from King's Lynn. In view of the fact that he was single-crewed, I decided to go with him as Observer.

It was still dark when we left the police station yard, with headlights, blue lights, and two-tone horns on. We left the town via London Road and Hardwick Road and took the A47 exit at Hardwick Roundabout and went up a stretch of road called Constitutional Hill towards the village of Middleton.

About half a mile King's Lynn side of Middleton on a straight piece of road we overtook three vehicles, one of them a Post Office van. Suddenly, it seemed that the whole World was spinning; I kept seeing verge, hedge, road, which was repeated several times then a ploughed field and then stillness. We had come to rest some distance in a ploughed field and neither of us was injured or shaken. What had happened was upon overtaking the line of three vehicles we had hit a patch of *"black ice"* in the centre of the carriageway, causing the unstable Ford Zodiac to spin in clockwise circles across the offside verge and into a farmer's field, still with blue lights flashing and two tones blaring. It was only through the calmness and experienced handling of the PCs driving which kept the unstable Ford Zodiac from overturning and there was very little damage to the underside of the vehicle; other than caked mud.

The driver of the Post Office van came to see if we were alright; we informed Headquarters of our dilemma and another car was despatched to the RTA at Necton; whilst we waited for the Early Turn Shift Sergeant who dealt with the police accident. The Post Office van driver made a witness account and the accident was written off due to the weather conditions and no error to the PCs driving.

Author: The Ford Zephyr 6 Police Special was a modification, its Spec was 2495cc, 112BHP at 102mph, manufactured between 1966 and 1971. It had a higher tuned engine, a heavy duty suspension, modified dashboard, a floor mounted gear lever with closer ratio than the normal column change. It was later found to be prone to easy swerving whilst travelling at high speed due to the car's modified weight distribution.

## *1969*

There was a Sergeant who transferred to "D" Relief both he and Peter Griffin had been Cadets with Wally Bunting and all were nearly thrown out due to their high jinks which seems strange when years later he was a real bastard as a Superintendent in Complaints & Discipline in the early 1980s; strange how suddenly butter doesn't melt! Pete and Wally became Special Firearms Officers and trained Norfolk Officers in this important field.

We had a new department set up to liase with the public after losing the Beat system it was called Community Relations and initially run by Sgt Malcolm Browne and PC Stuart Peters and later added to include Inspector Ivan Jordan and PC John Pond. We had a new intake in PC's George Dimmock, Dick Le Fevre and Pete Dennis. During the year I, with all of three and a half years in was the longest serving Constable on "B" Relief in August and fulfilled the first of many Acting Sergeant duties I was to perform over the next eight years. As I was not interested in promotion I had not bothered to take my promotion examination to

Chris Clark

*Derrick and Rebel with Stuart Peters Circa 1969*

P.C. Derrick PIMLOTT first Dog Handler in King's Lynn with "Rebel" the second of his 3 Police Aisation Dogs

Sergeant, so I couldn't be a Temporary Sergeant and get paid although I was fulfilling exactly the same role. I never did take my exam even though Fred Calvert at Staff Appraisals wanted me to I was quite happy at the sharp end. During this time I was also reserve Front Office/Control Constable for "B" Relief and was in there on a regular basis. I was still living in Single men's Quarters and unless you watched TV or went to the *"boozer"* every night single life was boring. So I started going out after completing late turn in uniform on a regular basis with either one of the night duty Traffic Officers or with my old friend Derrick Pimlott Dog Handler with *"Rex"* and later when he retired *"Rebel"* when Derrick was 6pm to 2am or sometimes with one of the Relief's who were on night duty following our late turn.

### *"Cash In Transit"*

On Tuesday the 28th of January after a late turn in the Control I teamed up with Bryan Edwards who was on nights with "D" Relief as a Panda Car Driver. At 11.03pm we were on routine patrol in South Wootton when we overheard over Force radio a call from HQ to Dersingham mobiles that a "999" report had been received of persons breaking into the RAC telephone box at Babingley near Sandringham. Although out of our patrol area we rushed to the scene and arrived at 11.10pm being the first mobile there and found the telephone box broken into and the coin container missing.

I then went on foot across the main road to a farm driveway leading to Neal's Farm where I saw an old style Ford Zodiac parked without lights in the darkness facing away from the main A149 Kings Lynn to Hunstanton road. As I approached the car tore off at a fast speed up the lane away from the road. I knew that it was a *"no through road"* and waited for the car to turn round which it did at a fast speed coming towards me with its sidelights on. I stood in the middle of the driveway with my dual light torch turned on red and it stopped about a foot from where I was I noted the index number was WBJ883. I went to the driver's side and got the driver out quickly searched him and found him to be a villain from Terrington St Clement. I looked and felt under the driver's seat and hidden there was the cash container coins and some screwdrivers took him back to the Panda car whilst Brian was dealing with the other two his Brother and Brother In Law.

We then with other officers conveyed them and their car back to Kings Lynn Police Station where they were each interviewed and admitted their part they also admitted and had taken into consideration (TIC) a spate of similar offences they had committed at telephone kiosks throughout the West Norfolk area and beyond.

On the 30th of January we received via a General Order regarding Port Security Scheme (This was in the light of recent activities over the water in Northern Ireland and The IRA and the start of 25 years of *"The Troubles"*) The Order carried stating that *"A National Port Scheme is being developed whereby passenger traffic in and out of the Country will be subjected to routine checks by local Police Officers trained in the field of security and criminal intelligence. As from the 1st February, 1969, the sea ports of Great Yarmouth, Wells-next-the-Sea, Kings Lynn and the airport at Norwich, are to be included in the Ports Scheme. All movement of passenger traffic including aliens, will be examined by selected officers in an effort to identify, and apprehend if necessary, travelling criminals and to obtain criminal and security intelligence. Headquarters Special Branch will be responsible for the administration of the work involved and circulation of messages involving port traffic."* The order then identified the Norfolk Officers who would operate this scheme and at Kings Lynn "F" Division it named Detective Sergeant Brown and Detective Constable Coady.

## "No Hindsight"

Frank Sampson the village *"Bobby"* of Magdalen and part time repairer of washing macines and suchlike was a really nice old boy and a WW2 soldier veteran of the North Africa Campaign. I remember one late turn when I was in the police canteen on mealbreak and Frank came in looking a bit flustered and out of breath, I ascertained that he had just cycled several miles in from his Beat.

Upon enquiring where his police mini van was he informed me that due to some minor mishaps he had been suspended from driving pending an eyesight test.

The mishaps were that during the same week at his Sub Div station of Downham Market whilst reversing his mini van in the police station yard he had:

(a). Collided with the cell block wall of the police station.

(b). Backed into another police vehicle.

(c). Reversed into Chief Inspector Arthur Jermy's private vehicle.

Frank then informed me that the previous evening he had been out on duty with his bike which was fitted with dynamo lighting and had been drinking whisky with a local farmer friend and in the meantime it had got dark outside. Upon bading farewell and leaving, Frank started cranking his bike up the long drive in complete darkness forgetting to adjust the dynamo against the rear wheel. The next thing is that Frank and cycle finished up arse over elbow in a ditch at the side of the drive; so he wasn't even safe out on a bike!

### *"Window Shopping"*

Sometimes the most innocent appearing of moments are when criminals are actually at work *"casing"* up premises for later burglaries, one such sighting was of two known criminals posing as a happy couple apparently in love looking at rings in a jewellers shop window. Well that's where the innocence ends and a *"copper's nose"* comes into use. He was an active shop burglar and she was a shoplifter and prostitute later to be his wife. On Sunday the 23rd of February I was on 1 Beat when at 14:25pm I saw this pair they were looking in H Samuel's window in the High Street and this would be one of a spate of jewellers that would some time later be burgled this turned out to be an invaluable sighting put into the new Collator system for future recall. (The story appears later).

### *"Not The Done Thing Dear"*

Now it's normally the bringing up and background that makes people into criminals but there are exceptions. On Saturday the 22nd of March I was on late turn foot beat covering the High Street area when at 2pm I was called to Boots Chemists where two thirteen year old girls had been caught shoplifting. They also had property stolen from Woolworth's and Terra Nova a ladies fashion accessory shop. One was the Daughter of a wealthy local businessman the other the Daughter of an Accountant and both lived in substantial homes and went to fee paying Boarding Schools one a Convent.

### *"Electrifying Stuff"*

I made another arrest whilst officially off duty. On Friday the 16th of May after a late turn in the Front Office/Control I went out with Roy who was on "C" Relief night duty Panda patrol. At 10.06pm we received a report of intruders at the Eastern Electricity Board premises situated behind the Pilot Cinema on John Kennedy Road (There would have been a lot of copper and other metals stored there). The intruders had made off in a Grey Mini XDM26 I recognised this number and requested a Collator's check to be made and it came back positive owned by a man of an address in North Lynn an associate of the "West Norfolk Mafia" referred to earlier. Roy and I toured that area and at 1015pm saw the vehicle travelling along Losinga Road towards the Discovery Pub and turn onto the forecourt of that premises and park. I saw the driver get out and the passenger was a Brother in Law of the main gang member B and referred to before. I said to the driver *"You are being arrested on suspicion of having broken into the Eastern Electricity Board premises behind the Pilot Cinema tonight"* He replied *"Can I get some cigarettes out of the pub first?"* Whilst I was arresting him Roy arrested the passenger and both were taken in for Interview.

I spoke to the passenger about the incident and then made him a cup of tea and gave him some biscuits whilst Roy was with the driver in a separate Interview Room. At 1140pm Det Sgt Ron Brown came and said to my man *"They tell me you and H are in for screwing the electricity compound behind the Pilot Cinema tonight what about it, is it true?"* T said *"I don't know anything about it Mr Brown, I'm on my way to have a drink with J and we get picked up"* Ron then said *"What were your movements tonight before they wheeled you in here?"* T said *"Well I left the Carpenter's Arms about 9.30pm and came into town, met J in Turbus Road and away we went for a drink"* Ron said *"Are you saying in fact that you haven't been to the compound or the Pilot Cinema Car Park tonight?"* T said *"Yes that's right."*

Ron Brown then left the room and returned shortly afterwards and said to T *"I'm not happy about your story, I've reason to believe you were on the Pilot Cinema Car park tonight and were in fact seen by a man."* T then said *"Well yes I was there; I was waiting for a bird."* Ron said *"Who is she? So that I can confirm the truth of what you say."* T said *"I'm not going to tell you who she is; I don't want her dragged into this."* Ron then said *"Was H with you?"* T replied *"No he wasn't with me and I didn't see him there."* Ron said *"Why did you deny being there in the first place? And now you come out with this after about waiting for a bird you won't name."* T replied *"Well when this bloke spoke to me and said he was sending for the police, I thought it was time I weren't there so I cleared off, you know what would have happened if I'd been there when the law rolled up, with my record I'd be the first one in."* Both T and H were charged with attempted burglary and later appeared at court and found guilty.

### *"The Saint's Anything But"*

During the Spring and Summer of 1969 and which continued unabated until 1970 there was a large scale organised theft of top of the range luxury caravans from the driveways of homes throughout East Anglia and the Home Counties. At the time the offender's were not known but eventually intelligence and good luck led to a travelling itinerant family by the name of Saint being involved. Often victims of these thefts would be awoken in the early hours by the noise of their holiday home being hitched up and driven away from their property and despite immediate police attendance to the scene and observation points mounted at strategic road locations in a given area, no trace of the caravan or fleeing victims with the getaway vehicle was seen.

During a routine check during the early hours of one morning during 1970 a large cattle float was stopped being driven in suspicious circumstances and the rear of the vehicle was inspected in connection with suspected cattle theft. Inside the cattle float was a stolen luxury caravan which was coupled to a Land Rover.

The method that this team of villains utilised was to have the cattle float parked in a quiet country lane about a mile from the pre-selected target caravan. The team would then drive up to the target caravan's location and hitch it up to the Land Rover then drive to where the cattle float was parked with the tailgate dropped and drive both Land Rover and caravan onto the float. The tailgate would then be closed and the driver of the Land Rover would get out and via a connecting door leading to the cab of the cattle float get into the passenger seat of it and the full load of stolen caravan and getaway Land Rover would drive off into the night to their *"Fence"* (Receiver of stolen goods). Many caravans were *"spirited away"* in this manner with the majority finishing up with new identities and sold through legitimate caravan dealers situated in the West Country.

### *"This One Sucks"*

Another example of the ingenious methods that some criminals from this era utilised. There was a lorry park situated just off the South Gates Roundabout in South Lynn, called the Hardwick Lorry Park. Up to 30 Heavy Goods Vehicles and assorted vans would park there overnight whilst their drivers would be booked into various Bed & Breakfast accommodation around the area. A pattern emerged whereby it was established that there was a regular spate of diesel thefts occurring from being siphoned from vehicles parked there and other lorry parks in the region. The normal method and science of stealing diesel or petrol by those engaged in it would be to carry a length of narrow plastic piping and a container force the fuel cap off insert the piping and physically suck the fuel out with the other end of the pipe inserted into the container and capillary action and gravity finishing the job.

Such was the volume and regularity of this type of theft it was decided to have plain clothes observations set up in a bid to catch the villains responsible. This was done on a rota basis and the officers would be on the lookout for anyone carrying a large can and length of pipng. However on one particular night a white Ford Transit van was seen to drive up close to fuel tank of a parked lorry and the officers could hear a small motor running. The officers went to investigate only to find that a hose had been inserted into the fuel tank of the lorry and a massive storage tank inside the transit van was being filled with the diesel from it and an electric pump was drawing the fuel. It was a bit like a petrol forecourt fuel pump only in reverse as it was taking and not delivering, fuel.

The occupants of the van were arrested and it was established that literally thousands of gallons (1 gallon = 5 litres) had been obtained in this way. Keith Holliday our SOCO (Scenes of Crime Officer) photographed the van and paraphernalia (excuse that no pun intended) and I circulated the photos and information on one of our Collator's Bulletins on one of the occasions that I was deputising for Clarence.

### *"The Case of The Butcher and The Baker but no Candlestick Maker"*

On Tuesday the 8th of July 1969 a murder was discovered at the former Chequers Public House situated on the main A10 road in the village of West Winch just outside Kings Lynn. The Victim a 50 year old Baker of Jewish extract with origins from Finchley, London after fleeing to England in 1939 from "The Nazis" in Germany was found dead at 6pm in a pool of blood with a pick axe handle lying nearby. He had purchased the former public house for just over two thousand pounds and was in the process of converting it into a restaurant to be opened the following year he also worked for four days a week at a Hackney Baker's In those days New Scotland Yard took charge of such enquiries for provincial forces and Detective Chief Superintendent Alfred known as *"Bill"* Moody was *"The man from the Yard"* on this occasion arriving at 4.20am on Wednesday morning after driving from London. That Friday's edition of the Lynn News & Advertiser carried the headlines *"Manhunt After Body Is Found."* Our Head of Norfolk CID Detective Chief Superintendent Reginald *"Reggie"* Lester worked with him on the case and between them quickly got a result.

On the following Thursday the 10th of July a twenty-two year old Butcher of no fixed abode was arrested for this murder and on Friday morning the 11th I and Inspector Lewis "Lou" Heavens escorted him to a Special Hearing at Grimston Magistrates Court in a White Police Triumph 2000 and he was remanded in custody; We then escorted him to Norwich Prison.

### *"The Grocer and The Factory Hand"*

That very same day and only four days after the first murder there was another sixteen miles away in Hunstanton. Jean Sadler aged 31 who worked at the local Co-Op was found dead in her first floor flat above a fish & chip shop on the corner of Church Street and Greevegate in the town. She had been indecently assaulted and an attempt made at raping her and then strangled she had been stabbed with a knife and she had also had an instrument forced inside her private parts. Messrs' Moody and Lester were quickly involved and other officers arrived during

Saturday including a Home Office pathologist from Cambridge and Forensic Science experts from Nottingham. I remember being sent to Dersingham Police Station on the Sunday following to assist local officers in this case and heard radio commentary that the suspect for the murder was driving and being chased along the A149 Road from Hunstanton towards Dersingham. Officers were scrambled and the man a twenty-three year old factory hand also of Hunstanton was arrested for this murder and brought into Dersingham *"Nick."* He then appeared at a Special Court at Hunstanton on Tuesday the 15th of July. When interviewed by The Press Mr Moody said *'This is the first time in the history of Scotland Yard where the officers at the scene have had two similar crimes in such a short space of time and to get two teams in such a large county as this arranged"*. This was designated as a *"Special Occasion"* with paid overtime being available.

A sequel to this story during May 1977 Alfred Moody was imprisoned for twelve years along with Commander Wally Virgo for having accepted very large sums of money from porn dealers when both were in charge of The Mets Obscene Publications Squad.
On Tuesday the 29th of July I was on duty with "D" Relief during the special occasion which I covered from the 28th of July until the 3rd of August with Ivan Soanes as Sergeant. At 3.30pm I was on town centre foot beat when I attended at FW Woolworth's in the High Street where I dealt with six, yes six! juvenile shoplifters there were three brothers each from two families, one lot from North Lynn and the others from South Lynn all aged between five and nine years. Although all were under the age of criminal responsibility all eventually became teen and adult criminals. Not long after the three from North Lynn were taken into care as their Father had been sexually abusing them.

From Tuesday the 5th of August until Saturday the 9th of August I was Acting Sergeant on "A" Relief and Supervising that Relief's officers including Barry John Wade and Dave Addison and then back on "B" Relief.

On Sunday the 17th of August I was on an 8am to 8pm Front Office/Control Duty when a member of the public brought in two boys aged 10 and 12 years from Gaywood Park Estate he had caught in possession of his Son's cycle which had been stolen earlier that day. This literally "snowballed" I finished up with a large amount of cycle theft detections and eleven yes eleven! Juvenile defendants. Three of these were each sentenced to 3 months Detention Centre and George Dimmock and I took them to Kidlington in Oxfordshire. Again most of the juveniles continued into crime during their teens and adulthood. You can take the individual out of their environment but you can't take the environment out of the individual.

### *"Long Sighted"*

In October a form C47 for reporting known or suspected persons and vehicles seen at night was devised and one sighting I put in not long after was to show how invaluable such information can be in the future. Sometime in late October after late turn I was out on traffic patrol with Sam Crookes and Mick Garwood and in a wooded area of Wolferton village. Around midnight we stop/checked three young Lynn villains whom we suspected were out petrol siphoning rather than buying it. Although we didn't have sufficient evidence to Nick them for going equipped I submitted full details of them and the vehicle they were using via C47. This information was to prove very valuable the following year during a night duty in the spring of 1970 when I was Front Office/Control Officer.

At 4.30am (on a date and time in 1970 not recorded) I received a telephone report of three persons disturbed siphoning petrol in the Gaywood area no vehicle had been seen and an immediate search by

Pete Keeley had proved negative. I remembered my sighting and located and circulated my original information from several months previously and within a quarter of an hour the same car and occupants had been located with siphoning equipment and a can partly full of petrol. All three were arrested admitted the offence and a spate of others. For this I received a "Good Police Work" from the Chief Constable.

We quickly found that information and intelligence concerning active or suspected criminals properly disseminated and indexed onto card system formed an integral part of our communications to patrol officers in our fight against crime, remember these were the days well before any national or local computerised systems in the police force. During this year the Collator left the Department and Clarence Hazelwood took over as Collator (and Constables Branch Board Police Federation) and I became his Deputy. One amusing story about the first one is that when he was Collator he was always trying to get notches on his belt to assist in his promotion (he eventually rose to the rank of Chief Inspector).

Someone conned him that the force were investing in a helicopter and they were looking for observers and he applied for the position, this was many years ahead even in thinking let alone coming to fruition. Norfolk Constabulary first had a police helicopter and observer crew in February 1994 some twenty five years after his report when both he and I were pushing 50!

Anyhow he put his report into Fred Calvert and the reply came back *"PC \* If and when we have a helicopter in this force you will be considered along with others for this role."*

**NORFOLK JOINT POLICE**

22/70

CONFIDENTIAL
For Police use only.

Telephone: Norwich 21234/7.
No.

Police Headquarters,
Martineau Lane,
Norwich,
NOR 07T.

21st May, 1970.

PERSONNEL ORDERS

GOOD POLICE WORK

P.C. 409 Clark "F" is congratulated for his intelligent understanding and interpretation of the collator's records, which led to the arrest of three men for theft of petrol.

At 4.20 a.m. the Officer received a report to the effect that petrol had just been syphoned from a vehicle. Panda cars were alerted; and in the meantime P.C. Clark searched the collator's records to confirm his suspicion that a vehicle had been checked late at night, several months beforehand, under circumstances which suggested the occupants were attempting to syphon petrol. He found the report and passed on the details of the driver of the vehicle. The address was checked and it was discovered that the engine of the vehicle parked outside, was still warm. The driver and two others were questioned and taken into custody.

## "Entrepreneurs"

Not everything was happy with morale in the new Joint Force two enterprising officers of the former Norwich City Force with a number of years service behind them were villains and when attending reported burglaries on night duty were adding substantially to their income and to insurance loss by clearing the premises out. They were caught when on one night duty they were called to an electrical shop alarm ringing where the premises had been burgled; they started removing many more items from the premises than had been taken by the original burglar/s and loaded them into the Police big van. Only on this occasion they were observed by a nearby resident and the following morning when the proprietor lamented to this person what had been stolen; he was informed by the witness that the police had removed items for safe keeping. Well that was OK until the proprietor telephoned Bethel Street Police Station and after enquiries resulted that no such property was present in the PSE (Property Subject to Enquiry); the two were hauled in and in September 1969, both were sentenced to 18 months imprisonment at Norwich Quarter Sessions after pleading guilty to burglary.

Going back to Peter on our Relief during night shift about 3am he would come into *"The Nick"* and start telling us the most dry boring self made jokes going like for example *"What do you call an elderly Egyptian?"* Answer *"Senile."* I quickly tired of this inane humour and using his own equipment would handcuff him to the radiator or sling him in the cells and leave him there until he promised to stop; or he had a callout. This was dedication to duty – Now I cannot remember when it occurred not that it matters it happened; "B" Relief used to follow "A" Relief's duties and "A" Relief having just completed 7 early shifts were weekend off on the Friday when we paraded for our first early turn. We thought that we had a transferee; it was a PC from "A" Relief reporting on duty in uniform! He had come in for his 8th early turn and wanted to know why we were there! And then the penny dropped and he slunk back

home to enjoy an early start to his well earned weekend.
This reminds me of another not completely dissimilar occurrence. One Sunday in March our beat bobby from West Lynn turned up at Shouldham Football ground to play for us only he had forgotten to put his clock forward to the start of British Summer Time and turned up near the end of the match.

Not to be outdone the following October at the end of British Summer Time he remembered but put his clock forward instead of back one hour so on this occasion he turned up two hours before the match and not seeing anyone thought that it had been cancelled! He was a good darts player and a first aider he was also a keyboard player with The 999's Pop group and a bit of a comic who somehow went on to the dizzy heights of Inspector.

Here is a riddle what connects Sir Robert Peel with David Bowie and Laurel and Hardy in the derision of police officers? Answers:

(i) Sir Robert Peel founder of *"The Met"* Police who previously kept pigs on his Drayton Manor Estate near Tamworth. Hence the words *"Pig"* and *"Filth."*

(ii) David Bowie aka David Robert Jones penned a song in 1965 *"Over the wall we go, all coppers are nanas"* which was changed by the yob elements to *"Over the wall we go all coppers are bastards"*

*(iii)* The Laurel and Hardy Theme whistled as an insult when two police officers are walking down the street together particularly in the case of two mentioned later who were dead ringers for Stan & Ollie!

Before leaving the subject Jeanne told me that the Police Station in St Ives, Cambridgeshire used to be situated in Pig Lane! And the police got the Council to change it. I looked it up and in June 1971 it made the *"Los Angeles Times"* in America: *"The policemen in the English town of St Ives might have saved themselves some embarrassment if they had thought first and built later. After all a new police station built on Pig Lane is really asking a lot of the long suffering British Bobby…..They asked the Town Council to rename it Eastfield Road." !!*

## "Viva Las Norwich"

On Tuesday the 18th of November I got up around 10am and worked a late turn in the Front Office Control and at 9.50pm just before clocking off I tore off a telex message from the machine which was now housed in the former Lost & Found cupboard and placed a copy on the night shift briefing board. I saw that it was a stolen vehicle report circulated by Norwich Division of a pale Green Vauxhall Viva 1967 model index number KCL983G stolen from Delves Garage Mountergate, Norwich during the early part of that evening and it was 6K of today meaning the sixth vehicle reported stolen in the County on that date.

I didn't think that it would be coming our way probably stolen for a later shop burglary in Norwich but for some reason best unknown to me I wrote the details down before going out on patrol as observer in traffic patrol car Alpha 16 with *"Harry"*. At 1010pm we went out on main trunk road patrol and at 1120pm we were called to assist the local Terrington mobile Foxtrot 28 containing two Pc's the scene of an RTA on the A17 at the *"New Inn"* Public House, Terrington St Clement. (This road is now a B class road since the A17 Clenchwarton to Sutton Bridge Bypass opened some years later).

On arrival by F28 they circulated that they had found 6K of today the stolen Viva from Norwich some sixty miles from where it was stolen! Having been involved in a head on collision the driver had done a runner from the scene. He was described as about 30 years, dark hair, wearing denim overalls and a donkey jacket and bleeding from the nose.

We made a search of the immediate area together with Derrick Pimlott who was in Foxtrot 19 with *"Rebel"* his new dog.

At 1145pm *"Harry"* and I stopped on the A.17 about three quarters of a mile the Sutton Bridge side of this incident in order to help a broken down lorry, the driver was from Gorleston. We got a local breakdown firm out and they attended. Before we left we asked the lorry driver and breakdown driver to keep a lookout for anyone on foot answering the description of the man that we were looking for and at 12:10am resumed patrol.

At 12:15am during the first hour of Wednesday morning the 19th we established that the wanted man had recently gone to the "New Inn" with a blood stained piece of curtain to stem the flow and he had used the toilet and then disappeared; we then made a renewed search of the area. At 1256am just when we thought the scent had gone cold and over an hour and a half after the accident we received a call from HQIR saying they had received a 999 call from the breakdown truck driver who stated the man wanted for stealing the Viva had now hitched a lift in the lorry which had been repaired and was heading towards Kings Lynn.

At 1.15am we stopped the lorry on Wisbech Road, Kings Lynn and I saw the male passenger was of the same description as the man who had ran from the stolen Viva. Not wishing to alert him to the fact that we had been tipped off by the lorry driver I said to him *"Are you this lorry driver's mate?"* He replied *"No I was picked up by this driver hitch hiking to Cromer."* I questioned the lorry driver who said *"No I picked him up in Terrington about 15 minutes ago I have not seen him before."* I then obtained details of the passenger and found him to be a thirty five year old man from Tuckswood Estate in Norwich who was a Welder.

I said to him *"I have reasonable suspicion that you were the person who stole a Vauxhall Viva colour Lime Green index number KCL983G from Norwich earlier this evening and were involved with it in an accident at Terrington St Clement. You fit the description of the man seen running from this vehicle and you are blood stained and have cuts to your face and hands. I am arresting you on suspicion of stealing this vehicle and other offences which will be explained to you later. You are not obliged to say anything but anything you do say will be taken down in writing and may be given in evidence."* He said *"How could I steal the car I can't even drive how could it be me I don't know how to drive. I cut my hands while at work filing, you fucking prove it and I'll fucking prove I was elsewhere".* He seemed to be drunk and apart from the obvious cuts he didn't complain of any other substantial injuries and when asked I asked him if he was injured he replied no and he refused medical treatment; we took him to Kings Lynn where he was seen by Sergeant Peter Griffin and Inspector Peter Farman at 1.20am.

Norwich Division CID was informed and the prisoner was banged up in the cells to sleep and await his interview with a DC from Norwich and myself at 9am; where he admitted all of the offences and made a voluntary statement. I then obtained a witness statement from the other person involved in the accident and at 1245pm went as escort to Norwich with the DC and the prisoner. He was charged at Norwich for TWOC (Taking a motor vehicle without consent of the owner) driving whilst disqualified, no insurance and driving without due care and attention. I eventually got back to King's Lynn around teatime and went to bed some 36 hours after I had got up!

The man had a substantial criminal record and later appeared at Norwich Crown Court and was disqualified for a further 10 years and received 3 years imprisonment.

This case clearly illustrates that you cannot police without the help of the public and that by stopping to help someone even when committed can bring forth valuable information and a good result. We asked Fred Calvert if he would write letters to both the lorry driver and breakdown firm thanking them for their help which he did.

## *1970*

The beginning of the year found me on regular foot patrol and just after 10pm on Tuesday the 20th of January I was on night duty in the Millfleet Bus Station together with another PC (this has since moved to the old cattle market site next to Sainsbury's supermarket). We were told by some people standing at a stop that a young man had threatened them with a knife and appeared to be drunk. As we were taking details one of the witnesses *said "Look there's that man who threatened us a short while ago with a knife."* and he pointed to a rather tall young man wearing a black leather jacket who was staggering about in the middle of the road.

He was shouting and singing and drawing attention to himself. I started to walk towards him and he went into the new block of flats at Hillington Square and disappeared from view, the PC and I then split up to search for him. A short while later I found this person crouching in a recess under a concrete staircase which led up to the first floor flats. I said *"It's the police come out from under there"* which after a short while he did. He was swaying about and his breath smelt strongly of alcoholic drink. I said *"I have received a complaint about your behaviour and have witnessed some myself I am arresting you for being drunk and disorderly in a public place and for having in your possession a knife which you used as an offensive weapon."* He shouted out *"I'm not fucking drunk, let me go or I'll do you"* I put a hammer lock and bar restraining hold on him and managed to locate a large sheath knife in a pocket of his jacket and remove it and threw it down for collection later. I then frog marched him to the Millfleet where I rejoined the PC who radioed for a panda car to take him in which arrived shortly afterwards.

As it did so my prisoner who had previously stopped struggling and seemed resigned to his fate, suddenly went berserk he kicked out and swung his fist at me which I avoided. But he then pushed me hard and I fell to the ground still holding onto him and as we went down he kicked out and caught me in the groin. Several officers had arrived by this time and tried to restrain him as he seemed to have gone completely fighting mad. It's a good job I had taken the knife off of him when I did! I then saw him punch one of our *"Specials"* in the head which started bleeding.

This twat was still going berserk and I thought to myself that's it *'I've had enough of being "Mr Nice Guy"* I grabbed him by the hair and with an arm up his back forced him to the open door of the Hillman Imp and deliberately banged his forehead on the top of the door frame and while he was dazed cuffed him behind his back and shoved him into the back seat of the panda car and he was raced off to the *"Nick"* and slung in the cells to cool down.

At 1.15am I interviewed him and found that he was a seventeen year old of No Fixed Abode staying at a B&B in London Road. I took a statement under caution and at 2:05am I charged him with the offences I had put to him and he was kept in the cells overnight and went to court the next morning and found guilty. A couple of evenings later I saw him on a bus with others and had to go on to warn them of their behaviour, realizing that it was me and our recent dealings together he shut up.

On Monday the 9th of March I was on night duty in Panda 2 with Terry Sturman when at 10:55pm we received a radio message from Control over our Pye Pocketfone to go to The Cattle market and we checked the phone box there. We arrived within 2 minutes and found considerable damage done to the telephone mechanism and the coin container was missing. We then spoke to a witness from WH Smith's who informed us that he had seen two youths run away from the attacked box. He described them as:

(i) 5'10", fair hair, wearing a blue denim jacket and trousers aged about 18 years and

(ii) Wearing an "Eton" type striped jacket.

We made a search of the area and just after 11pm we saw 2 persons who we knew as active criminals in Tennyson Road, one who was wearing denims and the other wearing a striped jacket. Our Sergeant arrived and spoke to one and arrested him.

Terry said to the other *"Where have you just come from?"* He said *"I took my girl to the Millfleet"* Terry *"Why are you walking back this way? It's a long way from the Millfleet."* B *"We got to Dodman's Bridge and thought it was quicker through The Walks."* T *"Why were you running through the Cattle market?"* B *"I haven't been anywhere near the Cattle market tonight"* T *"You answer the description of two youths seen breaking into the telephone kiosk on the Cattle market and I am arresting you on suspicion of this offence."* Caution Given. B *"I didn't fucking well do it why don't you pick on some other bastard I didn't know the kiosk was there."* We then took B in the police vehicle to the Cattle market and he said *"Well I may have come across the Cattle market with * I've been with him since 7pm this evening".*

Both prisoners were taken to DHQ in separate vehicles and upon arrival I searched B and found him to have a pair of woollen gloves in his jacket pocket and a cylinder ratchet spanner. Terry said to him *"Why have you got this spanner in your possession?"* B said *"It's just a bike spanner, I just forgot I had it on me."* He also had a large amount of coinage in his property; they were both later charged and admitted the offence.

*King's Lynn Magistrates Court*

This was located in the Town Hall. In the top photo The Bench is on the left, the large table is for Prosecution and Defence with the Witness Box on the right. The bottom one is the view from The Dock with Press Box on the left.

Commencing the 1st of April the 40 hour week came into being, it still meant shifts worked 7 shifts of 8 hours each as a norm i.e. 56hours and the Esso people (every Saturday and Sunday off) worked the 40 hours but we had 9 additional rest days paid for from April and 4 additional leave days taken off during the winter. That sounds fair enough until you realize that the Esso people were getting exactly the same as well as the same rate of pay that we in unsociable hours were.

# NORFOLK JOINT POLICE

Police Headquarters,
Martineau Lane,
Norwich,
NOR 07T.

63/69

Norwich 212347.

...NTIAL
... only.

23rd December, 1969.

GENERAL ORDERS.

40 HOUR WEEK

The Police Council's recommendation that there should be an actual reduction of working hours for the federated ranks as from the 1st April, 1970, has been accepted by the Police Authority.

At the moment however, with the existing manpower situation, this must be considered against the manpower available to maintain efficiency. Initially therefore, nine additional rest days will be paid for commencing in April and four will be granted as additional leave days during the winter to all federated ranks in the Force.

Full implementation of the 40 hour week will take place when the strength of the Force so permits.

Further instructions will be issued in due course.

During this month I joined the Divisional First Aid Team which consisted of Inspector Dave Pearson, PCs George Hooke, Keith Tuvey and WDC Daphne Williamson. DC Keith Holliday our Scenes of Crime Officer took photos of The Team on Thursday the 2nd of April.

# The Laughing Policeman

*Dave Pearson   Daphne Williamson   Me   Keith Tuvey   George Hooke*

### *"Front Office Confessional"*

Now it's not every day that you get a criminal dying to confess to you. On Saturday the 3rd of October I was on late turn Front Office/Control duty when at 4.25pm a 28 year old man I knew from my home village by the name of KB came into the station and asked for me he had been drinking and was crying but he wasn't drunk. He said *"Chris give me a pen and paper I want to confess to some break-ins and stealing a lot of money that I have done."* I said *"You don't have to tell me anything about this if you don't want to but if you do tell me and it's the truth I will have to arrest you and investigate what you have told me."* I then cautioned him and B said *"I want to admit everything it has been playing on my mind for a long time. About six weeks ago I was out of a job and had no money so I started stealing and breaking into places in the Dersingham area. I broke into Dersingham Secondary School and Potts School."* I said *"I'm going to arrest you for these offences K and make enquiries into the matter."*

I took him into the Charge Room and contacted Det Sgt Mick Farnham and DC Malcolm *"Joffe"* Brown for further investigation. At 6.30pm whilst doing a prisoner's visit I saw B in the cells and he said "Chris I want to tell you something those officers who are going to my house can you tell them that the stolen property is under my bed in a home-made fishing box". I then informed Mick and *"Joffe"* and they located and recovered the stolen property. B later appeared at court and pleaded guilty and I did not have to attend to give evidence.

Pete Valleley was promoted from Detective Constable and was our Station Sergeant prior to being a police officer he was in the Royal Air Force on 207 Squadron. John B and Mick H had also joined the shift when Mick transferred from Thorpe he looked like a refugee from *"The Three Musketeers"* he always wore his cape and his hair was long and he had a French moustache. He also incidentally had a Green Citroen car with running boards and front doors which opened backwards like the Citroen Big 6H in the *"Maigret"* French detective series which starred Rupert Davies. Pete Valleley took an instant dislike to Mick this laid back *"Hippy Looking"* cop who just didn't look right in uniform. I think they got on in later years when Mick spent most of his service as a Detective Constable.

Mick was at Thorpe when I was at Hellesdon and I used to see him at monthly probation classes along with Roger, another Mick H, Pete B and others; Roger must have studied hard as he eventually made Chief Superintendent. Mick was on duty in Thorpe one day when there had been a big freeze and as he came down the slope at Harvey Lane to the junction with Thorpe Road his police vehicle careered straight across the main road and collided with a large tree, this was pulled down shortly after.

Anyway Mick was on "D" Relief at Lynn along with others including a PC who later was HM the Queen's Beat Officer at Sandringham and taught the young Royals Prince Andrew and Prince Edward how to shoot; there was also Adrian who went on to be a Chief Superintendent in the Norfolk Force and then Deputy Commissioner of The British Transport Police. On nights they would go to Jim Donaldson's Fishmongers in Norfolk Street and buy whole kippers which they would grill for meal break and then deliberately boil the heads, tails and bones in a saucepan until the whole *"Nick"* stank of fish much to the disgust of the female civilian staff and the bosses who came in at 8am.

During my time in Single men's Quarters I thought that the place needed livening up so I applied to Fred Calvert and received permission to hold a monthly *"Singlemen's Dance"* this I published on a gestetner printer and circulated copies to the Relief's, CID, Traffic, etc as well as to female employees of the Banks in the town including the Trustee Savings Bank and to The Nurse's Home which had been built at the new Queen Elizabeth Hospital on Gayton Road. It was a *"bring a bottle"* affair and I used to chip in a quantity of booze as a starter. John B, Chris G and Mick H's wives would be in the Singlemen's kitchen on a Saturday afternoon making a mountain of sandwiches and other edibles ready for the do that night.

The Single men's Lounge would be cleared of furniture and resemble a dance floor the do's were very popular and the room would heave with writhing bodies to the *"Sounds of the Sixtys"* including Diana Ross and other Tamla Motown records which I had pre-recorded on my reel to reel tape recorder.

Many a policeman's romance started as a result of these functions and I was invited to several later weddings as a result. It may also have contributed to a couple of divorces from couples who had engaged in extra marital relationships leading from it.

## *1971*

During January there was a National postal strike which lasted for seven weeks and all Forces had to operate a Police Emergency Courier Service. In the Eastern Region three main sorting offices were set up at Mid Anglia Headquarters (now Cambridgeshire) Northampton HQ and Nottinghamshire HQ. GPO telephone kiosks were not emptied and became prime targets for villains.

### *"Not in my Nick"*

On Friday the 15th of January I was on a night shift and the sole person in Front Office/Control taking 999 calls, receiving and transmitting radio messages to King's Lynn Officers and to Divisional Officers via our HQ set. At 1130pm two prisoners were brought into the Charge Room and shortly after as I was taking a report of a man lying unconscious in Hunstanton when I was aware of a lot of shouting and swearing coming from outside the police station. Upon looking out I saw about seven local yobs who I knew. This group then came into the public foyer of the *"Nick"* still making one hell of a commotion and started to continually ring the enquiry counter button and banging on the counter.

I called out for them to be quiet and would see to them when I was free. I then went to attend to them and they were still shouting and banging and one who appeared to be the ring leader was leaning against the counter and I could smell that he had been drinking. He said *"We want to see JN and we're not leaving until you bastards let him go. If you don't there'll be trouble we know how you fuckers operate."* I was getting quite pissed off with his behaviour by now and I made a mental note not to add him to my Christmas card list.

I then said to all of them firmly *"Shut up and if you can't keep quiet you will have to leave you can't see N at the moment firstly he hasn't been charged and secondly there is no one to take you to see him and thirdly with your present attitude I'm not allowing you to come into the police station."* B said *"I want to see fucking Calvert."* I said *"The Chief Superintendent is not here get out of the station and stop shouting and swearing or you will be in trouble."* B said *"I'm not fucking going anywhere we're witnesses for N we want him out!"* The others were backing him up and chanting *"He said "I won't shut up to you or anyone you bastards are all the same we'll have you this time."*

I said *"Maybe so but you're going to leave my police station out! You can give your evidence in court."* They all remained in a standoff position. I then went into the public foyer and opened the main entrance/exit doors and said *"Right you lot out or you will all be arrested for obstruction."* They all refused to budge and I shouted out again *"Out! None of you can afford to get into any more trouble at the moment."*

All apart from B started to file out and he squared up to me, wrong move! I grabbed hold of his arm and shoved him out of the *"Nick"* and he turned and shouted *"Bastard! Bastard!"* This started the others up again and I said to him *"Right you've had more than enough warning you're in I'm arresting you for obstructing me in the execution of my duty and for disorderly conduct in a police station."* I took hold of his arm and he swung round and aimed a fist at me I countered by parrying the blow on my arm and put a hammer lock and bar on him and frogmarched him into the Station Charge Room. This resulted in the other six quietening down and dispersing, I had spent over a quarter of an hour with this prat luckily there were no urgent radio or phone messages coming in during that time.

Frank Leech who was gaoler put him in the cells at midnight. At 4.05am with Inspector Lewis Heavens and Sgt Peter Griffin present I charged B with being drunk and disorderly obstructing a police officer assaulting a police officer and resisting arrest he later went to court and pleaded guilty and was fined. The two he had come into the police station to see were each sent to Detention Centre for 3 months.

During January as a result of me researching both internal force and external force telex messages I realized that two travelling criminals could be responsible for a stolen vehicle from Wells being involved in burglaries at Dersingham and Hunstanton and Mansfield in Nottinghamshire and a further stolen vehicle from Mansfield being involved in telephone kiosk breaks at Kings Lynn near to a villian's sister's address and then being dumped near to their addresses in Tonbridge Wells, Kent.

I contacted the CID in the areas concerned and Maidstone Regional Crime Squad made them *"targets"* and after a surveillance operation they were eventually arrested.
At the beginning of February Olive Edwards old knitting machine of a switchboard was replaced with an Automatic Telephone Exchange at Kings Lynn, as well as others at HQ, Norwich and Great Yarmouth. General Order 1/71 stated *"All officers should familiarize themselves with the working of these exchanges as their correct use greatly increases the speed and efficiency of telephone communications throughout the Force area."*

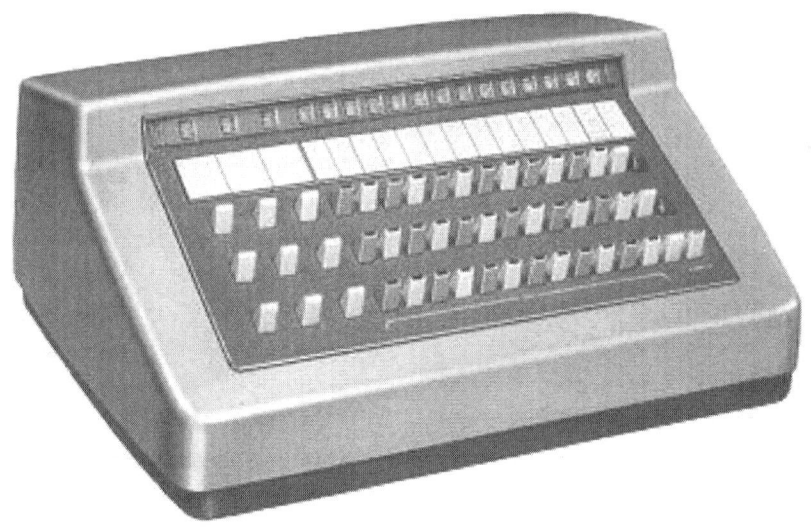

On Monday the 15th of February Decimalisation occurred in Great Britain when £.s.d, pounds shillings and pence changed to decimal currency all of the banks closed on the preceding Thursday the 11th and Friday the 12th in preparation of the changeover.

On Saturday the 20th of March I was late turn and at 4.05pm I came across what I thought was the dead body of a man lying on his back in College Lane near the South Quay he was unconscious and with a fixed stare on his face. I found that he had a faint pulse by feeling his neck pressure point and he appeared to be in a coma. I rendered first aid and thanked myself that I was in the team and up to date. I commandeered some blankets from a passing motorist and found that my radio transmitter wasn't working from that location so I dispatched this motorist to the telephone kiosk on Saturday Market Place to dial "999" for an ambulance (no mobile phones then) this turned up 10 minutes later and I went in the ambulance to the Kings Lynn General Hospital which was on London Road in those days.

My *"body"* eventually came round and I ascertained that he was a German Seaman a widower from Emden, North Germany and off the

Motor Vessel Luzia berthed in the Bentink Dock He was diagnosed by the Doctor as suffering from severe withdrawal symptoms following addiction to heroin and also with severe depression, he was detained in hospital.

From April I was the permanent Front Office/Control Officer on "B" Relief as well as Acting Sergeant during Pete Griffin's annual leave and other absences like firearms.

During June I went with my Dad on a day trip via Hovercraft from Ramsgate to France this was organised by his local the *"Albert Victor"* situated in Manor Road Dersingham. We had a very enjoyable day together and for the trip I had to have a day passport (not part of EU then) John Hansell one of our two Scenes of Crime Officers took the photo of me in uniform minus epaulettes.

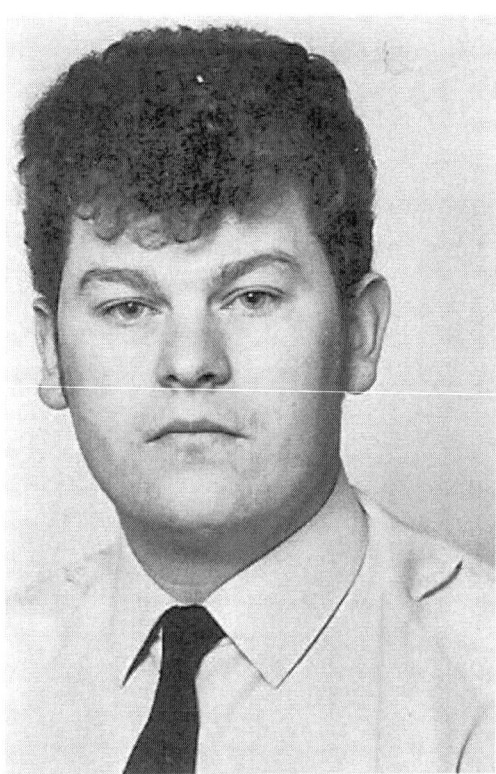

I was also Deputy Collator and covered Clarence Hazelwood's annual leave in August working 10am to 6pm duties during this year there was a spate of speedboat thefts occurring around the Norfolk coast from Great Yarmouth up to Hunstanton which leads me on to the next off duty episode.

### "We are not straw chewers"

On Friday the 6th August I completed a duty in the Collator's Office and at 1045pm I went out on a night shift in a traffic car Alpha 25 with Bryan Edwards. At 1.05am the following morning we were patrolling the B1153 Narborough to Gayton Road and heading towards Gayton and had just gone past Pentney Caravan Park when going in the opposite direction in the dark I saw a cream and green coloured Ford Thames 15cwt van index number, 932DYR. I recognised this vehicle as belonging to a London "overspill" criminal from the Fairstead Estate at Kings Lynn. This vehicle was towing a large speedboat on a trailer also displaying the index 932DYR making it look legitimate. I said to Bryan *"Quick turn round and go after him that boat will be stolen!"* He did and we eventually caught up with it on the old A47 road in Narborough village and stopped it. As we approached the vehicle I saw that there were two male occupants sitting in it and I went up to the driver's door and saw a large guy who I knew from his collator's photo as being BN he was holding the steering wheel with both hands and I could see that his hands were shaking nervously. I said to him *"What is your full name and address?"* N gave his correct name and gave an address on the Fairstead Estate Kings Lynn. The other gave his name and also from Fairstead Estate Kings Lynn. Bryan then said to N *"Who does this boat belong to and where are you taking it?"* N said *"We're taking it from Hunstanton to Stoke Ferry for a friend it's not our boat."* Bryan said *"Can you give me the name of this friend so that we can verify this?"* B said *"No I'm sorry I can't."*

I then said to N *"I think that you are not telling us the truth about the boat we think that you've nicked it and we're going to knock you off for it and take you back to Kings Lynn."* I cautioned him and said *"Where did the boat come from?"* N said *"We went out for a few beers and formed the idea of nicking a boat for some quick money we went to Brancaster and picked this up and we were going down to London when you stopped us. We were going to flog it or stash it away somewhere."* This version seemed highly unlikely as a spur of the moment thing as they had a spare number plate made up and I suspected that we had caught part of an organised team of speedboat thieves.

Both were taken to Lynn *"Nick"* and the boat was found to be a *"Fletcher Arrow"* seventeen foot high power speed boat colour cream with red upholstery, with a *"Mercury"* 1250cc outboard motor on a blue boat trailer. We circulated details of the arrests and the boat as it had not yet been reported stolen and went off duty to grab some sleep.
I returned to duty at 10am and liaised with Det Sgt Mick Farnham and went with DC Mervyn Clingo to do house searches of the two arrestees; when we searched the rented lockup garage belonging to N we found another stolen speedboat and trailer together with water ski's and other property the subject of beach bungalow breaks from Heacham. We were informed by N's wife that another *"overspill"* villain ML had done these breaks. This man referred to was later arrested for attempted murder and armed robbery. He went to Clarke's Filling station at Gaywood, hit the attendant over the head with a hammer wrapped in a sock and then stole money from the safe and till.

At 8pm that evening Mervyn and I interviewed N and in the course of it he admitted stealing the second speedboat from the outskirts of Nottingham during June or July the previous year, this he had repainted a different colour and was using it for his social life water skiing, etc. Both men later appeared at Quarter Sessions court and received custodial sentences, Bryan and I received a Chief Constable's Commendation.

# The Laughing Policeman

## "Black Magic"

Exactly one month later on Monday the 6th of September whilst again covering Clarence's absence in the Collator's Office for a Police Federation Conference, at 7pm I went out again with Bryan Edwards who was on a late turn traffic duty in the marked patrol car. At 1040pm he was driving back into Lynn down Gayton Road to the Gaywood Clock and the Gaywood and Wootton Road junction in order to book off duty. At this junction I spotted one of the main gang of burglars/receivers L who was a stepson to one of the main players, he was standing leaning against the crash barrier on the bend and looking up towards Wootton Road. The area was deserted and *"Gilberts"* the local fish & chip shop was closed. I immediately formed the suspicion that he was a *"lookout"* for something criminal happening or about to happen. We doubled back but by then he had disappeared and when we got back to the *"Nick"* I quickly located found Derrick Pimlott and we with *"Rebel"* went out and back up to Gaywood where I had seen this man.

At 1125pm having just got past the aforementioned fish shop we saw that the front door of Rosalind Bird's tobacconist and confectionist premises was hanging open and had obviously just been broken into. This was confirmed by a passer by who had seen it in that state a quarter of an hour previously, we found that a large quantity of cigarettes, cigars and boxes of chocolates, etc were missing from the store and that the burglars would have needed a vehicle to transport them in. I worked out that we were about ten minutes behind who had done it and with L being involved they would probably have gone down a dirt track called Salter's Road which would be a short cut from that part of Gaywood to North Lynn Estate where he lived.

I said to Derrick that rather than follow their trail it would be best to quickly drive the long way round town by normal road and try and cut them off at the far end of this track which we did going via Gaywood

Road, Loke Road and Losinga Road. We then turned into the North Lynn end of Salter's Road near The Discovery Public House and at once became aware of a vehicle parked in the darkness in a little bridleway at the rear of Losinga Road and we saw three people milling about near it. On seeing us all three ran up the bridleway and before Derrick could stop the police minivan and release *"Rebel"* all three had jumped over a barbed wire fence and disappeared into the maze of rear gardens of various private properties on the estate.

A lot were lived in by associate criminals and it would be fruitless to try and find them.

We found that the vehicle left at the scene was a Black Austin Westminster, index number 7456YG its doors were open and the engine was hot and we saw that the rear seat was laden with cardboard boxes which contained cartons of cigarettes boxes of cigars and boxes of chocolates. Upon closer examination of one of these, a box of *"Black Magic"* chocolates I saw some very fresh fingerprints on the shrink wrap plastic covering and a whole palm print and fingerprints on the boot lid of the vehicle which contained a lot more of their ill-gotten gain.

At 1am a street search of the area by Derrick Pimlott and by the newly promoted Sergeant George Hooke's "D" Relief night shift was negative and called off so we got a recovery vehicle out and had the Austin taken to Kings Lynn Police Station for full SOCO examination; I left Keith "Geordie" Holliday a note to check the prints found against those held on record of L and left full circumstances in the CID night log of whom I had seen prior to the burglary and full details of what later occurred and went off duty.

I was duty Collator the next morning and I saw that L had not been arrested or it appeared any further enquiries made into the burglary. That evening I went out with Derrick to an address in Turbus Road, North Lynn where I saw and spoke to L's step father we were invited in and there saw L and I said to him *"I'm arresting you on suspicion of burglary at Rosiland Bird's of Gaywood last night"* and cautioned him. Derrick said *"Where were you last night?"* L said *"I stayed home all night I went to bed early about half past ten."*

We then took him in to Kings Lynn *"Nick"* and about 9pm in the Charge Room L said *"What's this all about anyhow?"* I said *"You have been told why you have been arrested and you have been cautioned."*

L said *"How did you involve me in this?"* I said *"You were seen by two police officers K and positively identified at the Gaywood Clock at 1040pm last night keeping lookout. The place was deserted and you were leaning on the crash barrier on the bend so that you could see all three ways. We established that Bird's had been broken into and that's why you are here."* L said *"I've already told you I was home all night ask J and my old woman, they will tell you."* I said *"I don't care what they say you were seen there. I was one of the officers who saw you there."* L said *"Go ahead and prove it."* At 9pm he was placed in the cells overnight pending CID Interview in the morning.

At 9.45am the following morning to my dismay the CID had released him under Section 38 (2) of the Magistrates Courts Act to await the outcome of fingerprint evidence. In the meantime he committed further shop burglary offences and went to Quarter Sessions and he eventually received nine months imprisonment for those offences. Needless to say that the fingerprints on the box of chocolates came back an exact match for him, so not only was he lookout he had handled the stolen property and was physically involved in the burglary and attempted disposal of the proceeds.

During this year the Courts Act 1971 came into force and Courts of Assize and Quarter Sessions, which had been around since the 14th Century, were to be abolished by January the 1st 1972.

Sometime in October of that year I went to King's Lynn Quarter Sessions as L had pleaded not guilty to his part in the Rosiland Bird

Burglary or to Handling. He appeared in court in custody whilst already serving the nine month sentence mentioned above; he claimed false identity until the fingerprint evidence was given and then changed his plea to guilty.

I could not believe what the The Recorder said next *"Mr L I sentence you to nine months imprisonment for this offence which PC Clark and DC Holliday have proved beyond all reasonable doubt, however as this is an historical occasion being the last ever Quarter Sessions to be held at kings Lynn and yours the last ever case. I will be lenient and change the sentence to run concurrent with the one you are already serving."* As he was led down to the court cells L had this big wide grin on his face and looked straight at me with a smug expression. Well you could have knocked me down with a feather!

The bastard basically got off the burglary after slagging me off in Court, there was no good police work or commendation on this occasion for something I had achieved whilst *"off duty"* and to cap it all certain CID officers were going around puffing on the most expensive *"freebe"* cigars and I didn't get as much as a CDM Cadbury's Dairy Milk! There was no justice on this occasion.

### *1972*

From the 1st of January as previously mentioned Courts of Assize and Quarter sessions were abolished and replaced with Crown Courts in a Three Tier System, in the South Eastern Circuit a First Tier Court sat at The Old Bailey and Norwich, etc, to hear Murder Cases, etc whilst Kings Lynn became a Third Tier Court hearing lesser offences.

On Monday the 3rd of January I went to Headquarters for a two week Constable's Refresher Development Course, Mervyn Clingo who was at Hellesdon in 1967 and involved in the stolen speedboat case was on the course with me. In the photograph below I'm the one in shirt sleeve order as I was Acting Collator and Mervyn is standing next to me in civvies as he was a Detective Constable by then. Tom Braithwaite was Chief Inspector Training at that time he is seated centre front row.

Back to my story and 1972: PC 782 Dave Burton was on "B" Relief as a new lad during 1972 but he had previously been a Norfolk Constabulary Officer some years previously and had then joined The Royal Military Police became an Army Special Investigation Branch Officer and then on promotion an SIB Sergeant. Dave didn't stay in uniform long and by the following year was a Detective Constable.

I remember one time when he was night duty CID with us he was sitting in the Control Room/Front Office at about 4am reading the Eastern Daily Press which was a broad sheet newspaper and I set light to the bottom of it for a laugh. Well as Dave was reading the top of the paper and due to the hour he didn't realize what was happening until the paper was well ablaze and he suddenly jumped up shouting *"Clarky you bastard!"* before trampling the charred remains on the floor. Poor old Dave he didn't make it to retirement he died of a heart attack and was sadly missed.

## Drunk In Charge of a Uniform

On one really hot Monday in June two of my "B" Relief colleagues D and E and myself caught the bus from Lynn to go to Heacham we each took swimming gear and had a lovely day swimming in the sea and sun bathing. When evening came we walked into the village and spent the evening in The West Norfolk Public House drinking ice cold *"Carlsberg"* lager of which we each consumed twelve pints. We then staggered outside in time to catch the bus back to Lynn and get changed for night duty I was pissed as a newt when I reported for duty, this was completely out of character for me and I blame those two for leading me astray on that occasion!

I got out on patrol as quickly as I could before anyone noticed my condition and I remember swaying along checking property and the shops seemed to keep moving.

The next thing is that sometime after midnight Peter Farman our Inspector called me up on the radio for a point, no not a pint, a point! And I'm thinking *"I'm in the shit now."* When he arrived he had just turned out of his and soon to be mine "off duty" local *"watering hole"* at The Rummer Public House on the corner of Tower Street and St James Street and his breath smelt stronger than mine. Jack Cherrington the licensee used to have a *"lock in"* for special customers consisting of trusted police officers, The Mayor Eddie Edgley and others.

During this year due to the diabolical food still being served to us by Mrs Pink I found a rented house at 29 Checker Street which I rented from (Bron) who was one of our part time cooks and D and E who were in unpleasant lodgings shared this with me and I moved out of Single men's Quarters. We each paid a third of the rent and had a pool fund of money which we each put a third into for shopping, there were to be several changes of house mates from "B" Relief over the next four years as one by one they would get married and have their own place.

*29 Checker Street*

Now D and E and I all got on fine but after a short while during October 1972 D married P from the TSB and J moved in from Single men's Quarters and that's when the fireworks really started between him and E. It was like they were an unhappy couple always bickering and arguing and winding each other up, they were just like Laurel & Hardy; E would call J *"the fat monk"* J would insist that his hair wasn't receding but merely a double crown and they would go on and on.

Now J was an Ex Met Cadet and that tight with his money he would have to go to the dentist's to get his wallet out. He had this large Red Wolsey car but only ever put half a gallon in it and it was always running out and every time J would get the empty can out and walk to the nearest filling station and buy another half gallon! I think that he walked more miles than he drove.

J would say to me *"Let's go for a drink Clarky"* with his skin head haircut and dressed in his MPC (Metropolitan Police Cadet) T shirt jeans, braces and *"bovver boots"* he would look every inch a *"yob"* well come to think of it he was! We would go into The London Porter House just onto the main road from our digs and once inside he would put his hand into his jeans pocket in such an exaggerated way like someone putting their arm down a drain to unblock it. One of the regulars would call out "I'll get these J" and he would reply with pretend surprise "Oh! Oh! Well if you're sure." He would get away with this for four rounds with me having bought one and then sidle up to the one armed bandit put in the small amount of cash he had brought with him, make a profit and then call out *"I've got to go, goodnight."* He would do this time after time I don't actually remember you buying a round J you tight bastard!

We would also on occasions go to the China Garden and J would stuff himself with King Prawn fried rice which resembled a JCB digger tearing into an earth mound and guess who paid? His car reminds me of the day when J thought he would make his fortune out of selling crabs we had been down to G's Police House on Wisbech Road where the kitchen was full of crabs being cooked that he and some others from

"D" Relief had got from Holme-next-the-Sea.

J and I set off one sunny day having worked the tides out, you had to follow it out until the sunken peat beds were exposed where the crabs would hide in little caves and before anyone else got them put a gaff hook in which they would grab hold of and pull them out. We took the road to Old Hunstanton and just past The Le Strange Arms drove down a track about a mile past marshes and sand dunes until you come to the coast the last bit was actually travelling along a sand track.

Now having previously gone down this track with the others I knew that about half way along it the track broadened and there was deep sand in the middle but you could pass it on either side. I had pre-warned J of this danger but as we approached pig headed as ever he decided to drive straight through the middle and the result was up to our axles in soft sand, of course he made it worse revving the engine until it screamed and getting us deeper. He eventually tired of this and got out of the car in a fit of purple rage and went to the front offside wheel where with his Doc Martin *"bovver boots"* proceeded to kick in the chrome hub cap shouting out *"you fucking bastard"* to the poor innocent vehicle, it resembled the scene some years later from *"Clockwise"* when John Cleese from *"Monty Python"* thrashed his Mini with a branch after getting stuck in a pond.

Well I just sat in the front passenger seat with tears streaming down my face and helpless with laughter. After I had recovered we both set about finding pieces of drift wood to firstly dig out the mountain of sand which had accumulated by the rear wheels and then jammed them in front of these wheels to drive out from the sand tomb which we eventually did. When we got to the beach the tide had gone out and all of the crabs had been removed by other experienced beach combers or had got that bored waiting they had left home, we did a spot of sun bathing and returned to Lynn.

Before J left Single men's Quarters to move in with E and me his room there was full of spare parts for his car including a full set of wheels he had bought cheap or *"mumped"* off of some scrap merchant. C's room wasn't any better it was full of riding tack, including a saddle. Poor Edie and the other cleaners were always moaning about the state of their rooms. When E moved out his place was taken by S the Son of JB the village Policeman near Norwich and Nephew of PC SB from Docking Section.

S like C who was also on "B" Relief was heavily into early *"Pink Floyd"* and their album *"Relics"* is from that era, songs like *"Put down That Axe Eugene"* which at the time was an acquired taste and come to think of it, still is. They were always buying the newest Deck, Amp, or Speakers going and playing them at full volume.

On Sunday the 9th of January, due to the Miner's being denied a wage increase by Edward "Ted" Heath's Conservative Government, they went on strike for the first time since 1926. The strike went on for 7 weeks and The Government declared *"a state of emergency."* To economise on electricity generated from coal fired power stations, rotor power cuts and a 3 day working week were imposed. This was to be a similar picture in 1974 & 1978.

During March of this year several officers formed themselves into a *"Pop Group"* and they were called *"The Treble 9s"* Derek Stuart was on Lead Guitar with a Fender Stratocaster and a mean Hank Marvin imitator, Ron Elliott was on Rhythm Guitar with a Bison, Mick Hayman was on a Fender Bass Guitar, Trevor Bidle on Drums and George Hooke playing the Electronic Organ. I used to pre-record instrumentals and songs on the reel to reel tape recorder mentioned previously for them to practice to and I also recorded and played back their sessions. They went on to have great success at numerous *"gigs"* all over the County for a number of years, they were that good they could have turned professional.
Now again, because of the passage of time elapsing remember when this

next windup occurred or which recruit it occurred to. This particular lad, believe it or not confessed to us that he couldn't ride a bike! Well wrong thing to do with me around. I set about borrowing a Norfolk Constabulary permit to drive certificate, photocopied it and then *"doctored"* it with tippex. And then using a typewriter.

Where it said *"Is permitted to drive the following Police Vehicles"* I changed it to read Police Cycles and then changed as follows:

(i) Beat Car (Beat Pedal Cycle).
(ii) (ii) Beat Van (Trade Cycle).
(iii) (iii) Police Mini Bus (Tandem) but not
(iv) Traffic Car (Racing Cycle) until having passed the advanced course (test).

Then on one Sunday early turn a Sergeant from Dersingham who I knew was filling in as Shift Sergeant and I involved him in the plot so that the lad wouldn't suspect anything. He told this lad that he was giving him a *"Cycling Proficiency Test,"* we had cones placed in a chicane in the rear yard and this lad then set off wobbling between them whilst the Sgt looked official with clipboard and pen in hand. He then sent him off on a route from the rear yard up to Tower Street left into St James Street past the front of *"The Nick"* to the junction of St James Road with London Road. The Rookie was told that at some stage en route that the Sgt would step out into the road holding up his clip board and when he saw that he was to do an emergency stop.

Well the rest of us couldn't contain our glee we were like excited school kids waiting with anticipation in the confines of the Front Office/Control looking out of the windows waiting for the approach of our *"quarry."* Eventually we heard the squeaking of wheels and cranking of pedals emitting from the approaching under used unoiled beat cycle and just as it reached the best vantage point the Sgt stepped quickly off of the pavement in front of it whilst holding his clip board aloft. The ensuing result was that the lad braked violently came to an abrupt halt and fell of the too tall saddle! Helmet akimbo! A bit like Frank Spencer. We were all in fits of hysterical laughter and collapsing in a heap on the floor it's a wonder he didn't hear us, but the Sgt somehow managed to keep his composure and made notes on his clip board.

We then had the *"Official Presentation Ceremony"* in the rear yard with shift assembled and Keith Holliday our SOCO taking *"official"* photographs of the event. This lad stood to attention as the Sgt made a little speech about the award and how well he had done; he had more bull in him than I had! And then ceremonially handed over the authorisation *"Norfolk Constabulary Permit to Ride Cycles"* which we had had laminated. Needless to say this lad didn't make the grade as a copper and his services were dispensed with by the Chief Constable long before the end of his two year probationary period. Just think to this day he probably has his certificate and photograph framed above his mantelpiece to the admiration of his grand children. If you are the one concerned and read this *"I'm sorry, but only just a little bit."*

Fred Calvert was made a Chief Superintendent and during this year John Garth Williams *"the smiling assassin"* became our Sub Divisional Superintendent he was from County Durham and Charlie Nourse was promoted to Detective Chief Inspector.

During the first week of September amongst my other roles I became the Kings Lynn Crown Court Liaison Officer and was tasked with the preparation of all guilty plea files for Judge Adrian Head and the research and reading out in court of the accused's antecedent history and previous convictions before sentence. I was also the Court Officer for all not guilty pleas.

On Wednesday the 27th of September until Friday the 29th of September I was the Court Officer when I was to hear the Not Guilty Trial of a former police colleague who was accused of having broken into The China Garden Restaurant and stealing several large boxes of

King Prawns. His story was that one night at about 3am he was off duty on the multi story car park in New Conduit Street, Kings Lynn when he saw from the opposite side of the road a man walk along the first floor access to this restaurant and break in through an upstairs window as a result he then made a *"999"* call to the police station.

What really happened was that he burgled the place himself and to cover if anyone had seen him in the vicinity made the story up and rang in. Anyhow he was suspected of other crimes whilst a serving officer at Terrington and probably before whilst at Lynn having been on a Relief and the CID decided to check his story out and found that from the position he had been in on the car park he could not see the attacked premisesm, let alone anyone breaking in. He was arrested and lengthily interviewed by Senior Officers Charlie Nourse from the crime aspect and John Williams from the disciplinary code angle and between them got an admission of guilt.

But there was a lack of continuity between him being interviewed for the disciplinary code and the criminal case once he had seen a solicitor they put forward an allegation that his admission statement had been made under duress. Coupled with the embarrassing demeanour of these two officers in the witness box the defence latched on it and the Judge had no option but to instruct The Jury to return a Not Guilty verdict. After this he finished as a copper and changed sides and became a proper villain and got involved with the West Norfolk Crime Syndicate and with his inside knowledge of alarms and police units and response times led us a merry dance for a while. We had to develop special coded messages to pass over the radio in order to catch him and his co-burglars which we eventually did

The Crown Court sessions at that time were held in The Stone Hall which dated from the 14th Century and a part of The Town Hall, which had a multi-functional role; it was normally the venue for posh Ball's, Wedding Receptions, etc. When a court was convened The Bench, Dock, Witness Box, Jury Box, Prosecution and Defence areas which were built out of carved wood were brought out of storage and assembled like a giant jigsaw puzzle. I remember being present one day when Judge Head adjourned the Court in order for the wooden bench to be dismantled as his cherished fountain pen had dropped through a gap onto the stone floor below!

On Tuesday the 10th of October I went to Headquarters for a CID, Force Intelligence Section and Collator Conference and I was back in Kings Lynn Collator's Office catching up on new information put into the system. At 7.30pm I heard a message come over the Force Radio of a suspicious vehicle containing two men who had been disturbed stealing potatoes out at Clenchwarton. I went out with a traffic officer in his traffic car, call sign Alpha 13. On our arrival we saw near to The Victory Public House a light green Commer 15cwt van index number FNV297C it was unattended and the engine was warm and it had sidelights on. The rear offside wheel was punctured and raised off the ground with a wheel jack and an assortment of tools laying by it. Stacked inside the rear of the vehicle I saw a large quantity of 56kg paper sacks full of potatoes about 20 in total and I found a note book and papers relating to man who I knew to be a Seabank Estate, London *"overspill"* criminal, we then searched the area for our culprits.

At 8.15pm I saw P standing beside the A17 Road near to the Black Horse Pub in the village we pulled up and my colleaugue said to him *"I am arresting you on suspicion of the theft of potatoes this evening."* After caution P replied *"Come on now, you must be fucking joking."* With typical *"Cockney"* swagger and bluff he was adamant that he didn't know anything about the potatoes. I said to P *"Your van is loaded with nicked spuds and you match the description of one of the men seen to run away from it that's the score get in."* P was taken to Lynn and in the Charge Room he said *"You bastards have been after me for more than seven months ever since the last time I got done you are determined to have me for anything as I've got a suspended sentence hanging over me."* Nice verbals from his own mouth to put before a court. He was then placed by me into The Detention Room as the cells were full and when we were on our own he said *"Chris if I plead guilty, what's the chance of getting bail?"* I said *"All I can tell you is to tell the truth the question of bail is not up to me you are being held in custody pending further enquiries."* I then left him and had no further dealings he together with another man involved later pleaded guilty at court and both of them received custodial sentences.

## 1973

The year started with me performing a fortnight of Acting Sergeant duties on "B" Relief, Frank Leech was in the Front Office/Control and the shift consisted of Dave Burton, Alan "Sparky" Brighten, Brian Sayer, George Dimmock, Dick LeFevre, Eddie Cocking, Jim Hardy, Ken Canfor and Harry Evans-Hepple.

**Frank Leech and me as Acting Sergeant in the Front Office 1973**

I was again Crown Court Liaison Officer this year, from January to September as well as being Acting Sergeant and Collator Duties.

On Wednesday the 7th of March coming up to my 7th year in the job I had a Staff Appraisal Interview with Fred Calvert he tried at length to persuade me to take my promotion exam as he said that I was Sergeant Material. He also wanted me to learn to drive and find a girl and eventually get married. He eventually got his wish on the last two but promotion was not for me. I wanted to stay at the sharp end and by then there was far too much in-fighting and a *"dog eat dog"* free for all for any promotion position. The time of the University Degree Senior Officer material had arrived and dedicated experienced service was no longer the criteria looked for in promotion chasing candidates.

### *"I drove my tractor past your window last night"*

A rarity! On Thursday the 7th of June I was Acting Sergeant on "B" Relief and after dealing with reports and other admin paperwork I went out on patrol with Ken Canfor in Panda 2. At 9.10pm we saw this Blue Ford Tractor being driven through a built up housing estate at Riversway, North Lynn we caused the vehicle to stop and I recognised the driver as being 16 year old of Wootton Road, Kings Lynn. We stopped the vehicle and I said to G *"I am arresting you for driving a motor vehicle, namely a Ford Tractor, on a public road whilst disqualified from doing so by reason of your age which is sixteen years you have to be seventeen. Also for taking this tractor without the owner's permission and driving without a licence or insurance."* After caution he replied *"I understood that my provisional licence covered me."* I later ascertained that he had taken the tractor off a building site where he was working and did not have permission to use it or take it.

213

### "No it wasn't his f…..g day was it?"

On Thursday the 16th of August I was again Acting Sergeant and on early turn with "B" Relief and again out on patrol with Ken Canfor. At 12.20pm we were called to attend an injury road accident in a service delivery access road St James Court in Kings Lynn town centre. A Bedford TK lorry owned by a London firm had collided at a junction with a Morris Mini saloon driven by an 83 year old man from March and with his 80 year wife as passenger. These two were injured and we attended to them until an ambulance arrived. Ken then interviewed the lorry driver who was from Peckham in London and Mick Weatherstone obtained details of the accident and took measurements. The lorry had been moved to allow us to get to the trapped people in the Mini and then Mick parked our police Ford Escort, LVF726L in a position about five yards behind the parked lorry. After interview the lorry driver took a parcel from the back of his vehicle and delivered it to Court's Furnishers and at 1245pm I saw him return get in the cab start the engine and before anyone could move he had reversed it backwards into the parked police vehicle with the crunch of tearing metal and tinkling of broken headlight glass! The lorry then lurched forward and I could see that the front of our Police Car had been stove in. The lorry driver climbed out of his cab stared in disbelief at the damaged Police Vehicle and announced in a Cockney accent *"This isn't my f….ing day is it?"* and I had to agree no it wasn't. He later went to Kings Lynn Magistrates Court on two counts of careless driving committed on the same day within a matter of several yards apart!

To clear up any later confusion by the reader, we had two officers serving on the shift at the same time; one was Mick Weatherstone and the other Mark Featherstone.

### *"Caught In the Act"*

Now it's not often that you are in the right position to catch burglars in the act of committing a crime although I was fortunate to do so on several occasions during my career. One such event occurred on Monday the 20th of August when I was was Acting Sergeant on a night shift with "B" Relief and out on patrol with Ken Canfor when at 11.20pm we had a report over the radio of two men seen by Mick Weatherstone on the flat roofs of shop premises at the rear of Norfolk Street at the High Street end. As we were only round the corner in Chapel Street we were on the scene very quickly. Knowing the layout of the roads I set up a containment area and over the personal radio I instructed Mick to block off the Tuesday Market Place end and to wait there. At the junction with Surrey Street which runs from Chapel Street along the rear of Norfolk Street premises to the Tuesday Market Place I jumped out of the Panda Car leaving Ken to sit at that junction, that way we had the area cordoned off. I ran quietly down Surrey Street and about half way down I saw the shape of two people silhouetted on the skyline of the buildings. I stopped and listened and waited. Shortly after I saw two men climb down the fire escape of Marks & Spencer's from enclosed shop premises serving the rear of Norfolk Street and come into Surrey Street between Mick's position and mine. Mick closed in from his position and I did likewise, on seeing us the two men separated one ran towards Mick and the other towards me. I saw the one who was with Mick try to evade arrest but Mick held on to him.

The other one came steaming towards me like a hundred yard sprinter and I could see that his right arm was raised and saw him holding aloft a long metallic looking object obviously intended for me and he then as he got closer I saw that it was a jemmy bar (case opener) he then threatened me with the bar and tried to run past me. *"The bastard!"* I thought and with a mixture of fear and anger and with adrenalin pumping I launched myself at him like a quarter back and rugby tackled him at waist height pulling him to the ground whilst at the same time finding his right arm whilst still in mid air and managed to whip it up behind his back with such force that the object flew out of his hand and I heard it clatter harmlessly onto the cobbled street some distance away.

This guy then started struggling violently and by this time the red mist had descended and I pinned him to the ground by kneeling on his chest my right arm went back like a cocked gun and I released it like one of George Foreman's hammer blows and as my fist was about to bury itself in his cheekbone I just realized in time that the fight had left him and I managed to stop short of hitting him. I snarled *"Don't f….ing move you're nicked!"* He laid where he was and I then cuffed him arms behind his back and whilst doing so noticed that he had a red sock over his left hand and that the other was lying on the ground nearby and must have come off when he lost his grip on the metal object. Socks were worn normally by burglars then used over their hands at the scene of crimes so no prints were left and then replaced on their feet instead of carrying gloves which when found on a search they could be done for going equipped. I told him to stay where he was and then went across and examined the metal object that was probably intended to embed itself into my bare head, my helmet having been left in the Panda Car. I saw that it was a heavy tyre lever or case opener and returned with it to my quarry. I said to him *"You've been arrested on suspicion of burglary what's your name and where do you come from?"* He replied *"C from Bristol."* I then took C back to where Ken was with the Panda Car and searched him before putting him into the rear of the Hillman Imp. Another Panda car turned up for Mick's prisoner R from Wisbech who on being searched was found to be in possession of a long metal file and a screwdriver, so even if we didn't have a burglary as we had probably disturbed them in the act, we had got them for going equipped to steal.

When we got back to *"The Nick"* Charge Room and were booking them in I said to C *"Which premises have you broken into?"* He replied *"The Seed Merchants in Norfolk Street where I broke into last time. We were looking for cash."* I said *"By we do you mean yourself and the other person R?"* He replied

*"Yes."* I said *"Is there anyone else involved with the break-in that you have committed? As our dog handler is searching the area."* He said *"Yes there is one other G from Wisbech he is sitting round the Bus Station behind the garages in a White Vauxhall car waiting for us. He knows what we have been up to as we planned it together before we got out of the car when we came to Lynn."* I thought *"Nice one he can be nicked for conspiracy to burgle as he is hardly a lookout some half a mile away from where it happened."* I then relayed this information over the radio to Ken Canfor who then nicked the third one. All three later went to Crown Court pleaded guilty and each received a custodial sentence. Mick Weatherstone, Ken Canfor, I and others all received a Chief Constable's Commendation on Personnel Orders of the 25th of October.

This self generated proactive policing and clearing up crime was all very well, but the cases were then put together and dealt with by CID and it was their name on the file and not yours. I had already proven myself that I could organise major files preparation whilst being The Crown Court Liaison Officer but it wasn't my name on that either.

A card index on every serving officer of the Division who submitted a crime file was kept in CID and maintained by *"Ciddy"* our civilian Clerk/Typist, Maureen Caley. Mine forgetting my arrest turnover which wasn't recorded there was sparse, so when Senior CID Officers were looking for candidates for Central Crime Unit, Regional Crime Squad or Intelligence Gathering roles my name did not come to the fore.

It even stopped me getting the full time job of Collator/Local Intelligence Officer when that role came up on Clarence Hazelwood's retirement a couple of years later and I had to wait until the end of 1987 to get it, bearing in mind that I had helped start and develop it in the first place.

Additionally I was involved in many incidents whilst a Control Room Officer where I instigated an intruders on premises message to my patrol colleagues and because of my expert local knowledge of premises and villains, their words not mine, was able to quickly pinpoint the attacked premises, the most likely points of entry and those who may be involved and put the officers in a containment area and achieve a good team result. All of these I laboriously wrote up in the Station Occurrence Book with the headline *"B Relief Strikes Again."* Other Relief's then copied this method of entering up competitive thief taking until Kings Lynn was probably the best grounding *"Nick"* in the County for continually achieving good results. Unfortunately I was not able to get my hands on these O.B's when full up and archived and they have probably gone to book heaven via The Force Incinerator.

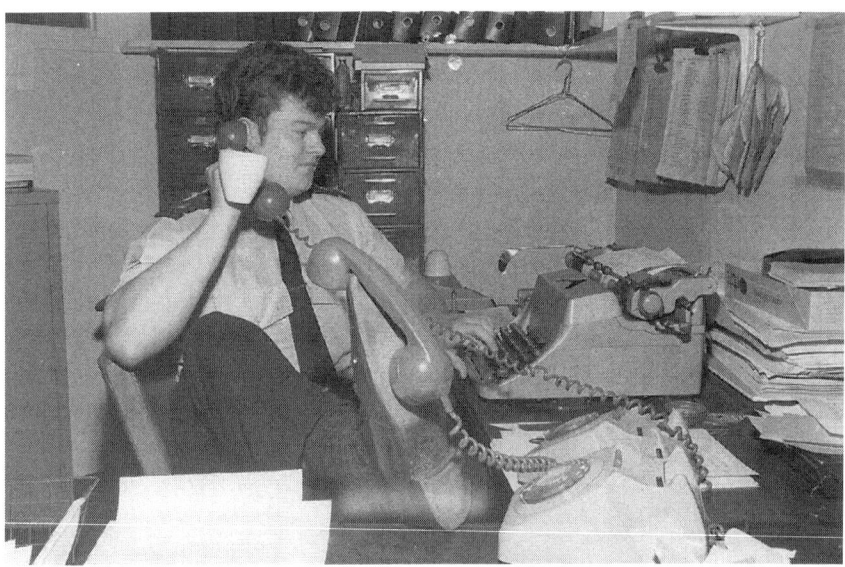

*Me Acting Collator and Acting the Fool Summer 1973*

The filing cabinets behind me contained the Nominal and Vehicle Index of known active criminals and all information that came in was typed onto a card and kept alphabetically and numerically and cross referenced. As a comparison look at the later photograph in my second bool taken during 1988 of the larger office and expanded system.

218

Another example of knowing your villains occurred on a night shift on Thursday the 23rd of August I was on foot beat and at 1.50am the Friday morning I was in Norfolk street when I saw two local *"players"* J and W both of Lynn emerge from Broad Street they were in a noisy mood and had been drinking but were not drunk. I said to them *"Where are you two now off to? I don't mind you drinking but don't go screwing"* J replied *"No we don't do things like that anymore he's taking me home"* and they walked off.

Around 40 minutes later a message was put out by another patrol that these two were believed up to no good in the High Street area by this time I had teamed up with Mick Weatherstone in Panda 2 and I instructed him to check the shop fronts by driving slowly past whilst I checked the rear of these on foot. A short while later he called me over the radio to Poysers where the premises had been entered via the door skylight measuring some 18" square and then forced the door from the inside this was J's M.O. The intruders had been disturbed and the cash till and float was still intact, about 15 minutes later J was nicked by someone else on the Relief and I continued checking other properties in the area.

### *"You Buy One You Get One Free"*

I got involved again on the following night shift when about 4.45am on the Saturday morning I was with Ken Canfor on Tuesday Market Place when we saw a vehicle drive down Ferry Street from the Common Staithe Quay and turn right into King Street it was a Grey Austin England index number 5691CR which had a roof rack with a load of wood strapped to it. We followed it through to Saturday Market Place along Church Street, Bridge Street and All Saints Street where we tried to pull it with our Blue flashing light. This was ignored by the driver and the vehicle continued without signalling left into Valingers Road right into North Everard Street and down South Everard Street stopping outside an address. I spoke to the driver and found him to be B a 39 year old Tides man for Kings Lynn Conservancy Board. I said to him *"Where have you got all this wood from?"* He said *"From where I work."* I said *"Have you got a bill of sale or receipt for this wood?"* He replied *"No they are only old bits which I've brought home to finish my conservatory with."* I said *"This wood is not old in fact several pieces are brand new timber and have been freshly been cut and planed see the wood dust is still on them."*

B then said *"Well it's my wood it doesn't belong to Kings Lynn Conservancy Board, I've been storing it down there."* I thought *"We've got a bright one here I will need to work at it."* I then said *"Where did you acquire it from then? As you haven't receipts from where you got it from."* He said *"Its stuff which floats down with the tide from where it falls off the boats we are allowed to have it."* I said *"None of this wood appears to have come out of the river it's freshly cut planed and completely dry with dust over it. You had better come down to the police station and get this sorted out. You are under arrest on suspicion of having stolen some or all of this wood."* He was cautioned and made no reply.

At the police station I informed Sgt Pete Griffin and our night duty Detective Constable Reg Bruce of the circumstances surrounding the arrest and at 5.10am I went together with Ken Canfor and the prisoner to his home address there I saw a partially completed wooden conservatory nearly ready for glazing. The wood of part of it was not of the same quality as that taken from his roof rack or of the most recent work done where he had painted over it I said to B *"How long ago did you build this part of the conservatory?"* He replied *"About* a year ago." I then said "And when did you paint it? As it's only partially completed." B replied *"About three months ago."* I said *"This looks like a freshly painted job to me."* I came to the conclusion that he had started the conservatory using salvaged wood and then had got greedy and starting taking home the Joiner's wood used for boat repairs etc from his employer. He was Bailed S38 (2) pending further enquiries and later found guilty at Court as well as being sacked by his Employers.

On Thursday the 6th of September Woman Police Constable 22, Therese Chadwick (My future Wife) joined The Force and started her 10 weeks initial training at Ryton on Dunsmoor, Coventry and she joined the Kings Lynn Policewomen's Department in the November. Her colleagues at that time are in the photograph below and from left to right Denise Lord, Janet Claxton, Daphne Williamson, Therese Chadwick and Pamela Betts her future Sister in Law.

On Thursday the 13th of September I was on Early Turn when at 11am I was with other members of the Relief presented to Her Majesty's Inspector of Constabulary Mr Stanley Peck during his visit to the Station.

During this time we had a prolific *"peeping tom"* and *"flasher"* called A who lived at Walpole St Andrew he was a milkman and would start his rounds about 4am. Anytime from late evening through to 2am or 3am we would receive numerous reports of a curly ginger haired man looking through windows at young women in various stages of undress and then exposing himself to them and driving off before they had time to report it. This would range from Caravans and Chalets at Hunstanton, through to Kings Lynn and the Downham Section. I used to literally file hundreds of these reports a year from all over the Division in our log kept in the Collator's Office.

On Thursday the 11th of October I worked an Early Turn at 1030am we had a briefing for a visit by Her Royal Highness Catherine the Duchess of Kent and between 11am and 1210pm was on a point duty at Saturday market Place, I resumed my point at 2pm and HRH left at 2.30pm.

PCs H and C were on "B" Relief at this time and when on meal break or off duty they were often in the Snooker Room of the Police Station and if they spied a man nicknamed *"Pepper"* walking by below they would shout out at the top of their voices *"Pepper!"* Now *"Pepper"* was an inadequate little man aged about 50 whom had a stutter and whatever the weather always wore the same beige coloured belted *"flasher"* coat, wellies and flat cap. For some reason he always homed in on me when I was on the Beat or in the Front Office and around the beginning of October he would call out if he saw me out *"Ha-ay! Clarky the guns will soon be singing."* It was a reference to the approach of the pheasant season when he would be a beater for Dougie Milton the Butcher from Grimston. Anyway if H or C shouted at him when I was in the Front Office *"Pepper"* would come in all a fluster and say *"Clarky why do those policemen sssscare me?"*

Now if you are beginning to feel sorry for this little man then think again. He had convictions for indecency with children and in the past had gone into The pilot or Majestic Cinema in the town and had sat next to a child and in the darkness put a paper bag with a hole in the bottom over his erect penis and then offer them a *"sweet"* and when they put their hand into the bag instead of finding a liquorice allsort they would feel a *"gob stopper!"* He was what Harold Steptoe would call his father *"A dirty little man!"*

During November Nationally Economic and Union problems were brewing, an Industrial Dispute had begun and a further Miner's Strike was on the horizon. Emergency Powers and conservation of petrol fuel and other forms of energy were imposed by the Conservative Government.

PCs Alan McGee and Les Neave were on the shift with us and covering the rural areas. We had the first Night Club opened in King's Lynn at the site of the former Grosvenor Hotel on the corner of Broad Street and Norfolk Street; it was originally called *"Annabella's"* and later changed to *"The Intercon Club."*

On Tuesday the 25th of December I was on a Late Turn and at 2.30pm I checked a man from Nottingham of No Fixed Abode who was sitting in the Snow White Laundrette in St James Street. After checking with Nottingham I found that he was wanted on warrant by them I arrested him and arranged a Nottingham escort for him, he spent the remainder of Christmas Day and Boxing Day in a warm cell and with hot food inside him which is more than I had as there was nowhere open.

## Chapter Four

## *"Into The Light"*
## *The First Police National Computer*

### *1974*

On Saturday the 9th of February there was a new Miner's Strike as the Miner's had been refused a seven per cent pay increase to bring them in line to their 1972 post strike position in pay; they had dropped from top to eighteenth position in blue collar worker pay in two years. A lack of coal to Power Stations meant further rota cuts in the electricity supply. In those days shop premises burglar alarms terminated at the local police station and at Kings Lynn we had four boards of Intruder Alarms each containing about twenty individual premises. Each board had a different continuous note and when the power cut they all went off together at different pitches, sounding like constantly wailing bagpipes and this for two whole hours at a time. Luckily both the Force Main VHF Radio and the Town UHF Personal Radio systems went down as well, otherwise we would never have heard any messages. As the cuts were pre-planned we adopted the old point system for conveying messages to beat officers verbally and their priority outside shop hours was to regularly check these premises as they were no longer protected by their alarms.

During this time Frank Leech as resourceful as ever rigged up two car headlamps to a 12volt battery and suspended them from the ceiling for lighting. The rest of the *"Nick"* had to make do with candle and torchlight. I remember people walking along the station corridors carrying a lighted candle it was eerie just like being in the cloisters of a Monastery. With regard to the radios going off I remember on one occasion just prior to a scheduled cut informing HQ by telephone that we were about to go off air and S the Force HQ Control Room Sergeant said *"What's wrong with your emergency generator?"* He had been in Training prior to this and had little concept of life in the real world and apart from HQ having one he was about two years ahead before any of the Stations had emergency generators installed. When I had picked myself up off of the floor I enlightened him as to what a 12volt battery could achieve and that was more than anyone else had.

During March Peter Griffin left "B" Relief and Sergeant M *"The Domino King"* took over on nights at around 3am he would summon the Relief into the Front Office/Control and play 3s and 5s dominoes. During this year Jim Hardy became a Detective Constable and on our Relief were PC 855Reg Pyatt, PC 266 Jim Englebach, PC 424 Keith Pearce and PC395 David Gerrard who had Pete Griffin's old collar number; also we had a PC who like Roy Jenkins *"What we want is a more pwospewus Bwitain"* could not pronounce his R's had joined us. That reminds me one Friday night duty he was on patrol near *"Sharkey's"* Fish & Chip shop when he called over the radio and said *"There's a Wukcus in Wailway Woad!"* Deciphered *"Ruckus in Railway Road!"*

PC 38 Phil Jones had come to Kings Lynn from Liverpool on transfer and PC 164 Roger Lord from Lancashire with his Wife Denise who was a WPC in the Policewomen's Department.

At that time on the relief we had a *"Wanker of the Week"* Award it was a carved wooden clenched fist with the middle finger extended set on a plinth with a plaque entitled *"The Fickle Finger of Fate."* We also had a medieval looking scroll to go with it entitled *"Wanker of the Week"* which under the title said *"For meritious conduct beyond and above the call of duty"* naming the week it occurred, who the officer was and for what deed it was won for. It had been running for some time and various officers had won it, for occasions like when an officer I cannot remember the name of when sent to Littlewoods following a hoax IRA bomb call. Somehow he went to Marks & Spencer and have them evacuate their premises! If I remember correctly it was Mick Hutchinson who instigated it on "B" Relief and then sold the idea to "D" Relief when he joined them.

Now turning to G he was probably the most gullible of all of the officers who joined "B" Relief, he was always winning the award and in the end we discontinued it as it had become boring with just his name re-occurring each week and he won it outright. One example I will quote, the idea all mine. This was the time when The IRA were at their height and Mainland Britain was a target to their atrocities, so there was nothing better than a *"bomb"* for G to deal with. All of the Relief and Jim Hardy who was Night CID Officer were briefed and all apart from Jim went and hid up in the target area. I then called G who was on Panda Two to go to The Central Electricity Generating Board (A potential IRA target) in Kettlewell Lane off of Littleport Street where there was a report of a suspicious object lying outside the main gates. This object was an empty 40 gallon oil drum which had wires and a battery strapped to it and in the darkness would easily be taken for a rudimentary bomb filled with fertilizer. G drove down Kettlewell Lane and saw the object in his vehicle's headlights, turned his radio off and then reversed back to Littleport Street where the next thing he was phoning me from a kiosk there and in a loud whisper said *"Chris there's a bomb outside the CEGB."* I said *"Stop winding me up you can't get me on that one."* He said *"No really there is a bomb there."* I said *"Alright wait by Littleport Street and I'll get Jim Hardy with the "Seek and Search" light to come to you."* This I did and a few minutes later Jim met G and they were walking up Kettlewell Lane with Jim shining this powerful torch which was like a car headlamp on full beam. They got to within a close proximity of *"the bomb"* and then Jim suddenly ran forward and saying *"Is this the bomb!"* and kicked it onto its side. At the same time G took off like an Olympic Swimmer and dived spread-eagled onto the grass amongst the dog shit. At this point the rest of the Relief burst out laughing from their various hiding places and G realized that once again he has won the prestigious award!

I last saw G in 2000 at Sandringham Park where he was with a Sergeant with their Community Relations Caravan, we had a reminisce and G said *"Chris, did you ever send me on any real jobs?"* Well G you certainly were game for a laugh.

A bit later on, another candidate for this award, had it still been running was W. There was a headline report in that mornings EDP (Eastern Daily Press), which we had delivered around 3:00am, of a body being found in the boot of a car on Mousehold Heath Norwich; so *"yours truly"* concocted a telex message purporting to have come from Headquarters Information Room that the suspect wanted for this murder was in a White Ford Cortina Estate and had connexions in the West of The County. The lads, apart from W had been briefed and Bob Mickleborough had put his personal White Ford Cortina Estate in a dark area of The Friars near to The Nar River, had left it with a door open and a *"bloodstained"* pick axe handle lying beside it; then he and the rest of the Relief together with Jim Hardy hid up in the area to wait.

When I was informed that they were ready I put a spoof message out about the contents of the telex, shortly afterwards Reg Pyatt called up saying he had spotted the vehicle and lost it somewhere in The Friars area. I then called W up on the radio and sent him on foot to search for it in that area. The radio was on *"talk through"* and there was a deathly hush for some time until a tremourless voice was heard to utter *"I think I've found the murder vehicle!"*

The next thing Jim Hardy leaped out of nearby bushes and shouted out *"Get down on the ground copper or you'll get it!"* W flung himself onto the potholed surface straight into a puddle and lay there, Jim walked up to him and dropped a green metal filing tray which hit the tarmac with a resounding crash right by his lughole! Then all of the lads came out of the bushes and W realized that it was a windup. I bet that if he had clean underpants on that night that they weren't after that experience.

Now a lot of minor crime was committed by children and youths from families who themselves were criminals or criminally minded and when I was a serving officer the same surnames came up time and time again, only the passage of time put a different Christian name or a different face to some popular surnames and in some cases I dealt with fourth generation culprits at the end of my service, having dealt with the first, second and third generation along the way. That class of person also seems to be more virile and produce more offspring, often with several partners, so you finish up with a hotch potch of the same blood and genes carried in several different directions. It would make family research of such individuals quite hap-hazard and confusing, not least to the to the persons themselves. It also made it extremely difficult for police officers in identifying family members in a criminal intelligence package.

The young members of such families learn their trade at very early ages and they are the most difficult and evasive to interview and one such example of this occurred on an early turn on Sunday the 24th of February. I was out on patrol as Acting Sergeant with Jim Hardy and just before midday there was a call from Dave Gerrard in Control to attend at Crusader Manufacturing on Oldmedow Road, Hardwick Industrial Estate where two youths were seen to be acting suspiciously.

We attended along with PC Hook in Panda 3 and Terry Duncan and Mick Weatherstone in Panda 2. Whilst en route there was a further call to say that PC Hook had located two youths at the nearby premises of Electro Carbon Diesel and he requested my attendance, whilst the crew of Panda 2 obtained full details and descriptions from the informant. Jim and I arrived at 12:10pm and I saw PC Hook talking to the two he had stopped and recognised both as being younger members of two well known Gaywood Families S and A. PC Hook said to me *"I've found these two by that pile of scrap,"* indicating to a quantity of metal in the compound of Electro Carbon Diesel. I also saw a black sack and a brown sack both laden with copper wire and other metal. A and S both claimed that they had been mucking about on the site and not stealing.

When asked their names not knowing that I knew them already, both gave false names and PC Hook then said that they were different false names to the ones he had been given. I then said *"Well I know that one is*

*A age fourteen years and the other is S age fifteen years, isn't that right lads?"* Both agreed that it was. I then said to both *"Right you two, now you've got the chance to explain what you were up to before we arrived"* S said *"Nothing, we were just going for a walk around the estate and then over to the bypass."* I said *"Well you are on private property here and I suspect that you have stolen that metal lying over there in those sacks."* S said "No we haven't touched anything, we were just going for a walk." I then took S to one side away from A and said *"I am going to give you one last chance to help yourself, we know that you were seen in a Ford Consul Estate car and then to approach other nearby vehicles at Crusader Manufacturing and I suspect that you have also stolen that metal in those sacks and had put it there ready to take it away."*

S then said *"Alright then I'll tell you everything."* I cautioned him and he said *"We did come out for a walk and as we came by the cars A took a car key out of his pocket and he got in and started it. He said that he would come back to the car later; I got a sack out of the boot and put some of the wire in it. We also had a lorry tube which is over there."* He indicated to the front right hand side of the building against the fence, where I saw a Black lorry tube. I then said to him *"Where is the car ignition key now, is it still in the car?"* S said *"No A has got it in his pocket."* I then said *"You stay there in the police car with PC Hardy while I go and speak to A."* I then walked over to where A was standing with PC Hook and cautioned him. I then said *"Right let's have no more messing about, S has told me everything, where is the car key that you used to start that car?"* A said *"I threw it away in the grass when I saw the police car coming."*

Mick Weatherstone made a search and within two minutes located the ignition key which A confirmed was the one he had thrown away and had brought it from home with him. I then said *"Right tell me what you have both been up to this morning?"* A replied *"Well okay as he's told you, we took a tube from ATS and wheeled it down the road, then we got in a car, S took a sack out of the boot while I got into the driver's seat and started the engine by putting the key in it. Then we put some wire and other stuff in the two sacks over there and that's when you came."*

A was placed in PC Hook's Panda car and then I retrieved the two sacks containing wire and other metal and put it in the rear of the Ford Escort Estate police car along with the lorry tyre which Jim had retrieved. The two youths were taken to Kings Lynn to await arrival of an adult person for each. Both made full admissions in the presence of adult family members and also made voluntary statements. Both were reported for Theft, Attempted Theft of a motor vehicle and additionally A for going equipped to steal. PC Hook then dealt with the crime file.

On Monday the 25th of February, I worked a 6am to 6.30pm shift and at 1.30pm went with Clarence Hazelwood to a Collator's Conference at Headquarters.

Ted Heath the Conservative Government's Prime Minister called a General Election, hoping that the country would back him on his stand, but the British Public were fed up of being in the dark and Labour under Harold Wilson were elected into power and the strike ended shortly after. On General Election day Thursday the 28th of February, I performed an early turn duty at St Margaret's Ward Polling Station.

## NORFOLK JOINT POLICE

TELEPHONE: 21234 (7 LINES)

CONFIDENTIAL

For Police Use Only.

POLICE HEADQUARTERS,
MARTINEAU LANE,
NORWICH
NOR O7T

20th March, 1974.

GENERAL ORDER No. 14/74

NORFOLK CONSTABULARY

On the 31st March, 1974, the Norfolk Joint Police ceases to exist and the new Norfolk Constabulary comes into existence on the 1st April, 1974.

The Norfolk Constabulary will police all the area formerly policed by the Norfolk Joint Police and those parishes transferred from Suffolk to the new County of Norfolk.

These parishes are:-

>Belton
>Bradwell
>Burgh Castle
>Fritton
>Hopton
>Herringfleet (part)
>Corton (part)

The new parishes will be policed as part of the Great Yarmouth Division from the existing beats of Bradwell, Belton and Hopton. The three resident officers transferring to the Norfolk Constabulary. (See Personnel Order No. 12/74).

On Sunday the 31st of March Norfolk Joint Police which had ruled for five years, ceased to exist and was replaced by the pre 1968 name of Norfolk Constabulary, this in advance of the April Local Government Boundary Changes, we gained some parishes and lost others to neighbouring County Forces, Mid Anglia combined with the Isle Of Ely area and this County then had one Police Force called Cambridgeshire Constabulary, some of Suffolk's boundaries were changed, as were Lincolnshire's.

**NORFOLK JOINT POLICE**

TELEPHONE: 21234 (7 LINES)

POLICE HEADQUARTERS,
MARTINEAU LANE,
NORWICH
NOR O7T

CONFIDENTIAL.

For Police use only.

12th November, 1973.

GENERAL ORDER No. 59/73.

POLICE NATIONAL COMPUTER.

The planned starting date for the first vehicle registrations on the new central licensing scheme at the Department of the Environment, Swansea, was to have been 1st January, 1974. The Swansea computer is behind schedule and the starting date has been deferred to 1st April, 1974.

The present plan was for the Police National Computer to go live with vehicle owners application on 1st January, 1974 and to follow this with the stolen vehicle application in April, 1974.

The Police National Computer will now commence a vehicle owners service in practice and testing mode from 1st January, 1974, changing over to operational running when the Department of the Environment system goes live.

The present system of obtaining details of vehicle owners will continue up to the 1st April, 1974.

The Police National Computer, still in its infancy, went into full service on the 1st of April for vehicle owner checks. I went on a PNC Course and trained as an operator. It was marvellous, typing in a vehicle registration on a keyboard and getting a result back on a Green screen monitor within six seconds, what a boon it was in our fight against crime as we were now entering a new phenomenon.

### *"The travelling Criminal"*

During the 1960s crime in the main was parochial and most burglaries were committed by local villains and the chance of detection made more achievable. After the clearout of London "Overspill" villains and the ensuing toing and froing of these to carry on their criminal activities, other criminals cottoned onto the idea that the further they travelled to commit crime, the less chance there was of getting caught as they were anonymous in other Divisions and neighbouring Force areas, until the advent of PNC, which greatly helped to keep track of their movements.

One team we had was made up of the leader B of Peterborough and two brothers H from Wisbech and P from South Lynn. They also had associates including from South Lynn. They were safe blowers and targeted various national companies as far away as Bristol where substantial sums of money were kept on the premises. Their Silver Fox coloured Ford Zodiac was sighted in many counties where they were casing premises for future break-ins involving explosives. At 3.30pm on Friday the 10th of May I saw P with his car having new tyres fitted and the wheels balanced at Sudbury Tyres, Friar Street, Kings Lynn, obviously about to embark on another lengthy trip, I submitted my information in the normal way. It would then be graded and entered onto the person's nominal card index and evaluated, if felt worthy, a copy of my information would then be forwarded to officers with interest of that individual to build up intelligence and his profile.

In order to tackle this type of criminal, Forces like Norfolk had a Central Crime Unit operating within the County to target local based criminals committing crime within the County. If the criminal travelled across a Region i.e. several different Force areas then this came under the remit of the Regional Crime Squad and each large area of the country was divided up into Regions comprising of several Forces, and each Force from within that Region had officers seconded to The Squad. Superimposed on this system was a three tier Intelligence System,

Local Intelligence Officer, Force Intelligence Officer and Regional Intelligence Officer and it was their job at each level to identify targets for surveillance.

However this did not deal with the problem of the National travelling criminal and it would be more than two decades before we had a National Crime Squad and National Crime Intelligence Service during 1992. (This was in June 2007 superseded by the "SOCA" Serious Organised Crime Agency a merger of the National Crime Squad, National Crime Intelligence Service, The Investigation Arm of HM Customs and Immigration and the National High Tech Crime Unit. This organisation dealt with drug trafficking, organised immigration crime, professional company or individual fraud, money laundering, proceeds of crime, terrorist finance. Now in 2016 we have the National Crime Agency).

From May throughout the year, I did further duties as Acting Sergeant, Deputy Collator and Crown Court Liaison Officer.

### *"One unknown turned up, Another known went missing and never returned"*

At 7.15am on Tuesday the 27th of August a farm worker and his son on their way to work at Brakehill Farm on Sir Peter Robert's Estate at Cockley Cley near Swaffham found a badly decomposed trussed up headless body of a young woman lying in undergrowth beside a lover's lane; about 200 yards from the Swaffham to Cockley Cley Road, opposite RAF Marham's shooting range. The arms and legs were trussed up behind her back and it was covered by a large brown plastic NCR (National Cash Register) dust sheet; later enquiries revealed that only six were made by a Scottish company between 1962 and 1968. The body was of a well built woman aged between 23 and 35 and 5'00" to 5'2"tall. She was wearing only a short pink Marks & Spencer nightdress with a frilly low-cut neckline.

Because the body had lain in the middle of an area of dense bracken and willow herb for two to three weeks, it was in a decomposed state – further complicating efforts to identify her. According to the pathologist she died during the first two weeks in August and had been murdered and decapitated elsewhere.

**Nightdress of victim on a manikin**

About 100 Officers, made up of sixty Uniforms and forty CID, were drafted into the area as the search for the brutal killer began. Leading the investigation was Detective Superintendent Ivan Mead; Deputy Head of Norfolk CID. He went on to be Chief Superintendent at Kings Lynn in the near future, then later became Assistant Chief Constable South Yorkshire and Deputy Chief Constable of Dorset, retiring in the mid 1980s. He was quoted as saying *"The person who killed her obviously went to very great lengths to make sure that police could not identify her."*

Det Supt Ivan Mead, who led the initial murder hunt. (MC 8506)

Detectives Ted Worby (right) and Adrian Horn, later to become police chiefs at Lynn, on house-to-house inquiries during the murder hunt. (MC 8508)

Detective Sergeant Ted Worby and DC Adrian Horn pictured above were also involved in this investigation. Ted went on to be a Chief Superintendent. Adrian gained the rank of Chief Superintendent in Norfolk and then went on to be Deputy Commissioner of British Transport Police.

There was no sign of any murder weapon at the scene so police teams began a toothcomb search of the surrounding area using six of Norfolk Constabulary's Dog Section , including Pat Rout and Derrick Pimlott;. Fields, hedgerows and hollows were searched; also a nearby field of barley was cut that afternoon, in the search for clues.

A murder hunt detective looking for clues from a combine harvester cutting a field of barley near the spot where the headless body was found. (MC 8484)

Home Office Pathologist Dr Alfred Lintoft carried out a post mortem examination and further tests were made in the days following – but without discovering the cause of death.

Regional Crime Squad Officers, Forensic Scientists and even an expert in Botany assisted the investigation, while nationwide enquiries were made in an attempt to discover the woman's identity. House to house enquiries were conducted and thousands of people interviewed as they visited virtually every house at Cockley Cley and Swaffham. The net later widened to include homes in villages to the south such as Gooderstone and Oxborough and to the North and West of Swaffham in a 10 mile radius.

An Incident Room was set up at Swaffham Courthouse and more than 1000 separate lines of inquiry were investigated in the early stages and even The FBI and Interpol became involved. Again at this time there were no computers, so like the *"Yorkshire Ripper"* enquiry which came later, everything was on card index and had to be cross referenced. The Force Bedford Mobile Headquarters was used as a base in a stubble field near to where the body was found. It later joined the stalls at Swaffham Market as part of the Police appeal to the public.

A mobile police station was set up on Swaffham Market to widen the appeal for information about the murder. (MC 8637)

To this day, over 40 years later we are no closer to solving this woman's identity and then exposing her murderer, than we were in 1974. There was some suggestion that she may have been a Leeds prostitute now that would open all sorts of hypothetical thinking"! If you linked it to the name Peter Sutcliffe who I believe committed this crime and forms one case in my book *"Yorkshire Ripper: The Secret Murders"* By Chris Clark and Tim Tate under John Blake title.

The Norfolk Cold Case Investigation Team later re-investigated this unsolved crime and it was aired on BBC Crimewatch in September 2008. Information was received concerning the possibility of a missing woman who lived at RAF Hemswell during the time of the finding of the body. Also during late 1973 to 1974 a possible theft of a NCR cover from the RAF supply unit at RAF Scampton also in Lincolnshire.

Three days after the discovery of the headless body on Friday the 30th of August, Pamela Exhall aged 21 years a Law Graduate from Fleet in Hampshire who was on a motorcycling holiday with her 17 year old Brother and staying at Diglea Snettisham Beach Caravan Park disappeared after dinner at around 10:30pm when she told her Brother that she was going for a walk on the beach in the moonlight. Diglea, situated on Snettisham Beach Road is an isolated spot some two miles from the village and a good 400 yards from the beach and well off the beaten track; inland of the two sea walls.

***Pamela Exhall***

Norfolk Police succonded helicopters and Police Frogmen and Dog Handlers joined an extensive search of beach, caravan sites and gravel pits. At the time there was a feeling that Pamela had walked into quick sand and drowned, or was suffering from amnesia, but with unsolved abductions and murders abounding around the country who knows? She could easily have been the victim of a local bait digger who frequented the mud flats between tides digging lug worms and was then raped, strangled and buried in the sucking mud.

Two days earlier on Thursday the 28th of August two colleaugues from "B" Relief and myself took three prisoners sentenced to 3 months detention each by King's Lynn Magistrates Court to Kidlington Detention Centre in Oxfordshire, close to Eynsham where I had trained; on the way back we stopped in Oxford and jointly purchased a Chinese take Away which we shared in the back of the police minibus.

Chris Clark

*Diglea Camp A*

242

We were like *"The Three Musketeers."* I remember one hot Sunday in summer one early turn when the three of us were on separate foot beats in the town centre. There was absolutely nothing doing and it was like a ghost town, I think that everyone had gone to Hunstanton for the day. The three of us met up near The Princess Royal Public House in Blackfriars Street around noon and as none of us had bothered to go into the Station for a meal break so we decided to grab a quick pint. We went into the rear yard of the pub took our helmets and epaulettes off and walked in the back door, the few regulars there must have thought it was a raid. Anyway each one of us bought a round in turn and then three quarters of an hour and three pints each later, we left like we had never been there.

As from the 1st of September my annual pay went up to £2,232.

On Thursday the 19th of September I was performing night duty on Cycle Beat 2 when at 11.35pm I cycled into the new Vancouver Court Bus Terminal from Railway Road as I had heard the sound of car gears being crunched and a scraping noise and as I approached the corporation footway separating the bus station from Sainsbury's Car Park I saw a Blue Hillman Minx with a White roof straddled and stuck across the raised 5 inch kerbed footway with the front wheels and sill on the raised area and the rear wheels on the road surface. The vehicle contained four persons. On seeing my approach the driver hurriedly put the car into reverse and jolted backwards off of the raised footway and turned around and as I signalled it to stop the car was driven quickly off into Railway Road, I took the index number, VTL321 and followed on my cycle.

At 11.55pm I re-located the vehicle outside *"Johnnie's"* Fish Shop renamed from *"Sharkey's"* and saw that the last person in the queue was the person I had seen driving the Minx. I took him to one side and said *"I witnessed you driving VTL321 at 11.35pm tonight on Vancouver Court and Old Sun way in a careless manner and I suspect that you have alcohol in your blood,* have you been drinking tonight?" The man replied *"No."* I then said to him *"I am now going to request you to take a breath test as I suspect you of having excess alcohol in your blood."* I then took him to a Panda Car driven by PC 38 Phil Jones and at 11.55pm the man took a breath test which was positive. I found him to be C of Kings Lynn and I said to him *"I am arresting you for having excess alcohol in your blood and you will also be reported for careless driving on Vancouver Court and Old Sun Way."* After caution he said *"I suppose I'll have to come along then, I was taking a short cut to get out that's all."*

Phil then took him to the *"Nick"* where 20 minutes later he took a second breathalyser test administered by Sgt Barrie Myhill; these were the days before the Lion Intoximeter breath testing machine. Sgt Myhill said to him *"Alright Mr C, at 12.15am you have the opportunity to take a second test. You commit no offence if you refuse, but I will then go on to ask for blood or urine samples. If you take this test and it is negative, you will be free to go. If it is positive I will then go on to blood and urine samples."* C said *"Alright, I'll take it."* Barrie assembled the kit and told C how to inflate it; this second test was also positive, C elected to have a blood specimen taken and a doctor attended and took blood.

This blood was divided into three samples and C was given the choice of the three samples and when he had picked one I placed it into an envelope and sealed it and C was informed how to look after it and who to take it to for independent analysis. The other two samples were sealed in a tin put into an envelope and placed in the SOCO Refrigerator for forwarding to Home Office Forensic Science Laboratory. I then reported him for driving without due care and attention and after caution he said *"Fair enough Yes."* and Brian Sayer took him home.

In October we were contemplating further winter economic problems and General Order 55/74 dated the 23rd of October stated *"Having regard to the present economic situation, it will be necessary to plan for economies in respect of fuel throughout the winter months and of the use of stationary at all times."* The order went on about electricity and fuel consumption at Police

Buildings *"Whenever possible office and corridor lighting should be kept to a minimum required for comfortable working conditions. Police Station signs and courtesy lights to remain on. All unnecessary radiators should be turned off and every effort must be made to conserve all types of fuel."*

### "Ron Brown's Retirement"

The following presentation photograph was set up in the Parade Room at King's Lynn Police Station to mark Ron Brown's retirement during 1974; and John Hansell SOCO asked me to press the camera. All members of CID, Scenes of Crime, Crime Prevention, Special Branch and Drug Squad were there; including the head of Norfolk CID, Det Chief Superintendent Reg Lester.

Top Row left to right: DC (later Det Chief Supt) Ron Elliott; DC (later Supt) Steve Swain; DC (later Det Sgt) Tom Walton; DC (later Chief Supt) Adrian Horn; DC Ernie Bean (transferred) DC (later Det Chief Insp) Ivan Thompson; DC (later Chief Insp Royalty Protection) Dick Curtis; DC John Hansell.

Third Row: The late DC Dave Burton; Det Sgt Jack Locke; DC Jim Hardy; DC (later Det Insp) John Barnard; DC Mick Hutchinson; DC Keith (Geordie) Holliday; DC Dave Barnes.

Second Row: DC Keith Davey; DC Tom Humphrey; DC Ray Hansen; DC (later Det Sgt) Dave Dingle; DC Chris Garner; Det Sgt Mick Farnham; Det Sgt Gerry Norton.

Front Row: Det Sgt (later Insp) Ray Wright; the late Det Chief Insp Charlie Nourse; the late much loved Det Sgt Ron Brown; Det Chief Superintendent Reg Lester; Det Insp Ken Watling; DC Peter Coady.

Chris Clark

### *"Don't Take The Piss!"*

On Saturday the 21st of December I was on late turn town centre foot beat when at 4.55pm I was at the junction of High Street with Norfolk Street when I heard three males and a female making a lot of noise, shouting, etc. I told them to be quiet and they carried on walking down Norfolk Street and when I was out of sight I heard them start to shout again and they were laughing loudly and started whistling the *"Dixon of Dock Green"* theme tune. I caught up with them and re warned them about their behaviour. Again when I was out of sight they started up shouting laughing and this time whistling the *"Laurel and Hardy"* theme tune. This time I took their names which the female and two of the males did and one male refused and started arguing with me and he took no heed to a further warning.

I told him that he was under arrest for threatening behaviour and obstructing me in the execution of my duty and after caution said *"I don't have to tell you anything."* I then told the others that they also would be arrested if they carried on in the same manner and told them to move on. I then called up a panda Car to take my arrest and me to the police station and there found the 16 year old youth to be H of an address on the Fairstead Estate at Gaywood. As he was a juvenile he was taken home and reported for the offences in the presence of his Father. I had a number of runins with this lad over the next 20 years right up to my Retirement, when he was a 36 year old dealer of class A drugs.

## Chapter Five

## *"By Royal Appointment" 1975 – 1981*

Before I move onto my story here are a few stories associated with The Royal Family holidays at Sandringham and The Police guarding them over the years.

During the severe winter at the end of 1962/1963 which I mentioned in the first chapter Sandringham suffered the same conditions and HM the Queen went into The Police Lodge one day and asked PC 396 Barry Osborne *"Is everything all right Officer? "No Ma am"* came the reply *"It's bloody freezing in here!"* With that the Queen ordered more coal for The Lodge. Then during Christmas 1966 PC 72 Chris Cushion was on duty one day when the Royal corgis *"Whisky"* and *"Sherry"* were let out. The official line was that they were playing in the grounds and went onto the ice covered lake the ice gave way and both animals fell into the water and then were unable to get out unaided.

What actually happened was the same that has befallen many a serving Officer, the corgis came out snapping and snarling and latched themselves onto Chris's trouser bottoms and in trying to free himself from their jaws by shaking his legs violently he inadvertently tossed the dogs into the lake! Realizing that he would be better in deep water than in deep shit Chris and AN other at first tried unsuccessfully with a ladder to get the dogs to scramble onto that.

Failing this he then took off his helmet and coat and waded into the lake breaking the ice as he went up to his chest in icy water. This is the moment when HM the Queen came out and witnessed the event luckily she hadn't seen the prequel and she was full of admiration for her gallant Officer saving her beloved dogs from drowning.

On Friday 29th December 1967 during her Christmas Holiday at Sandringham, HM the Queen arrived by Royal Train at Kings Lynn

Railway Station, I was on early turn and performed special duty there at 1.40pm. On Saturday 20 January 1968 I was on late turn and from 8:40pm I was tasked with traffic control at Gaywood Clock to facilitate the journey of the Royal car carrying HM the Queen Mother from Sandringham to The Fermoy Centre to watch a performance. (This was the original position of the clock tower, a number of years later it was dismantled and moved about 50 yards South on Gaywood Road to make way for road widening and traffic lights at the junction of Wootton Road with Gayton Road.)

On Friday the 24th May 1968 I did a 7am to 7pm shift and went to Norwich for a Royal Visit HM the Queen visited City Hall, County Hall, and Police Headquarters and had lunch at The Assembly Rooms. On 15th August 1969 from 6pm until 10.30pm I did traffic duty and guard duty at The Guildhall of St George, The Fermoy Centre, where HM Queen Elizabeth the Queen Mother was attending a performance.

During another cold spell in the 1970's there had been a fresh fall of snow whilst a particular night shift were on duty and just before the end of their tour they went onto the back terrace lawn and in large lettering that even a helicopter would spot, they spelled out *"F..K OFF"* in the snow. This was intended for the early turn which upon finding it would have erased it before daylight; however the first person to witness these hieroglyphics was HM the Queen Mother as she opened her curtains in a first floor bedroom and to quote her Daughter's Great Great Grandmother, Queen Victoria, *"She was not amused!"*

## "Kidnap Attempt on Princess Anne 1974"

### Ian Ball born 1956

I have added this account as it was pretty close to my heart during the time that I was a Royalty Protection Officer. During the late evening of Wednesday the 20th of March 1974 HRH Princess Anne and her first husband Mark Phillips were returning to Buckingham Palace from a London charity event in one of the royal cars driven by the chauffer Alex Callender in the back with the royal couple was Lady in waiting Rowena Brassey and her personal protection officer Inspector James Beaton was in the front passenger seat.

On Pall Mall their Rolls Royce was forced to stop by a Ford Escort driven by 26 year old Ian Ball a burglar with mental health problems. The direct speech included here was released by the National Archives under the 30 year rule. Ball jumped from his car firing a loaded hand gun and Inspector Beaton responded by jumping out to shield the Princess and he tried to disarm Ball by firing his gun however Beaton's gun jammed and Ball shot him in the head and chest. Alex Callender was also shot as he tried to disarm Ball as well as a journalist who was passing by and saw what was happening and tried to intervene, he was Brian McConnell and he was shot in the chest.

Ball then told Princess Anne of his kidnapping plan and tried to get her out of the car. He said *"Come with me for a day or two I want two million."* Princess Anne retorted *"Not bloody likely and I haven't got two million."* The Princess in a document later written for Prime Minister Harold Wilson said *"It was all so infuriating I kept saying I didn't want to get out of the car and I was not going to get out of the car... I nearly lost my temper with him but I knew that if I did I should hit him and he would shoot me."*

Eventually Princess Anne dived out of the other side of the royal car and a second passer by Ron Russell then punched Ball in the back of the head and led Princess Anne away from the scene. PC Michael Hills came across the scene and was also shot in the stomach by Ball but managed to put in a call for help on his personal radio and another nearby police officer Detective Constable Peter Edmonds gave chase and brought Ball down with a flying rugby tackle and he was finally arrested.

At this time HM The Queen and HRH Prince Phillip were on a state visit to Indonesia a letter was found penned to *"The Queen"* outlining a ransom demand of £3 million for your daughter back. Ian Ball was prosecuted for attempted murder and attempted kidnap and pleaded guilty and was sent to Broadmoor where he remains.

Inspector Beaton was awarded the George Cross and went on to be a Superintendent in Royalty Protection (I met him at Sandringham) Alex Callender, Brian McConnell, PC Michael Hills and DC Peter Edmonds were awarded the Queen's Gallantry Medal.

After this incident royal security was stepped up but that did not prevent Earl Mountbatten's later murder by the IRA in 1979, the Queen being shot at during Trooping of the Colour in 1981, Michael Fagan entering her bedroom in 1982; or Prince Charles being shot at in Australia during 1994.

I must say that I found royal security during the time I spent involved in it during the height of the IRA campaign a bit of a farce it seemed that we were there to deter *"nutters"* and that's about all. More on these events and my royal experiences now follow.

On Wednesday the 1st of January 1975 I started a month's Royal Duty at Wood Farm, Wolferton on the Sandringham Estate. This particular Royal Christmas Holiday was taken here because Sandringham House was undergoing a major overhaul and about a third of it including the kitchens was being renovated and modernised and reduced in size. Our Police Lodge consisted of a large static caravan situated at the top of the drive opposite Wolferton Church. Cecil Rowe and Nigel Blower were the Sergeants in charge of our Relief and both were adept with a frying pan and at cooking a full English breakfast for the lads, the smell of it cooking came wafting on the breeze and it was like manna from Heaven after three hours patrolling outside.

On the first day I was on early turn together with Cecil Rowe and another PC a recent transferee from The Midlands and others who were guarding the farm house and I was walking down the drive towards Wood Farm when cycling along in the opposite direction coming towards me I identified the figure of Prince Phillip the Duke of Edinburgh . He was done up in a Norfolk Jacket with his trouser bottoms tucked into long woolly socks and neatly set off with a deer stalker hat. He was using this mode of transport to cycle from Wolferton the two miles or so to Sandringham as petrol rationing and conservation was still in force and he had ordered the chauffeurs to set a good example. As he went past me he said *"Good Morning Officer, Happy New Year!"* I saluted and said *"The same to you Sir."* I then called up on my radio which was on "talk through" to warn the other PC who was the caravan side of me of the impending approach of HRH. I said *"Watch out M here comes the Duke of Edinburgh!"*

At that moment in time this PC was completely bored with life, waiting for his breakfast and to pass the time was kicking stones about with his wellies on and hands thrust in his greatcoat pockets looking like *"Compo"* from *"Last of the Summer Wine."* He then turned around looked at the approaching figure that looked to him like a gamekeeper and with his Sherlock Holmes mind deduced wrongly that I was trying to wind him up. He answered back over the radio *"Piss Off!"* and as Prince Phillip got to his position the PC deliberately turned his back on him.

HRH then said to him as he had to me *"Good Morning Officer, Happy New Year"* and he still thinking it was a Royal employee, said *"The same to you mate!"* He still wouldn't believe me until when we later went into the caravan for breakfast and Cecil Rowe with a cracked grin confirmed that it had indeed been HRH. He was quite worried then and thoughts of Ravens and The Tower of London sprang into his mind!

On another occasion I was on duty at the back of Wood Farm, Prince Phillip had gone out either bird watching at Wolferton or driving his horse and carriage at Sandringham. Her Majesty the Queen came out dressed in head scarf, wellies and coat and after bidding me *"Good Morning Officer"* and me responding and saluting went off down the lane into the woods with just her dogs, there were no Personal Protection Officer or game keeper with her. Anyone watching could have abducted The Monarch and we would not have known, we were left guarding a royal house with no royals inside, only *"flunkeys."*

About an hour later Her Majesty came hurrying back carrying one of her dogs whose mouth was bleeding it had got caught in one of the keeper's snares, it could so easily have been her who needed help; when you think that it was only some ten months after her daughter was nearly kidnapped.

On Monday the 6th of January 1975 I worked a 7.30am to 1.30pm before my full night shift at Wood Farm commencing at 10pm, this was in order to travel to Headquarters for an interview with The DCC Gordon Taylor who I saw at 11.30am. He was to become Chief Constable on the 1st of April, following Peter Garland's retirement; Peter Smith ACC became Deputy Chief Constable and Ch Supt John Hall became Assistant Chief Constable.

*DCC (later Chief Constable) Gordon Taylor*

### *"It's Only Me Officer!"*

On another occasion during this Royal Visit at Wood Farm in the week commencing Monday the 6th of January, I was on night duty when one night well after midnight I was walking up the long driveway from the farm towards the police caravan when a vehicle turned into the lane from the public highway and drove at speed towards me and the Royal Abode, thinking that it might be an IRA *"Hit Team"* and that I would be dying shortly guarding Her Majesty and that my Mum and Dad would be proud. I assertively signalled the vehicle to stop with my right arm extended in the time honoured fashion whilst shining the red reflector part of my police lantern and much to my relief the vehicle ground to a halt. As I approached the driver's door a young man with familiar protruding ears leaned his head out of a personalised number plated Green Range Rover and said in a cheerful voice *"It's only me Officer!"* I had just stopped the Heir Apparent HRH Prince Charles. He thanked me for my vigilance, bade me goodnight and made his way home to his bed.

On Wednesday the 25th of July 1979 I was on duty at Sandringham for the Annual Flower Show attended by The Patron Her Majesty Queen Elizabeth the Queen Mother a week before her 79th Birthday; Catherine Duchess of Kent was also in attendance.

Therese took this photo of Her Majesty Pete Coady our Special Branch Officer is on the left and Fred Waite my old work colleague at Sandringham and later Head Gardener President of the Sandringham Flower Show is on the right

### *"Sleeping Partners"*

I remember an occasion when I performed duty at Wood Farm during January 1980 less than a year after Lord Mountbatten had been murdered by The IRA. On this occasion I was the driver of a Police Ford Escort Estate, I was unarmed and my two colleagues who were both armed with .38 revolvers. Our brief was to sit at the top of the drive by Wolferton Church and stop anything that tried to go down towards Wood Farm where HM The Queen and HRH Prince Phillip were staying. Not long after we had arrived both settled down for the night one reclined his front passenger seat and was soon fast asleep the other was lying full length on the rear seat; having firstly unbuckled his gun belt containing both holster and pistol and having carefully wrapped the belt around both placed the weapon in the vehicle glove compartment, making sure that the first chamber was empty to prevent any accidental firing.

Can you imagine the scenario? There was I the only outside protection for the Reigning Monarch with just a lump of wood to protect her with whilst my two colleagues were fast asleep snoring and farting. As I sat there I thought of The IRA's current arsenal of weapons which included fully automatic pistols and rifles and our life expectancy should an ASU turn up. I would have been shot first even though fully awake and alert my front passenger might have reacted to the noise and wake up in time to draw his weapon but the one on the back seat would have stood no chance, having firstly to clamber over his sleeping or dead partner's body, unravel the belt, draw the weapon out of the holster then go *"click "bang!"*

Looking back it was nothing short of lunacy, perhaps they both thought that no one but a *"nutter"* would attack the Queen, but the PIRA assassinated Lord Mountbatten and they planned to assassinate HRH Prince Charles & HRH Princess Diana in June 1983 some three years later. The latter plan was only foiled when the "Bomber" turned "Super Grass" this was some sixteen months before the Brighton Bomb and the attempt to overthrow the British Government by force.

On Wednesday the 31st of July 1980 I performed duty at Sandringham Flower Show Therese who was off duty took my parents to this event and during my break I joined them for a Pic Nic. Just think, if I hadn't joined the police force I would now have over 40 years service at Sandringham and might have become Head Gardener its strange how life pans out. Anyway I now had a nice new white Ford Fiesta police car which replaced the van as my beat vehicle.

*HM Queen Elizabeth the Queen Mother*   *HRH Catherine Duchess of Kent*

257

Chris Clark

Sandringham House from the Lake taken on my Canon Sureshot

## *"Nicely turned out for The Queen Mother's 80th Birthday"*

On Sunday the 4th of August 1980 Her Majesty the Queen Mother's 80th birthday, I was on duty at Sandringham Church for the 11am service which was attended by HM the Queen, the Queen Mother and other Royals. The Queen made this a very special day for her mother by allowing The Press into the grounds for the first time, previously they had to make do with taking long range telephoto lens photographs from behind the church gates. The photograph below shows both of the Queen's leaving the church at 12 noon and somehow *"yours truly"* got stuck in the centre of the photographer's viewpoint; there was no bribery involved, I can assure you.

## *"Specials"*

Now I must write a paragraph on the Special Constabulary, a lot of older coppers hated the fact that unpaid civilians came out on a weekend dressed in a police uniform and performed duty at village fetes, carnivals, Remembrance Sunday parades and the like and in their eyes stopping us from getting full recruitment and a decent wage. My own personal experience at King's Lynn and generally within West Norfolk, both as a patrol officer and control room operative, viewed the dedicated bunch of people that we had with admiration; particularly on a Friday and Saturday night when we had a lot of public order incidents to deal with and due to poor recruitment we had depleted manpower to deal with large numbers of yobs fighting; they were putting their feet and shoulders where it mattered, beside us. On one dreadful night one of our special colleagues was hit over the head with a heavy bar stool and hospitalised by an amphetamine fuelled RTT, the boxer mentioned earlier. So my heartfelt thanks goes out to people like Massey Banks, Brian Hooks, Trevor *"Whisky"* Warner, Roy Backham, Bob Dye, Richard Smith, Bill Cox and countless others who gave us, and some who are still serving, excellence service. A big thank you to all of you, wherever you served in the Lynn Downham or Hunstanton areas.

## *Back to 1975*

Around this time there was a spate of jeweller's shops being broken into in Kings Lynn and other towns in the area, the MO bypassing the alarm, removing roof slates and then cutting a hole in the loft and dropping into the first floor of the attacked premises. The Detectives had little or no idea who was responsible and we had a Divisional CID Conference at Lynn and certain names were bandied about, it was even thought that *"out of towner's"* were involved. I mentioned my sighting earlier of G outside H Samuels, but it was dismissed out of hand.

It was during a week of night shift when I was doing a combined Acting Sergeant and Control dual role due to manpower shortage and I only had three Constables to cover the whole of Kings Lynn when at about 3am on one particular date (details were in the Station Occurrence Book) when I received an alarm activation at Kings Lynn of the window display at Dryden's Jewellers, which was then on the corner of Tower Street and Blackfriars Street. I put out a message to our three lads, told Headquarters that we had an alarm and that I was closing the police station temporarily and ran the 300 yards or so to Dryden's where the other lads had arrived at. On my arrival I could see that one of the intruders was inside the shop and moving about and he eventually sat down on a chair and folded his arms, I recognised him as being G that I had mentioned to CID.

I set up a containment area so that the block was sealed off and we awaited the arrival of the key holder. In the meantime we saw another intruder walking about on the high roof of the attacked premises who then went and hid behind the large advertising board of *"Poysers Flowers"* on the adjacent roof. When the key holder arrived some 20 minutes later and we went into the premises and arrested G. He cheekily said to the key holder *"You took your time getting here!"* He then told me that when he made the hole to get into the premises the joists were just wide enough to allow him to drop through, but when the alarm went off he couldn't squeeze back through to escape as he was stockier than the other slim burglar. We then gained access to the roof and arrested the other man involved B.

What had happened we later found out was that the intruders had removed the roof slates dropped into the first floor loft, bypassed the main alarm linked to Police Headquarters at Norwich, then cut a square hole in the loft floor and then drop feet first into the premises. Having

261

achieved this they then set about clearing the shop of stock.

As there were some nice items in the window display these were also removed. This was their downfall, Dryden's had a window *"scare"* alarm fitted, to alert police if a *"smash and grab"* occurred and as they reached into the window recess this alarm activated and terminated in the King's Lynn Control Room. Both G and B admitted the spate of jewellers shops burglaries committed in Kings Lynn and the surrounding areas and both received hefty sentences after their guilty pleas at Crown Court. Once again a valuable sighting submitted by me into the system had made a large future gain in our battle to win the war on the streets.

### "Haway The Lads!"

On Saturday 8 March I was on late turn footbeat which covered the High Street area our shift was deplete of men as most of the Relief and others on duty had been deployed to police the Norwich City v Sunderland AFC football match at Carrow Road in Norwich.

Barry Richards a colleague of those days takes up the story. *"I was on duty that day, the only time I had overtime. I was taken by bus to Norwich where we were briefed at Bethel Street station. I had been looking forward to it, a great match, great atmosphere, standing behind the goal and watching the game for free whilst being paid O/T. Then reality struck. The inspector said the following officers will be on car park duty. Sure enough P.C.323 Richards was assigned to the car park. When I arrived there was another inspector there. There were several coaches with the Sunderland supporters in. The inspector went on each coach in turn and told them they would all be searched when they got off the coach and anyone carrying an offensive weapon would be arrested and miss the match. By way of amnesty any weapons could be placed in the aisle, an officer would collect them and no further action would be taken. I was ordered on the first coach, it was like going into the lions den. They were all shouting at me, one grabbed my arm and started jabbering at me but for the life of me I couldn't understand a word they were saying, it was like a foreign language to me. Anyway it was an eye opener, knuckle dusters, knives, scanners in socks, you name it I picked it up."*

The Author continues: That day Norwich City FC were hosting Sunderland AFC in League Division Two and luckily it was a 0-0 draw as at around 6.30pm all 500 Sunderland Supporters coaches pulled into the Southgates Lorry Park, Kings Lynn in order for the supporters, who were mainly from mining stock to refresh themselves in certain ale houses throughout the town.

At around 7.30pm I was positioned at the Tuesday Market Place end of High Street when I heard this almighty roaring noise ensueing from the Saturday Market Place end and endless chanting of *"Haway The Lads!"* and thought that some alien country had invaded us. As the noise got closer and build to a crescendo I could see an endless horde of Red and White striped shirted men marching up the pedestrianized High Street towards me and realised that it was all 500 Sunderland Supporters who were fairly well oiled up by this time.

My immediate reaction was to run and hide up until this tidal wave of red and white had passed but no it was my job to uphold the peace and show neither fear nor favour to anyone; especially foreigners with a strange dialect! So I stood my ground like some Sheriff in a Western where a gang of outlaws have ridden in to take the town over.

As the first and obvious *"leaders"* got to me I picked out the biggest and tallest one who was about 6'8" and towered over my 5'10" frame and said in a loud voice

*"I don't want any of you messing about on my beat otherwise you will miss your coach back to Sunderland!"*

He replied in his Mackem dialect "

*Whe-Aye man! Alreet meert am off doon tha pub leek man, aye aye yall get nah sheet oot us, al buy ya a drink if we do, good neet."*

Then all 500 swept past like a herd of Wildebeest and disappeared into the local hostelries and true to their word there was no trouble from them. It's a good job that I wasn't wearing a black and white Newcastle scarf otherwise I wouldn't be writing this now!

On Saturday the 3rd of May Dudley Hubbard replaced Barrie Myhill as Sergeant on "B" Relief and Barrie went on to be Prosecutions Department Inspector after being a Patrol Inspector. Maurice Ayres took over from Gerry Dunn as Chief Inspector; Maurice hailed from Stanhoe and he and my Mother went to the same school, his nickname then was *"Motsy Ayres."* John Garth Williams remained Superintendent and Ivan Mead took over as Chief Superintendent after Fred Calvert retired.

### "Don't Mess With Me Boys"

On Friday the 27th of June 1975 I was on night duty on town centre foot beat patrol, when at 11.15pm I was in Norfolk Street when I saw P and H two teenage burglars who were known to me, one of them H who I had *"Nicked"* the year before for public order offences. They were standing against a large display window at Carter's TV and HI FI shop together with two girls. They started jeering and trying to be the big boys to impress their female aquaintenances and I warned them of their behaviour. I then continued patrol and in Old Market Street I cleared out the Lord Kelvin Pub of Irish Students who were drinking after time. During this time at 11.45pm I again saw this pair in company with another known person N. H and N went off together towards New Conduit Street and twenty-five minutes later, at 12.10am early Saturday morning, I saw H walk from Broad Street into Norfolk Street eating fish & chips from paper near Goodchilds Photography.

Suddenly from nowhere N appeared and joined him. They were obviously up to no good and I circulated over my personal radio to the other lads on the relief that they were probably testing us ready to do a burglary.

When I reported for duty at 10pm Saturday night the 28th of June, I discovered that overnight Bambers Outfitters in Broad Street had been broken into via a 1st floor toilet window, but the intruder/s had been disturbed; obviously by me as this is where I had seen N emerge from and join H, the latter a lookout. At 1140pm I checked Bambers and found the premises secure, the bastards had obviously been hiding up waiting, because some 25 minutes later, at 12.05am early Sunday morning we had a report of the burglar alarm sounding there.

I immediately attended together with George Dimmock and Reg Pyatt, but the intruders had been disturbed by the audible alarm sounding and we received information on the identification of the suspects involved and searched the area around the Bus Station, which had moved from The Millfleet and was now in its current location, and saw N and G walking together towards paradise Lane where they split up. N walked towards Norfolk Street and then left into High street and G walked towards Railway Road. At 1210am the Sunday morning, I said to G *"I am arresting you on suspicion of burglary at Bambers."* After caution he said *"What burglary? I haven't done a burglary."* He was searched and put in the back of our police car and then George and I searched the area looking for P, H and N in connection with crime over the past 48 hours.

At 1220am as we were driving past Jackson's Shoe Shop in Chapel Street near to the junction with Surrey Street, I looked to my left into the illuminated premises and saw the front door hanging open and inside the shop and on their way out were the aforementioned three burglars, with N in front, followed by H and P. I leapt out of the police car and went to arrest the nearest one to me who was N, as all three ran off down Surrey Street. P being the quickest runner was in front, H next and N and me bringing up the rear. I saw N drop a black radio he had been carrying from the shop and it was recovered later.

It was at this point I realized that I should have done the cross country runs at Eynsham as here I was nine years later on aged nearly thirty and having lived on takeaways was fat and out of condition and chasing after young fit teenagers which was for the younger members of the Relief. It was a bit like a four man relay race, only the last one held the baton. That gave me an idea and as I was running flagging behind and shouting out *"Stop you three!"* I drew my truncheon out of its sheath pocket sewn into my right trouser leg and shouted to the nearest one in front *"N stop or I'll drop you with my stick!"* This was totally ignored and I went to throw my truncheon to catch his legs up so he would fall over, I threw it and it took off like a javelin and homed in like a possessed exocet missile straight towards his head. As it did so I thought *"I'm in the shit now!"* It was with immense relief that the rear wall of the Midland Bank jutted out further than the others in the street and stopped the truncheon from embedding itself in N's head.

At the end of Surrey Street H turned left into High Street and the other two right into Tuesday Market Place and then towards The Globe Hotel. At this point after having run about 300 yards I gave up the chase as George Dimmock was in hot pursuit in the Panda Car. I returned to the scene of the burglary, collecting the dropped radio on the way. The door to the shop had been kicked open and several pairs of shoes and trainers were strewn about on the floor and the till was lying in pieces.

At 12.35am George returned in the Panda together with G and N was also in the back, who he had *"nicked."* I got in the front passenger seat and N started shouting and swearing and kicking violently on the back of my seat, he was endangering the driving of the car and George pulled up. N was still going ballistic so I reached with my right arm behind me and grabbed a handful of his long hair and whilst still in my seat I physically pulled him out of his seat and up and over my shoulder and into my side foot well of the car and held him with my foot jammed on the side of his head whilst George continued driving to the *"Nick."* On the way N was saying that he was going to report me and when he grew up he was going to *"pop"* me (shoot me). Both prisoners were left with DC Keith Davey to deal with. Later at 2.30am we went to G's address in North Lynn and collected his Father and at 2.40am interviewed G who admitted his part and made a voluntary statement and at 4.15am we took both him and his Father home.

During the middle of July I started dating WPC Therese Chadwick and in September moved out of 29 Checker Street into her ground floor flat at 69 Gaywood Road, Kings Lynn. We were to be married in March 1977. It was during July and August when walking home from her flat to my digs when I noticed two officers from a certain relief were abusing their position as police officers in uniform and using their police vehicle for nefarious deeds. Both were on night duty in the Riot Van and picking up females leaving The Intercon Night Club and driving off somewhere to sow their wild oats, this was just one thing as this pair were up to all sorts. Years later after they had left Lynn these two plus one other were arrested for conspiracy to commit armed robbery. One had left the job and planned a wages van robbery using cast police uniforms which the other had managed to get hold of from Headquarters Stores; they even had the sketch plans of how they were going to do it. One was eventually reinstated much to the distaste of fellow officers and posted out of King's Lynn and met his maker years before he should have.

During August Ray Wright who had been a Detective Sergeant was promoted to uniform Inspector and was our Shift Inspector for a while.

## *A Vintage Year*

On Saturday the 20th of September, 1975, I was on night duty and in the *"Riot Van"* call sign Foxtrot 25 together with Jim Englebach who was driver and Reg Pyatt, when at 1.35am on the Sunday morning I saw a male running from the Southgates past The Lord Napier PH into Goodwins Road, I recognised him as S and he was carrying a bottle of wine in each hand. I got out of the police vehicle and examined the bottles, they were good class and full and had *"Peatling & Cawdron of Bury St Edmunds"* on the labels. I said to him *"Where did you get these bottles of wine?"* S said *"I bought them earlier this evening."*

I said *"I'm not satisfied with that and I am arresting you on suspicion of burglary at Peatling & Cawdron London Road."* After caution he replied *"Oh No!"* and he was taken into Lynn police station. In the meantime I had radioed to a Panda patrol to check Peatling & Cawdron and they confirmed that a plate glass window was broken and there had been a *"smash & grab"* at the premises. At 2.30am S made a voluntary statement admitting the offence and as he was of no fixed abode he was kept in custody awaiting CID follow up in the morning.

## *I Had A Nose For Trouble*

On Wednesday the 15th of October I was on night duty foot beat when at 10.35pm I was at the rear of Kennings Tyres in Stanley Street, when I saw a dark blue Ford Transit van come up Stanley Street and reverse up to the wall of Kennings so that the rear of it was flush with the wall and three men got out of the vehicle. The driver was about 6'2" and wearing spectacles. I noticed that the vehicle didn't have a front number plate and I called out to the driver *"Hey I want a word with you!"* The man who had been the driver came back from Railway Road junction leaving the other two and said *"Yeh! What's up?"* I said "What's the index number of your van that you have just parked here?" He said *"I don't know but it's an F registration I think, I haven't had it long."* I said *"Well I don't either, because there's no front number plate for it."* He said *"Yeh! Well it fell off it's inside the van."* I then looked inside the van and lying on the dashboard against the windscreen I saw the front number plate it read HCE138E, I checked the tax disc and it also read the same index number. I dealt with loads of this type of minor traffic offence and normally said *"Get it sorted"* but with this one I instinctively knew that something wasn't quite right. I decided to check further and said *"What is your name and where do you live?"* He said S and he gave an address at Tilney All Saints. I said *"If you drive about at night with your number plate off where there is vulnerable property like a tyre company it makes us suspect that you might have a safe or something in the back. Get it fixed as soon as you can."* I then resumed patrol.

I was still completely unhappy about this person and vehicle's presence in town and shortly afterwards I liaised with WPC 22 Therese Chadwick (My Fiancé) at Vancouver Court Bus Station who was on a 4pm to 12 midnight shift and asked her to keep observation on the van and informed Control of its presence. I then went on foot patrol checking vulnerable property in the area. Half an hour later I came from the rear of Sainsbury's onto the Car Park and saw the van HCE138E start up and leave the area heading towards North Lynn I informed Control and carried on checking property.

At 12.07am early Thursday morning I was on foot beat in London Road when Control reported an alarm at Marston Radiators Hardwick Road and sent Panda 1 and Panda 2 to it, they called up at 12.10am *"Intruders at premises."* I hailed a *"Geoff's Taxi"* that was passing and got a lift to the scene to act as backup and arrived at 12:15am. On my arrival I saw the same dark blue Ford Transit Van HCE138E, parked with its lights off at the attacked premises and in the rear of Keith Pearce's Panda car I saw and recognised S the driver I had spoken to earlier that evening. I said to Keith in S's hearing *"This is S who I checked earlier in that van at Kennings"* S said *"Oh it's you is it?"* I got in and went as escort to Lynn police station.

At 1220am I went into the Matron's Room where S was and said *"Right S unless you are in any doubt about it you have been arrested on suspicion of burglary at Marston Radiators."* After caution he replied *"I've told the other one we sat there discussing Go Cart Racing and then you lot came and picked us up."* I said *"When I got to the premises there was an alarm ringing there did you hear it?"* He said *"Yes I thought that you lot set it off when you arrived."* I thought to myself *"I've got a wide boy here!"* and I said *"No we attended because you lot set the alarm off by screwing the place. The reason why it didn't ring straight away was to give us time to get there before scaring you off."*

He said *"I don't know anything about screwing the place, I got out to have a slash and the others had one as well. We were all sitting in the van when you lot turned up so you've got nothing on us."* I said *"How do you explain that there was a window that had been forced only a couple of yards from your driver's seat where the van was and this is what set the alarm off?"* He said *"I don't know anything about that as I said the other two P and D got out for a slash I don't know what they were up to when they were out of the van as I was inside then."*

I then said *"You mean to say that you knew nothing about the burglary at Marston Radiators?"* He replied *"No."* I said *"Did you see anyone else there when you arrived or while you sat there?"* He said *"No, mind you we were talking about the Go Cart so we wouldn't have noticed."* Again I thought *"This bloke is full of shit!"* I said *"How long were you sat there before the police arrived?"* S said *"Only a matter of a few minutes."* I said *"Well the premises were entered at 12.07am that is when the window was broken as there is a contact on it and this set the alarm off at our police station at that time. There is a delay before the alarm sounds at the premises and when we get there we find you three sat there. You can see what the score is you've just got to have this one haven't you?"* He said *"If you say so but I think that it's worth having a run for my money I've got nothing to lose."*

I said *"That's up to you sit tight I'm just going to check if you've got any form. Have you ever seen the inside of a police station before?"* He said *"Yeh! A few months ago when I was living at Mattishall, I got pulled in for a garage break when my grand father died I wasn't too pleased they had me in and let me out on £25 bail. When I got back to hear the charge I wasn't in there more than a quarter of an hour and they dropped the charge."*

I left S with DC Ray Hansen and did a CRO check. I then interviewed S using contemporaneous notes (these were the days before tape interviews) and then wrote out my statement of evidence. He later appeared at court along with the other two and was found guilty and all received a custodial sentence.

On Monday the 27th of October I commenced a Police Learner Driver Course at Headquarters where I lived in HQ Single men's Quarters, Sergeant Ernie Stutterford was my driving instructor and I completed this and received my full driving licence and police driving permit on Friday the 21st of November.

On the Saturday following Therese handed me a set of car keys and outside stood my very own first vehicle which she had bought as an early birthday present, I was the proud owner of a dark green Singer Chamois the deluxe version of the Hillman Imp index number NRT193E.

### An Authorised Police Driver

On Friday the 28th of November I was on early turn and after nine and a half years in the job I had my first shift as a Police Panda driver in a Hillman Imp, index number KVF875P and from Saturday the 27th of December I became the full time Unit Beat 2 Panda Driver on "B" Relief. Being a fast response vehicle life was even more busy and varied from now on and I dealt with just about everything there was in the case book.

Here is just a sample of one ordinary late turn:

2.30pm commenced patrol UB1 with PC424 Pearce.

2.35pm Boots High Street report of woman collapsed, ambulance attended. 2.53pm Attended non Injury RTA Loke Road, voluntary statement and report for careless driving.

4.33pm Attend non injury RTA Columbia Way, voluntary statement and report for careless driving.

5.05pm Articulated lorry broken down St John's Terrace, severe traffic congestion, did traffic duty.

5.25pm Meal break DHQ.

6.10pm Called out from break to report of an alarm at Bawsey Feedstuffs, false alarm insecure rear door, secured by key holder.

6.30pm conveyed female from RTA on B1145 to QE Hospital for treatment, dealt with by Dersingham Section Officers.

6.55pm Bevis Way ref keys locked in car, managed to get into vehicle for owner.

7pm attended Dow's North Lynn, Industrial Accident, man fallen off storage tank. A Loader employed by Dow Agro Chemicals was loading acid on top of a Malaysian Tanker and had slipped on the wet foot rail and fallen 12 feet to ground, back injury, bleeding from wound at base of scull, conscious and alert, no guard rail on tanker. Taken by ambulance to QE Hospital A & E. Message left for Health and Safety Factories Inspectorate.

8pm DHQ Reports.

8.10pm resumed patrol.

8.12pm Hillington Square re yob trouble, warned them and they moved on. 8.30pm in Norfolk Street, sighting C47 re known burglar H seen riding a pedal cycle.

8.40pm Tennyson Avenue junction with Gaywood Road sighting C47 re another known burglar M riding a black trade bike with a step ladder carried on his shoulder.

9pm Parked Panda Car and carried out vulnerable shop property check in South Lynn.

10pm completed duty DHQ.

## *1976*

The year started with me again performing Acting Sergeant duties on "B" Relief. During February the former Policewomen's Department disbanded as a result of the Equal Opportunities Commission and all of the staff transferred onto the four Relief's thus ending the long specialist history of a proud Women's Constabulary. Therese joined "B" Relief and we worked on the same shift until the end of 1977 when I moved to Gayton and she stayed on "B" Relief.

Also during February computerisation of a Wanted/Missing Index was being placed on the Police National Computer and preparing to back record conversion from card index and in March descriptive searching for vehicles used in crime and stolen checks were in force, that was where full details of make, model, colour, registration mark, engine/chassis number, were not known and you could search on each of these fields. For example if you were looking for a White Ford Cortina with part index of ABC1??D, the computer searched on 1 to 199 and came up with all White Ford Cortina's in that number range and year, thus narrowing down to a researchable quantity.

## *This didn't warm the cockles of their heart*

On Friday the 2nd of April, I was on a night shift in Unit Beat 2 Panda together with PC 288 Bob Mickleburgh, when at 10:35pm there was a report of intruders at the wholesale fishmonger premises of Albert Balls Cockle Store in Hextable Road. We attended and arrived within three minutes, coming in from John Kennedy Road and about half way down this short road, nearly opposite the junction with Lansdowne Street. I saw a Black Ford Cortina, index number, ELK741C, parked without lights and containing two people.

As we drove closer I could see from the headlights of our vehicle that the driver was FG and the passenger his brother MG both active criminals from a large *"traveller"* family; and as we drew level I saw two large polythene bags of cooled and shelled cockles lying on the rear seat, there was also a length of rubber tubing and a petrol can lying behind the driver's seat. I said to FG Where did you get the cockles from?" He replied *"From an old boy down the road."* I said *"I'm not satisfied with that, I suspect that you and your brother have stolen these cockles from Albert Balls yard and you are being arrested."*

After caution neither made any reply and we took them to the *"Nick"* and I later took their car into our bulk PSE property yard and obtained a statement from the witness to the burglary. I then interviewed both defendants who admitted the offence and did a house search and charged them. DC 427 Chris Garner was our Night Detective who dealt with the file. When the two brothers subsequently went to court, with their previous convictions they *"went down"* but not only that, they had their car confiscated and sold by the court as they had been additionally charged with going equipped to steal with a motor vehicle!

## *The 1976 Drought*

The long hot summer of 1976 which eventually ended in September was the culmination of a 16 month dry spell – the longest recorded over England and Wales since 1727. It had its origins in the weather of 1975 when dry warm sunny weather dominated from May throughout that summer, and the autumn and winter of 1975 were also drier than usual followed by a dry March and April of 1976. The period of May to August, 1976 was again exceptionally, dry, hot and sunny and Heathrow recorded an unbroken spell of 16 consecutive days from the 23rd of June to the 8th of July when there were temperatures in excess of 30% centigrade. Without sufficient rainfall and scorching hot weather the grass in many areas of the country turned brown, there were countless heath and forest fires, many rivers dried to a mere trickle and an enormous amount of ponds and small lakes completely dried out, a lot of them never to come back to a water course apart from temporary water holes in time of heavy rainfall like the summer of 2007 and 2012 and winter of 2013.

As the ground dried out particularly in fen peat and clay areas thousands of subsidence claims poured into insurance companies at an overall cost of £60 million and agriculture suffered £500 million worth of failed crops. The peak of the drought coincided with the holiday season and much of the south west of England could not cope with the record amount of holiday makers and the huge increase in demand for water. A drought act was passed and there were numerous cuts in supply, at Hunstanton and other locations on the east coast there was an invasion of swarms of lady birds along the promenade.

I was on annual leave from Tuesday the 10th of August until Tuesday the 24th of August. Therese and I hired a Commer Highway Motor home and in that fortnight toured from Cambridge, Oxford, Stratford on Avon, Somerset and Minehead, Devon and Torbay, Hampshire and The New Forest, Chichester and Brighton, Ampthill Forest, with overnight stops at various locations en route. The grass was brown wherever we went. I have never known an English summer like it, with wall to wall sunshine, very hot days and balmy nights like in the tropics.

During this summer someone was taking advantage of the weather in a different way, along the south side of Gayton Road there were numerous large detached properties set in their own grounds which were being broken into whilst the owners were away and substantial amounts of property being stolen from them, including silverware and jewellery.

There was no intelligence on who was committing these and suspicion was on Brighton Antique Knockers the only clue being olive green paint left on an ornamental fountain of one such property where a vehicle had scraped against it leaving the driveway. Before going on leave I performed a week of night shift from Monday the 19th of July until Sunday the 25th of July and during that week did observation duty in Panda 2 in the burglary area from 10:45pm to 2:00am nightly, I had a combination of observers including PC 825 Nigel "Smokey" Thomas, PC Kelly Seaman and PC 779 Lionel England, but nothing transpired or connected with what was going on and the burglaries continued on into late autumn.

During the week of nights commencing Monday the 11th of October I persuaded Sgt Dudley Hubbard to allow me to do observations in the Gayton Road area in my private vehicle, the Singer Chamois Therese had bought for me the previous year. Nothing happened Monday night, Tuesday night, Wednesday night or Thursday night.

On Friday night the 15th of October I staked the area out from 10:15pm as I had done the previous four shifts. At 1:55am on the Saturday morning I saw an olive green Ford Zephyr coming from the Fairstead Estate along William Booth Road and turn left into Gayton Road and towards town, driving along slowly. I could see that the driver was the only occupant and he was looking to his right at the drive ways of the *"posh"* houses and as he went past I could see his face illuminated by my headlights and recognised him to be a local active burglar O.

I informed Control and followed the vehicle at a discreet distance so as to not scare him off and radioed his direction of travel to uniform patrol officers. He eventually stopped outside an address in Gaywood Hall Drive. And at this point Dick Curtis and Dave Bulmer turned up and nicked him on suspicion of committing the spate of Gayton Road burglaries, his vehicle was impounded and Keith Holliday our SOCO confirmed that the paint sample on the Ford Zephyr was identical with that found on the fountain.

O received a term of imprisonment for the burglaries which he cleared up, directly due to me using my initiative and carrying out covert observations as opposed to sticking out like a sore thumb in a Panda car. There is a sequel to this story O and I were due to meet up again in 5 years time during 1981 when again whilst on observation I rumbled him and put him away for a further 4 years and a paint sample was again to be his downfall; more on this later in the book.

Ivan Mead was promoted to Assistant Chief Constable of South Yorkshire and John Williams replaced him as Chief Superintendent and Maurice Ayres became Superintendent. I remember sometime after Therese and I doing Football Duty at Carrow Road, Norwich City v Manchester United and we went into the foyer of Bethel Street Police station the Norwich Divisional Headquarters. There were a group of very senior uniform officers in a huddle all with *"scrambled egg"* on their cap peaks one of them left the group and with a big beam on his face exclaimed *"Watchyer Fanny!"* to Therese, it was Ivan now ACC and he stood and spoke with us *"mere constables"* for a while asking how we were doing and that's how he was very down to earth.

I also remember one previous Control Room duty at King's Lynn when

I was letting rip into one of the younger recruits when Ivan popped his head in whilst I was in full bore and promptly closed the door again. He came back some time later and I apologised for my outburst that he had been caught in. He replied *"Not at all, I hope you sorted the problem out and showed him the error of his ways?"* I replied *"Yes Guvnor"* and he said *"These young ones need to have someone on their case."* Many years later the PC in question confided to me that I had helped in shaping his career, during half of it he was a good Dog Handler and thanked me for putting him on the straight and narrow.

## *1977*

### *Force Disorganisation*

As from Monday the 3rd of January whilst I was still performing duty at Sandringham, Norfolk Constabulary re-organised and was divided into four separate Divisions, with the DHQ's situated at Norwich, North Walsham, East Dereham and King's Lynn, the latter having Sub Divisions at both King's Lynn and at Dersingham. It is never a good idea to have a Divisional Headquarters and a Sub Divisional Headquarters situated in the same building like a two tier wedding cake and this would cause identity problems at King's Lynn for years to come. An example being the Divisional Chief Superintendent and the Sub Divisional *"arm wrestling"* for territorial information from the combined Divisional and Sub Divisional Control Room staff. It would manifest itself in years to come and would do poor old Superintendent Robin *"Bob"* Humphrey's head in when the Chief Superintendent would race in before 8am to pick our brains on the overnight events not only in the Division but *"Bob's"* Sub Division as well and then inform the Assistant Chief Constable at Headquarters.

The Traffic Department was split into two separate Divisions, Eastern

Area operating from Bessemer Road, Norwich with a Sub Div at Acle and Western Area operating from King's Lynn with Sub Divs at Dereham, Swaffham and Attleborough.

During February I was back at King's Lynn on "B" Relief, showing round our two new recruits *"Nicky"* Baron and Pete Newton who along with Dave Bulmer had joined the shift. Ray Wright had been promoted and was our Shift Inspector, Maurice *"Jack"* Rix had been promoted from Terrington St Clement Beat Constable and was Patrol Sergeant for a short time before becoming Station/Custody Sergeant.

During 1976 I and Reg Pyatt, who had been a Sergeant in the Royal Anglian Regiment used to regularly visit the Army Recruiting Office in Wellesley Street as part of our beat work, these sort of premises were high on the IRA *"Hit List."* We got to know the Recruiting Sergeant TR very well and had tea with him not realizing that his family would later be hit with a tragedy of enormous proportion.

During December 1976 Ts daughter a14 year old schoolgirl went missing from Downham Market and for the first few weeks she was considered to have gone off for her own reasons. Some six weeks later on Tuesday the 8th of February her naked body was found in a ditch a couple of miles from her home she had been raped and strangled and there were strange cut marks on her back like a "Criss Cross" pattern in the game "OXO". She had obviously been murdered on the day that she went missing when she should have got a taxi to her boyfriend but instead hitch hiked.

Now with all of the national highlighted cases it would be easy to assume that a serial predator had taken her but following good local detective work involving *"Ted"* Worby who was Detective Sergeant at Downham Market and Detective Sergeant Peter Valleley of Thetford and others, a local dustman was arrested and later sentenced to life imprisonment. He would never admit to having left the cut marks on the body however which was a method used to dispose of animal carcases if quick lime were added would speed up decomposition particularly in a cold climate.

Therese and I took annual leave from Wednesday the 16th of March to Thursday the 31st of March and we were married on Saturday the 19th of March on her 24th birthday at Norwich. Our guests included serving and retired police station colleagues, Fred Calvert, Peter Griffin was my best man, Frank Leech, Derrick Pimlott, Olive Edwards, Janet Claxton, Denise and Roger Lord, Dick Lefevre, Jim Hardy, Stuart Bray, Simon and Ann Dixon.

During April/May we had a new intake of probationers joining "B" Relief, Barry Richards, Bruce Appleby, Liz Craig (Later Liz Appleby after marrying Bruce and sadly she died as a young woman from Cancer) Rick Aldous and Mick Knight. Dave Bull also joined the shift; he had originally been on "D" Relief then transferred to Cambridge and then transferred back to King's Lynn. Alan Steward was on the shift under sufferance from his beat at Terrington St John, due to his drinking habits.

The summer of 1977 was also hot like the two preceding ones and this increased the volume of drink related Public Order offences, people only fight in nice weather and heavy rain of a weekend was always the *"best policeman."* Anyway the hot sunny weather certainly helped the Queen's Silver Jubilee during June, streets were closed off and people brought out tables and chairs and mountains of sandwiches and home baked sausage rolls, pies, quiches, pastries and cakes and urns of tea and coffee and there was dancing and singing well into the night and after. It was probably the most public togetherness event since "VE" day in 1946.

On Monday the 8th of August the Criminal Names Index came into operation on the Police National Computer.

On the 1st of September, 1977, my annual pay went up to £3,360 and during this month we gained a new Shift Inspector on "B" Relief, and what a bundle of joy he was! Luckily I only had to put up with him for four months, before I moved to Gayton; but that was four months too long, all was not well with the Relief or with the Country.

The economy was weak and in August there had been 1,600,000 people unemployed and that is unemployed, as opposed to the work-shy and those who deliberately live on benefits from our taxes which is not what the welfare state was introduced for. The economic situation carried on into the following year when there were similar undertones which was to boil over by the end of 1978.

On Sunday the 2nd of October I was Acting Sergeant on early turn together with PC Bob Mickleburgh when Therese called us to the scene of a particularly unpleasant suicide, not that any are pleasant. A middle aged managing director of a local hardware and gas bottle supply company had committed suicide during the early hours whilst staying at a friend's house. He had gone out to the shared garage and driveway complex between semi detached properties, put a double barrel shotgun into his mouth and blown most of his head away. We found him lying in a massive pool of blood of about a gallon in all and bits of congealed brain and fragments of skull everywhere, including stuck to the up and over door of the garage where they had dried hard.

After dealing with the sudden death and a doctor to certify that death had occurred! And Keith Holliday our SOCO taking photographs; we moved the body and found a suicide note and a length of rope coiled up under the body, so he had contemplated more than one way to leave this planet. We then got buckets of water with copious amounts of mild green *"Fairy Liquid"* and washed away all of the blood and set about the difficult task of removing the mess from off of the garage door whilst singing the West Ham FC anthem *"We're for ever blowing bubbles"* to try and detract our minds from this gruesome task and it was a bit like trying to get dead dried insects off of the front of a car in the summer, anyway *"Fairy"* worked on that, so it should work on baked on crockery.

We then set about retrieving as much of the scattered skull and brain fragments that we could find from off of the lawn and flower beds.

### This ones mind was blown too!

On Friday the 14th of October 1977, I commenced a 10:00pm to 06:00am tour on UB2 Panda with PC691 Nick Baron and commenced a property check of our designated area of patrol. Not long after midnight we were called to The Millfleet with regard to a drunken person seen near The Lincoln Tavern PH. We located this man in Stonegate Street near the rear entrance Of Mann Eggerton Motor Dealers and saw that he was staggering about on the footpath and bumping into the wall. He was obviously drunk and he then supported himself against the wall with his arms in a raised position and his head resting against the wall and with his legs spread apart; he then threw up on the pavement and then staggered along in the direction of Church Street. As we got closer I immediately recognised him to be H a local burglar and druggie. He seemed to know where he was going and able to look after himself so we allowed him to continue his meandering journey.

At 12:40am we received a report of a dark coloured Ford Cortina seen leaving the Tuesday Market Place some half a mile away from Church Street, the vehicle had damage on its front off-side and its headlamp was broken; the driver reported to be under the influence. At that time we did not know the relevance of what was about to unfold and we conducted a search of the Loke Road area for this vehicle.

At 12:50am Nick and I received a report to attend outside 83 Columbia Way, North Lynn regarding a fail to stop hit-and-run (RTA) road traffic accident, where the offending vehicle's registration number had been taken. We arrived at the scene at 12:53am and saw a Ford Cortina Estate parked on the near-side close to a lit lamp-post, facing north towards Lady Jane Grey Road. This vehicle had a large dent in its rear off-side wing and the complete rear off-side lighting assembly was demolished. Left at the scene by the offending vehicle was a complete buckled nearside wing and a large amount of the same coloured paint debris smothered over the rear off-side of the Estate car. Nick and I followed the route north which the offending vehicle would have taken and about 200 yards further along Columbia Way we found the offending vehicle a dark blue Ford Cortina with the registration number which the witness had given us.

The rear lights of the vehicle were on and it was stationary at an angle on the nearside of the road. I went round to the front of the vehicle and located the driver of the vehicle who I found to be H of North Lynn the drunken pedestrian mentioned earlier. A member of the public had taken the car keys off of H and I took possession of them from her. Nick then took H to the police vehicle and administered a breath-test whilst I inspected the Ford Cortina which resembled something out of Jimmy Bacon's scrap yard and I found damage other than the impact with the Cortina Estate. I went back to the police car and established that Nick had given H the breath-test which was positive (I would have been very surprised if it hadn't been) and we then drove H to The Nick.

En-route he became very belligerent and disorderly he was swearing and being abusive and kept rolling about on the rear seat of our police car. Finally we managed to get him into the Charge Room, where he was completely stripped and searched for drugs (even in these early years it was common for drug dealers/users to conceal their deals in the natural orifices of the body). Dudley Hubbard came into the Charge Room due to H's demeanour and I left to return to the RTA scene where inside the Cortina Estate I found a quarter sized bottle of Bell's Whisky hidden under the driver's seat. We didn't know when we took H in that he had defecated in his trousers and he was too out of it to realise. Whilst I was away from the Nick I was later told that when H was allowed to get dressed he suddenly yelled out *"Some dirty bastard's shit in my trousers!"* It's a good job that I didn't witness this otherwise I might have needed urgent medical attention for split sides.

I then obtained witness statements and at 3:50am returned to Lynn Nick where Nick Baron and I Interviewed H. I asked H *"How did you have the accident with the other estate?"* He said *"What accident man?"* I replied *"Your car was involved in a non-stop accident in Columbia Way about12:50am with a Ford Cortina Estate you hit the rear offside of it with your front nearside wing and left your complete wing there. You then drove on about another 200 yards before coming to a stop and you were given a positive breath-test and arrested".* H said *"How many charges are there against me?"* I said *"Six; positive breath-test, driving without due care and attention, failing to stop after an accident, failing to report an accident, provisional licence holder driving unaccompanied and without "L" plates."* H said *"How much will I get for that lot?"* I said *"I've no idea."* H said *"Well I might as well do a bunk then, as I am bankrupt for four thousand pounds now."* I then said to H *"How did the damage on the driver's side of your car happen?" You have hit a wall somewhere with it. It was not done in Columbia Way and your car was seen earlier in the Tuesday Market Place area with one headlamp and damage on the driver's side. What did you hit before the accident in Columbia Way?"* H said truthfully *"I can't even remember the accident in Columbia Way."* Nick Baron then said to H *"You will be reported for being drunk in charge of a motor vehicle with excess alcohol in your blood; driving without due care and attention; provisional licence holder driving unaccompanied and without "L" plates; failing to stop after an accident and failing to report that accident."* After caution H made no reply.

I then drove H to where his car was in Columbia Way in order to get his insurance certificate and MOT certificate and then dropped him off at a girlfriend's in Stag Place. The following night duty on Saturday 15th October 1977 H attended King's Lynn Police Station at 10:15pm and at 10:20pm Nick Baron interviewed him under contemporaneous notes after caution (this being some ten years before tape interviews).

PC691 *"What time did you start out last night?"*

H *"About eight o'clock."*

PC691 *"Where did you go?"*

H *"I went to West Lynn to see my children; my wife had come back to Lynn for the weekend."*

PC691 *"Where did you go from there?"*

H *"We had a bit of a row so I went to the Jolly Farmers"* (a South Lynn public house)

PC 691 *"Where did you park there?"*

H *"I parked in a side street."*

PC 691 *"Do you mean Portland Place?"*

H *"Yes."*

PC 691 *"What time did you leave the Jolly Farmers?"*

H *"I got there about a quarter to nine, because I was looking for a friend and I left after having one drink at about nine o'clock."*

PC 691 *"Where did you go to next?"*

H *"I went to the Maids Head and parked on the Tuesday Market Place dead opposite the Maid's Head about two rows back."*

PC 691 *"What happened at the Maids Head?"*

H *"I decided to stay in there to see if my friend came in there and obviously while I was there I was drinking; one thing just lead to another and I was so drunk I didn't realize how much I had had to drink until it was too late and from then on I can't remember anything until after the accident and I was coming up the steps of the Police Station. I realize that I shouldn't have attempted to drive in that state; but it was only because I was in that state that made me drink to start with and I would just like to apologise for everything."* H declined to make a voluntary statement and at 10:35pm the interview ended and Nick and I then made up our account in our pocket note books.

## Chapter Six

## *"Pastures New"* 1978 – 1982

## *1978*

Form A/84   NORFOLK CONSTABULARY            9764.

## MEMORANDUM

From   Chief Constable.

To     C/Supt. "D" Division.

---

TRANSFER                       3rd January, 1978

P.C. 409 CLARK "D" from King's Lynn to Detached Beat, Gayton.

(Police House, Gayton).

P.C. 922 CLARK, wife of P.C. 409 CLARK will continue to work at King's Lynn, commuting at her own expense, as suggested by her.

*[signature]*

Chief Inspector,
for Chief Constable.

On Thursday the 29th of December, during an early turn I completed my last tour of duty at King's Lynn where I had been man and boy for the past ten and a half years and Therese and I took annual leave I from Friday the 30th until Friday the 13th of January 1978 and she up to Tuesday the 10th giving us time to move from our rented ground floor flat at 69 Gaywood Road, King's Lynn, into our new home owned by Norfolk Constabulary at Gayton Village police house and try and get it into some order of semblance and decoration before going back to work.

The Police House, Lime Kiln Road, Gayton was to be our home for the next eight years and I was to be the *"Village Bobby"* on Gayton Beat for the next four and a half years. I would have direct responsibility for the parishes of Gayton, Leziate, Ashwicken and Bawsey as well as a Section Patrol Officer for the Grimston Section. Therese continued to work in King's Lynn on "B" Relief and and she became Acting Sergeant in Dudley Hubbard's absence and became a full time Control Room operative as well as George Courtney Green's Local Intelligence Officer Deputy until I re-gained it in 1982 when posted back to Lynn.

### *"The 1978 East Coast Floods"*

On Wednesday the 11th of January Therese was on late turn and I was still on leave finishing off the decorating, during that day the weather had become quite horrendous and the wind was blowing from the North East at nearly force 12. Having been on winter tidal flood watch at King's Lynn for the past 10 years and been involved in many close calls; I knew instinctively that on this occasion King's Lynn and The Wash area was in for a pasting. I telephoned DHQ to offer my services during the early afternoon and this was rejected, the attitude was that nothing was going to happen. In the meantime a massive tidal surge was sweeping its way down the North Sea from the North of Scotland to the shallower and narrower part between Holland and Belgium and the North Norfolk coast which then squeezed the surge and the inevitable occurred and that evening the River Ouse burst its banks and there was severe flooding in many parts of the town.

At Heacham the high tide was half an hour later and the force of wind and water suddenly tore a large hole through the outer sea wall and contained between this and the inner sea wall a six foot high bore of sea water raced the two miles to Snettisham beach. Ray Beeston and David Dingle were on tide watch in a police minivan on the top of the outer sea wall at Snettisham Beach Caravan Park when they were alerted by colleagues at Heacham of what had happened. They started to drive back down the sea wall towards the safety of the inner wall when they got by the club house and shop of the caravan park, the tidal bore of flood water hit their vehicle and it was tossed around like a cork in a millstream. The pressure was too much for them to open the doors, so they opened the sliding windows of the vehicle and bailed out and managed to swim and scramble to the far side wall and onto dry land, whilst their vehicle was swept away towards the shingle pits.

These were the severest East Coast floods since 1953 and the warning systems set in place since then, mainly by Fred Calvert, helped a great deal in saving many lives on this occasion.

Further around the coast Wells next the Sea didn't fare any better, the sea defence bank was breached under the weight of the storm water and carved out a 100 metre wide gap and many parts of the low lying areas of this picturesque little tourist town were flooded. Many large boats were washed from their moorings onto the quayside and a trawler battling her way to port alongside the sea defence, which is a mile from the lifeboat house to the quay was carried through the breach and finally came to rest on what was the football pitch!
The famous pier at Hunstanton which dated from Victorian times and

had withstood the 1953 flood had been ripped out by the force of wind and tide and was washed away, bar a few steel girders. I saw this and other devastation on Saturday the 14th of January when I commenced my new role as Gayton Beat Officer, but was immediately posted with Chris Dann on a 2pm to 11pm shift onto Section Motor Patrol to the Heacham and Snettisham areas on further storm tide flood watch and anti looting patrol to prevent theft from flood damaged gift shops, beach huts and caravans (there is always somebody ready to cash in on someone else's downfall). The scene at both Heacham and Snettisham resembled a battlefield, some static caravans at Heacham had been blown off their concrete pads and had finished up at the Snettisham Beach Caravan Park well over a mile away from their original position and then only stopped by a barbed wire fence or other obstruction. Some were squashed together and left in grotesque positions, resembling cattle when herded into a tight corner.

I did further similar duties on the Sunday and Monday following. The damage to West Norfolk and King's Lynn ran into many millions and the flood waters were higher than the 1953 floods. The normal predicted high tide at King's Lynn for the 11th of January should have been 26.6 feet, but it reached 31.4 feet, some 5 feet higher than prediction and overwhelmed defences put up after the 1953 great flood, it left a new record pencil line on the wall of St Margaret's Church, which has all previous flood marks back into the dark ages.

Chief Superintendent John Williams at Saturday Market Place knee deep in flood water outside St Margaret's Church helping to push a flooded Mini out of the water.

Water flooded St Margaret's Church, Lynn.

On Thursday the 19th of January, I commenced a week of night duty Section Motor Patrol with Chris Dann and during that week met Keith Manship my Dersingham Sergeant and Keith Swanson who was Acting Sergeant while Nigel Blower was at Sandringham. My Superintendent was Harold Parkinson, the Inspector Terry Finbow and my section colleagues were Phil Hales at Great Massingham, Peter Thompson at Grimston, and Martin Middlebrook at Pott Row and Peter Dennis at Middleton. The Section Motor Patrol I have already mentioned I worked one week of night shift every two months and alternated between Chris Dann and Brian Greenacre who were both from Dersingham. We were responsible for policing the royal residences of Sandringham, Wood Farm, Anmer (The Duke and Duchess of Kent's Norfolk home) as well as the Dersingham Section.

Previous Beat Officers and occupiers of the Gayton Police House were in descending order, Roy Daynes, Rodney Atkins, Ron Ravenscroft and Harold Parkinson. That first winter in our new home was really cold, we had snow blown under the Norfolk Red Pan tiles into the loft, which was not felted and all of the pipes and plumbing froze up. There was no central heating, just a small coal fire in the lounge which was supplemented with a portable gas heater and the windows were single glazed; with Therese and I working different shifts to each other there was no one to keep the fire burning and we invariably came home to a cold house, and to cap it all coming home one evening I found that a lump of coal had rolled onto the brand new carpet and burnt a hole in it.

On Wednesday the 31st of January I did a gash night shift Section Motor Patrol with Mick Staff who was at Dersingham and at 4:15am on Thursday morning the 1st of February I dealt with the sudden death of Doctor Ansell who together with Doctor Jolly, had been the Clark family doctor and who had been a regular visitor to our house since the mid 1950's.

During the first few months of my new posting I went around familiarizing myself with the locals, which included beef, turkey and arable farmers, a static and mobile caravan centre and a landed gentry in the shape of Julian Charles Marsham, the future 8th Earl of Romney who resided with his wife and young family at Gayton Hall. (He became Lord Romney in 2004 after the death of the 7th Earl) I quickly integrated into the local community and having met as many Gayton Parishioners as possible on a "hello" basis, before having to deal with any official business they came to know and trust me and that I would deal with them fairly and impartially and I already had the majority as allies, having won their "hearts and minds". I became a Committee Member of Gayton Social Club and the Gayton Village Hall Management Committee and as well as being Parish Liaison Officer for Gayton, Leziate, Ashwicken and Bawsey; I also became a Parish Councillor for Gayton, which I had sought permission of the Chief constable for and at the time was a rarity for a serving officer.

I dealt with all of the normal tasks which befell a rural beat officer, including issuing pig licences and renewing firearm and shotgun certificates. Any young offenders were in the main dealt with between myself the victim and their parents and on this basis I was able to keep everyone and the village ticking over as a community without outside interference. However this did not help with police statistics which people and politicians rely on so heavily nowadays and after I was replaced in 1982 the beat was swallowed up. It appears that if you look after an area and don't have escalating crime figures and anti social behaviour problems as performance indicators, then a community loses its police presence.

When the Force had a Beat Census in 1981 and my crime and other related figures were low, the Planning and Development Department carved up beats like mine and those of other colleagues, like Rodney Gooderson at Outwell, for example and when I moved back to King's Lynn in 1982 Gayton was swallowed up in part of the Middleton Beat.

However in 1978 I was responsible when on duty for calls in over 12 parishes in the Section and I had a Blue Morris Marina Van, which was fitted with a blue light but no Police/Stop as the King's Lynn Panda Cars had and together with my colleagues from the other beats, mentioned above operated a 5 man beat to cover the area 24/7. As I have previously mentioned, Grimston Section in 1967 would have operated with twelve men, an Inspector and a Sergeant, the former Grimston Police Station and Courthouse where in 1969 I had taken a murder remand suspect had since been sold and was now *"Highlight Film Studios"* run by a former pupil from Dersingham School. Therefore my home police station, apart from the dining room of my police house which housed a police cupboard for forms and paperwork, was the Sub Divisional Headquarters at Dersingham.

Over the years I came to the conclusion that I had a jinx on the Norfolk Fire Service, even though one of my old school chums Francis Lane had aspired to being one of the Norfolk Brigade's chief officers. At 3:30pm on Wednesday the 29th of March, I attended a large shrub and grass fire at East Winch Common adjacent to the village playing field, where the King's Lynn Brigade had gone on to fight the blaze which was under control by 4:30pm.

But there was a further problem, despite advice from me to the contrary one of the fire tenders had driven straight across the soft turf of the playing field, instead of skirting around the edge and had got stuck to its axles in mud. I then suggested calling out a local heavy lorry breakdown garage service which was poo pooed by the officer in charge, instead he called out the brigade's heavy lifting recovery vehicle from Hethersett near Norwich which arrived just before 6:00pm and that too got stuck! He then asked me to call out Sid George from Middleton who I had originally suggested and by 6:15pm both brigade vehicles were freed with the faces of the firemen the same colour as their tenders.

On another occasion I was travelling along Columbia Way following a fire engine *"on a shout"* and around the corner from Lady Jane Grey Road came an elderly couple in a vintage Morris Minor which collided with the fire engine and was written off.

One classic one was in 1976 when I was on a late turn at King's Lynn with Barry Richards this was doomed to failure from the start. I had just changed over from a Ford Escort Estate into a Talbot Horizon when we got a fire call to Gaywood. We jumped in and roared off out of the rear yard into peaktime traffic with blue light turning headlights on full beam but no *"two tone horn"* and the traffic lights at Blackfriars Road junction with Railway Road were red against us. Just for good measure I pressed the car horn whilst going over the junction and suddenly the windscreen was full of water making visibility temporarily nil! I had pressed the windscreen wipers lever where the Ford Escort horn would have been!

Undeteered we made our way to the scene in Bagge Road which turned out to be nothing more than a chimney fire and en route were following the two tenders sent out. As we arrived at the scene the first tender overshot the address and promptly reversed backwards into the front of the arriving second tender!

King's Lynn Ambulance Service were a far more genteel lot and I got to know most of the paramedics over the years and had Sunday breakfast with them when on early turn when at both Lynn and at Gayton.

The large garden which I had inherited at the police house was a wilderness and referred to by colleagues as a *"third of an acre rough shoot."* That first spring and summer I set about transforming it and one area I made into a lawn and patio and the other into a large vegetable and fruit garden, with two greenhouses for growing salads. I also had a dozen laying hens and we became fairly self sufficient and always had fresh produce as well as two large chest freezers stocked with the vegetables and fruit.

Additionally we sold any remaining produce and eggs at King's Lynn Police Station Canteen and always had orders for it. My little friend *"Timmy"* Turrell, who lived opposite at number 83 Lime Kiln Road with his wife Mildred helped me a great deal in my enterprise and was caretaker when we were on holiday, God Bless You Timmy. Both are now sadly departed from this life and *"Timmy"* is now one of God's Angels.

Talking of holiday's that summer Therese and I went to Torbay and stayed in a static caravan and took in all of the local sights. n the Wednesday after returning from a bay boat tour we berthed at Paignton Harbour and for some strange reason I had a rush of blood and tried to hurdle a chain link fence on the slipway and this got caught in the heel of my trainer. I went up in the air with the greatest of ease like the man on the flying trapeze, until the earth's gravity took control and I crashed to the ground right arm first. The resulting impact smashed my elbow with an excruciating pain and the tip became like a floating knee cap, with which I have problems with to this day. Therese took me to Torbay General Hospital by car and after X-Rays I was admitted overnight ready for an operation to set the bones the following morning, having endured a fitful night, including locking myself in the toilet when a gay male nurse wanted to give me a bed bath! The following morning I was informed by the surgeon that the wound was infected, caused by crab and fish bacteria from boats using the slipway and that I would have to stay in until the following Monday for the operation. I quickly discharged myself and spent the rest of the holiday with my arm in a sling.

We ended our holiday and Therese drove us home the 295 miles back to Gayton which I felt every bump of and I was eventually given a tetanus injection and my arm put in plaster by King's Lynn London Road Hospital staff. I was then stuck at home bored and it was during this time that I one handed laid a large crazy paving patio in the back garden whilst on sick leave. After 17 days I asked Harold Parkinson if I could work light duties at Dersingham police station, he said that there was nowhere that I could fit in but he arranged with John Williams at Lynn that I could travel in with Therese and work whatever duty she was doing, thus I returned to "B" Relief somewhat prematurely, albeit only temporary and helped out in the Control Room and Collator's Office, with my left hand getting used to answering the telephone and writing.

I remember at the end of one particular week H who had been recently been promoted to uniform Inspector on "B" Relief coming into the Control Room and saying to Therese *"You're off the shift next week on Collator Duties"* He then turned to me and said *"Chris you'll be in the Control Room."* I replied *"No I won't! I'll be in the Collator's Office with Therese."* He said *"I am ordering you to report for duty in the Control Room."* I then said *"You had better check with the Chief Superintendent (John Williams) as Superintendent Parkinson my boss has cleared it with him for me to do light duties wherever Therese is working and so that she can drive me backwards and forwards, I am only at work on light duties with my say so."* He checked and had to concede that I was right.

There was a plus to me breaking my elbow as that year the force had started PSU Training with the impending Miner's Strike looming and Norfolk Officers being seconded to South Yorkshire, Derbyshire and County Durham for it. I never got trained or had to go to those areas, I could not identify with being a human uniform crash barrier between striking miner's and *"scabs"* and had a lot of sympathy with their plight and the main argument was between Arthur Scargill and Margaret Thatcher's government.

On Sunday the 17th of December Patrick Joseph "Mad Dog" Magee the future Brighton Bomber, travelled to England and planted sixteen bombs in Cities across the country, including Bristol, London, Manchester, Liverpool, Coventry and Southampton, we were put on high alert at Sandringham during this time.

From the 1st of September I had a pay increase and my annual salary rose to £4,611. the Force establishment was 942 Constables, 190 Sergeants, 64 Inspectors, 24 Chief Inspectors, 15 Superintendents, 7 Chief Superintendents, 1 assistant Chief Constable, 1 Deputy Chief Constable and 1 Chief Constable. By this time the British Economy was so weakened that the Labour Government under the leadership of Jim Callaghan had to seek a loan from the International Monetary Fund. Harsh conditions were imposed which included cuts in public spending and this peaked in the *"Winter of Discontent"* when a number of trade unions went on strike. The dead were not buried and were kept deep chilled in mortuaries, rubbish was not collected and left in huge rotting piles on street corners, lorry drivers and key hospital workers were also involved. When asked about a crisis, Jim Callaghan famously replied *"Crisis what crisis?"* This all helped bring about the demise of the Labour Party as the Government and the following May they were defeated by the Conservative Party and thus started the reign of Margaret Thatcher as Prime Minister. On a local level, West Norfolk seemed to reflect the countries views and there was a constant tussle every four years between Henry Bellingham (Conservative) and Christopher Brocklebank-Fowler (Labour).

## "The Phantom Crapper of Old Dersingham"

Dersingham Police Station like other Divisional and Sub Divisional Headquarters had a separate toilet marked **Superintendent** and the Superintendent RHIP (Rank Has It's Priveleges) kept it locked; however all of the the lads had skeleton keys and could get in anywhere. It was not uncommon for the officers on night Section Motor Patrol to sit on the high seat of office and use the facility; one in particular deliberately refrained from flushing it after use leaving the resulting spectacle for the Superintendent's morning attention.

Thinking about it Headquarters had several toilets reserved exclusively for senior executive; perhaps that's where the lateral thinker's dreampt up their force reorganisation plans utilising the special A4 sheets of toilet paper specially formulated to be photo copied and distributed force-wide.

## *1979*

### *"Let It Snow, Let It Snow, Let It Snow!"*

During the late evening of Wednesday the 13th of February at about 11:30pm Therese and I were returning home to Gayton having visited my parents at Dersingham, en route it started snowing very heavily with a strong North Easterly wind blowing it through the hedgerows which immediately caused it to drift. On the B1153 Hillington to Gayton Road I had to drive completely on the off-side to avoid being stuck in a drift and we just got home before the road was completely impassable. The next morning the area resembled the North Pole, the main road which we had travelled along the previous night was filled with snow right to the top of our boundary hedge which was some twelve feet from road level! And there was about four feet of the stuff lodged in our driveway which took me all day to dig out, I needn't have bothered though as that night the wind blew it all back in again! It was the heaviest snowfall since 1947, although it was nowhere as cold as the Siberian Winter I had experienced during the winter of 1962/3.

The story was the same all over West Norfolk, villages cut off for days at a time, at Narborough 37 people were ferried to safety having been stranded on the A47 Road and Swaffham Police Station was used to house 15 people for the night. At Docking local officers including Les Neave crossed fields in a tractor & trailer to a bakery at Burnham Market to collect bread for cut off villagers. Closer to home it took two whole days and nights working continiously for a JCB to cut a single carriageway through the hard packed snow filled B1153 from our house the one and a half miles to Grimston. I spent several days marooned in Gayton and spent my time looking after the elderly and disabled, making sure that they were warm and fed and clearing driveways of snow and ice.

***"He flew through the air with the greatest of ease***

***The traffic man in the flying Capri's"***

A few weeks after this I was out on patrol one Sunday morning during an early turn, 8am to 4pm in my mundane Morris Marina van, which had to have a sack of sand in the back to make it stable during icy weather and although the morning was bright and sunny, there had been a hard overnight frost. Driving along the B1145 King's Lynn to Gayton road between Bawsey and Ashwicken I was overtaken by this flash top of the range Police Ford Capri traffic car driven by G formerly on "B" Relief and mentioned earlier who has now aspired to Traffic Department. A couple of minutes later I was winding my way down Brow of the Hill at Leziate and going round a sharp left hand bend, there in the middle of the road upside down and no longer looking like a flash top of the range, but more a heap of junk, was the Police Ford Capri, with appropriately, accident signs, bollards and other equipment strewn around and at that moment G was crawling out from underneath this mangled heap, injury only to his pride!

He said *"I hit a patch of black ice on the bend."* I kept my thoughts to myself but wondered how my unstable Morris Marina van with a tendency for the *"arse end to try and meet the head end"* had just safely negotiated that very stretch of *"black ice"* bend and why G's vehicle had tried to become a *"Red Arrow!"*

In May police houses owned by the authority had an increase in wallpaper allowance for redecoration, Constables to Chief Inspector rank were allowed £3.50p a roll, Superintendent's £4.00p a roll. I also had a substantial increase in my annual salary, it rose from £4,611 to £5,450 in April and then rose again in September to £6,186 that was nearly a 30% increase.

## *1980*

On the 4th of January a General Order was issued by Chief Constable Gordon Taylor, with regard to Parish Community Liaison Officers, the first paragraph of which stated *"The closure of detached beats causes much concern to the local communities in the areas affected. The parish policeman has been part of the rural scene for over a century, but during the past two decades his role has changed considerably in that he has been given mobility and communications and is required to police a much wider area."*

During the first quarter of the year the PNC was expanded to include a national disqualified driver index and in February a G.O. came out on the use of search and rescue helicopters covered by two *"Sea King"* helicopters from RAF Coltishall. The Order stated that their primary role was the search and rescue of military and civil aircrew in distress, other duties fishery protection, rescue of crew from vessels in distress, evacuation of sick personnel from lightships/houses, transfer of patients between hospitals, assistance to the general public in snow, flood, etc. The order went on to describe the procedure for obtaining RAF helicopter assistance and the selection of landing sites.

During the spring Gordon Taylor retired and George Charlton replaced him as Chief Constable, Peter Smith was his Deputy Chief Constable and John Hall was his Assistant Chief Constable. When Peter Smith retired in 1983 John Hall became DCC and Peter Howse ACC. Later in 1989 Peter Howse became DCC.

**Chief Constable George Charlton**

### *"No Hiding Place"*

During the early hours of Friday the 6th of June a window was smashed at a Greengrocer's Shop in London Road, King's Lynn, close to the Butchers premises referred to below. Two witnesses living in a flat above it were alerted by the noise and upon looking out saw a man nearby wearing a T shirt and "long gloves".

During the weekend of the 13th to the 15th of June, Therese and I were on rest days and entertaining one of my brother's and his fiancé at Gayton and during the early hours of Sunday the 15th were driving them to their home in King's Lynn.

At 1:25am whilst driving through the Southgate's Arch On London Road into town and towards the junction with Checker Street, under the bright street lights I saw and recognised one of Lynn's active burglars M of the *"West Norfolk Mafia"* and a nephew of B. I knew that he was professional in his method of operation anti surveillance and hard to follow. He was wearing a bright red T shirt and I saw that he was wearing black or dark blue woollen gloves or socks over his hands. This is a method he had used before to avoid leaving fingerprints and not get found with gloves for going equipped to steal and would then replace the socks on his feet after the burglary.

He was walking along a row of shops between Smith's Bakery and South Lynn Post Office on my offside and seemed to be concentrating his attention on these premises. I immediately suspected that he was about to commit a break-in at one of these. Upon hearing and seeing our car he made out that he was walking towards the Southgates.

I then turned left into Checker street and drove to the nearest telephone kiosk which was in South Lynn Plain and phoned the "Nick" and spoke to Dick Curtis the night shift "A" Relief Patrol Sergeant and told him what I had seen. I then dropped my passengers at their nearby destination and left Therese in the car in Friar Street car park and walked through the deserted streets from there into Checker Street towards the junction of London road and took up an observation point on the corner of some flats in Checker Street.

GREENGROCERS  AS THEY WERE IN 1980  LONDON ROAD SHOPS 2010  BUTCHERS  FISHING TACKLE SHOP

BUTCHERS SHOP  M's FIRST POSITION  SECOND POSITION  MY FIRST AND SECOND POSITIONS

Almost immediately I again saw M he was still in the area where I had originally seen him, this time between a Chemists and Colin Stevens Fishing Tackle Shop and I had to move back into the darkness to avoid showing out. He then must have heard a vehicle, probably a police car searching for him and walked across London Road to the corner of

Checker Street, using The London Porter House pub wall as a vantage point and a short time later retraced his steps back to the shops which held his interest, which included a Butchers and I heard a loud noise. What I didn't know and had not seen at the time, was that he had smashed the glass front door of the Butcher's shop with his shoulder, firstly placing masking tape over the area first to diminish the noise of falling broken glass he had cut his left arm in the process and had then hid up to see if any attention was drawn to the noise.

Also unbeknown to me a witness living in one of the flats was awoken by the sounds of breaking glass and saw a man in a red T shirt and wearing gloves walk from the direction of the shop into Checker Street. Shortly after I heard the sound of a vehicle travelling along London road from the police station direction and saw M ran across the road back to his vantage point and then ran up Checker Street towards my position and took up a further hiding place just a few yards from where mine was. He stood looking towards London Road and appeared to be listening.

I then saw that the objects on his hands were definitely socks as I could see the heels sticking out away from his wrists. He then seemed to sense my presence and turned his head towards my direction and recognised me and he was about to run off. I quickly closed the distance between us and shouted his name and said *"You're under arrest!"* and grabbed hold of his right arm he then swung his free left arm and tried to punch me at which point I put him in a headlock and he struggled violently. We were prancing around like a pair of ballet dancers and I applied more pressure and he stopped struggling, we stood there for what seemed ages with no sign of police assistance arriving.

If I had hindsight, at that moment I would have got him on the ground and restrained him properly but I was in a difficult position. It is a completely different set of circumstances being on duty and in uniform and knowing a crime has been committed as opposed to being off duty and a crime possibly about to occur. Eventually he shouted out *"Alright you bastard I give up you're hurting me I hurt my arm earlier"* and held up his left one.

I then had to make a decision and relaxed the pressure of the headlock a bit as I was in danger of cutting off his air supply and at that moment he seized his opportunity and broke free and ran off up Checker Street and down an alleyway. I ran after him but I was slowed considerably by the fact that I was wearing smooth leather sole and heel shoes which afforded little grip on the road surface and was a bit like running on ice.

He then made off into some rear gardens and through an old peoples home and houses in Southgate Street and out of view. Shortly afterwards I bumped into two Lynn foot beat officers and together we searched the area where M was last seen to no avail. I then rejoined Therese at 1:50am and went to Lynn Police Station to make a statement, it was there that I noticed blood on my shirt which I assumed had come from M's injured arm. A search of the shop premises by DC Ray Hansen the night duty CID officer revealed the attempted burglary at the Butcher's shop with blood on the glass of the door and a stolen vehicle was found parked at the rear doors of the premises in Guanock terrace in readiness as a getaway vehicle.

On Saturday the 5th of July, a red Austin van was stolen from Guanock Place King's Lynn, which is in close proximity to the first two attempted burglaries. During the early hours of Sunday the 6th an alarm activated at the Modern boot Repairing Company premises in Norfolk Street and PC Dick Ellis attended and found the stolen van parked round the back, two other officers, Janet Tsang (later Thomas) and Nigel *"Smokie"* Thomas then helped him search the shop where he disturbed the burglar who ran off and after a chase by the three officers was found to be M and arrested. He had also been wearing socks on this occasion and threw them away whilst running.

Whilst on bail for this latest offence M went into hiding and was circulated as wanted and on the run for some time, we eventually caught up with him a year later. The three

cases came to King's Lynn Crown Court during October 1981 with M pleading not guilty to all charges, the red T shirt and pair of black socks which he had worn at all three crime scenes were shown as exhibits.

The Jury convicted him of the Modern Boot Repairing Company burglary but his QC said that there was no direct evidence to place him at the attempted burglary of the Greengrocer's or the Butcher's as no-one had seen him smash the glass! M gave evidence from the witness box to say that *"I was just walking home when I heard a big crash of breaking glass and went back to have a look and saw a man running across the road then a police officer approached me and held me in a headlock."* The Jury were taken to the scene and took a copy of the sketch plan that I had made, together with my statement. The Jury came back not guilty on this one, however Judge Adrian Head gave him two years three months and gave four awards of court, two in the sum of £25 each, one for £30 and £50 to me!

Here is an extract from Personnel Order 42 dated 22nd October, 1981:
*"At the conclusion of a trial involving five offences of burglary, going equipped and taking without owner's consent, Judge Adrian Head made awards to three civilians for their assistance and also made the following commendation and award in respect of PC 409 Clark, "D" Division. Having been active in or towards the apprehension of M. In the ordinary way awards are not made to the Police, because they are regarded as doing their duty for which they are paid. This Police Officer was off duty, and we are frequently reminded that Police Officers are ordinary citizens wearing uniform. On this occasion PC Clark was not wearing a uniform and he went to considerable trouble and risk in the pursuit of his duties as a Police Officer at a time when he was off duty. I think he went beyond the call of duty going back down Checker Street and taking the steps which he did. I direct therefore that he be commended for that to the Chief Constable. I do not see why I should treat PC Clark differently from any other*

*ordinary citizen and I direct that he should be given an award of £50."* Very nice this was too which I received on the 14th of November and remember fifty pounds was worth a lot more then in value compared with today's value.

On Friday evening, the 12th of July the Dersingham Police Station civilian Public Enquiry Office Clerk/Typist, Daisy Dye retired, Therese and I went to her leaving do at The Feathers Hotel. In the photograph following she is being presented with a carriage clock as a retirement gift by Superintendent Harold Parkinson; and from left to middle are her former bosses, retired Superintendents Ernie Francis and his successor Sid Burton and to the right is retired Traffic Constable Arthur Barrett. Also pictured in the background are from left to right Constable Lionel Hewitt from Fakenham, Detective Sergeant Mick Farnham from Downham Market and formerly at Dersingham, Detective Sergeant Gerry Norton at Dersingham and retired Constable (and Special) Fred Beales from Docking.

On the 1st of September I had a pay rise from £6,186 to £7,503 per annum, another substantial increase.

## *1981*

On Saturday the 1st of January, following various surveys and statisticcal census, (the toilets were working overtime and someone had diarrhoea) the Norfolk Constabulary was again disorganised, the people responsible, the force executive of the day called it *"reorganisation."* The old adage of *"If it ain't broke it don't need fixing"* sprang to mind. Grimston Section became D10 Beat, some villages formerly in King's Lynn Division, were lost to other newly formed Divisions and we gained others not previously policed by us. The police map of the County was transformed into a giant jigsaw puzzle. Overnight our reporting police station moved from Dersingham some six miles away to Hunstanton some twenty miles away, we were totally confused so you can work out how the public felt.

An example of this new change we gained Castleacre which was formerly policed by Swaffham only four miles away in Dereham Division and that parishioner's new point of reference was Hunstanton over twenty-five miles away. This same situation was repeated all over the County, additionally a lot of beat and other police officers formerly in *"tithe"* police house or rented police accommodation, suddenly found themselves posted a long way from their pre 1981 patch, some having been there many years.

All local knowledge of the areas and people which takes some time to develop was lost overnight and these officers had to start over again from scratch. So both the public and the police officers tasked to serve them, suddenly felt cut off and remote. So much for centralised policing which didn't gain one extra body where it was needed most, at the grass roots where they had been previously. Luckily, I was to remain a local beat officer for the D10 and Gayton area for a further 15 months, before it was my turn to be severed from the village beat scene.

At the time both Therese and I loved village life and wanted roots, so during May I submitted a report on the future of Gayton Police House and the desire to purchase it whilst a sitting tenant, if and when it became available on the market. The house was subsequently sold to us on the 15th of October, 1982.

During this year Alan Smith became Detective Chief Inspector and Kevan Coyle Detective Inspector, both having previously served on the Regional Crime Squad, Cecil Rowe was a Uniform Inspector and Terry Finbow was Temporary Chief Inspector both now at Dersingham.

### *"Temporary Crime Squad"*

During my preceding three years on the local beat I had built up a very good knowledge of B's activities who I have earlier mentioned he was West Norfolk's main receiver of stolen property who lived in a nearby village and I had supplied a lot of grade one intelligence on him and his associates into the system. At the time during February and March 1981 there was a spate of burglaries of off licences, tobacconists and garages occurring all over Norfolk and in the neighbouring Counties of Cambridgeshire, Lincolnshire and Suffolk.

The team committing these, known as *"The SAS"* because of the fact that they wore full face balaclava masks to avoid detection on shop premises CCTV systems whilst committing the crime. They comprised of B's nephew arrested by me in June 1980 whilst I was off duty and O another who I was the instigator of for his arrest in October 1976 for the Gayton Road house burglaries and who I was to be involved in the arrest of later during July 1981 and two others who I was involved in the arrest of for shop burglaries previously in June 1975.

Alan Smith and Kevan Coyle both nominated me to work with the Norwich area of the Regional Crime Squad under the leadership of Detective Sergeant Bernie Kerrison (who I had done my basic training at Norwich Division with) who had a surveillance package on B and I was written off normal uniform duties until further notice. I worked permanent nights and kitted myself up in dark *"all terrain"* civilian clothing, complete with haversack which contained a torch, truncheon and handcuffs, area plans, a flask of coffee, food, a small bottle each of whisky and brandy. I was collected from Gayton each night by RCS personnel in one of their four covert vehicles we operated in four teams and had two officers to a car and they included Terry Glister and Pete Boucher who have since sadly died, also Bob Adams who was promoted not long afterwards.

For the first part of the night we staked out the various known burglar's addresses, including the ones previously mentioned for movement and details of vehicles in use in order to build up to date intelligence. Then we would all rendezvous at the village playing field and four of us would walk through fields, rough ground and alongside a stream, the one and a half miles until we got to the rear of B's property.

One car would be hidden up at the village end using night vision binocular, acting as a forward observation post for vehicular and foot traffic and two out on foot hidden in a wood at the front of the target address, also with night vision equipment. I knew B's regular routine and it included going to bed about 10:30pm and getting up around 6:00am to tend to his pigs and poultry.

The information presented to The Squad by Lynn CID was that the *"SAS"* team would burgle a premises using a stolen vehicle to transport the stolen property in then go to B's premises where he had a bonfire in readiness, burn any incriminating and identifiable wrappers etc and then leave with the property. B himself had volunteered this information which was in effect placing a noose around his own neck. For me this information did not add up with my suspicion that he would actually receive and dispose of the property himself at a later date. Also I knew where the information had come from a serving detective and that source was too close to the target for my comfort and in the past it had been tested by me and found to be unreliable.

At this point I will break from the present to previous occasions that I have direct knowledge of concerning the activities of this Informant and his Handler. Some years previously in the late 1960's due to the knock on effects of swine fever and foot and mouth disease putting the meat prices up there was a large scale organised theft of fattened pigs in the Region. B and his then *"West Norfolk Mafia"* team were in the thick of it together with two of his long term associates.

A *"Pig Squad"* comprising of local beat officers was formed and had several small successes. When the heat got too much for him B fingered his own son who was caught in the act of stealing four pigs found in the back of his Ford Consul with the rear seat removed; so he would drop anyone in order to save his own skin. This same detective was always getting smaller criminals locked up on the information of the big one, for me the reverse has always applied, go through the tiddlers as bait to get the big fish landed.

The next examples are more sinister, information came in from the same source that B's two main men then who the Crime Squad had previously targeted intended to burgle *"The 77 Club"* at Brancaster and they were to pick up an unregistered car from B to commit the job with. On this particular night plain clothes officers secreted themselves in the *"target"* address in Brancaster some sixteen miles away from B's, awaiting action. I was on a late turn 4pm – 12mn local Gayton/Grimston patrol in full uniform in a marked Morris Marina Van. I decided to test the information and drove down B's lane and hid my van in a field behind a hedge not far from his address and waited hidden in the hedge. It was a black foul night with torrential rain, shortly after taking up my position I heard the *"swish"* of waterproof leggings and the two main men who were both very anti surveillance minded passed just a couple of yards from my location, talking quietly to each other.

They went to a Nissan Hut garage that B had and I heard them start up a motor and shortly afterwards drove along the lane past me.

I allowed them 100 yards before following them at a discreet distance with the lights off on my van; I followed them like this through several villages and onto the A148 King's Lynn to Cromer Road where I followed them for about three miles before I aborted as it was unsafe to follow further without showing out. They had gone by the B1153 Coast Road junction so I knew Brancaster was not their intended target, but had gone towards Fakenham instead.

I went to a kiosk and reported to the Headquarters Information Room of what had transpired for them to alert the officers staked out at Brancaster by telephone. What I found out later was that on this night the two had gone to RAF Sculthorpe Base and their intended target was the Club there, however they saw an MOD Policeman doing his rounds and aborted and went instead to the Village Store at West Rudham and burgled that of its stock of spirits and cigarettes and the proceeds obviously went to B. Whilst I was covering the Collator Duties during this time I catalogued they had committed over £66.000 worth of burglaries in Norfolk and the surrounding border Counties, that was a tidy sum then when you think that my annual wage was just over £4,500!

On the next occasion the information was again crap designed on the face of it to be helpful but again to keep B out of the frame, but on this occasion they hadn't accounted for the uniform lads. Half of Fakenham town centre had plain clothes officers secreted within shop premises awaiting the two but they went in undetected and committed a burglary at a clothing shop and were back out on the A148 before you could say *"Hey Presto!"* PC *"Nicky"* Baron & a colleague were in a marked night patrol car on the outskirts of the town around 3am when they saw this old Bedford Van leaving Fakenham and decided to pull it.

On seeing them it sped away and they followed it along the B1145 towards Great Massingham when about a mile outside the village the van slowed and two figures jumped out of the sliding doors, one on the driver's side and the other on the passenger side, before splitting up and running in opposite directions. The two officers gave chase the passenger got entangled in a barbed wire fence and *"Nicky"* Baron was able to arrest him, the driver managing to outrun the other officer. I was on night duty Control Room at Lynn and sent out assistance. After this these two took *"Early Retirement"* from being active burglars and became handlers instead leaving the fitter up and coming younger ones to learn the trade like their sons and nephew's team.

On another occasion I was on another late turn and saw this detective officer's private vehicle parked up at B's I took up my previous observation point and kept watch, it was still there at 2:00am and I knew that this detective was on annual leave and I reluctantly went off duty as I was on early the next day. Around the same time I was called to two large trailers full of baled straw which had been deliberately set fire to and owned by another villain. He alleged that B had lost the straw carting contract to him and he would be the one behind this arson. He said *"One of your detectives is as bent as he is, you want to be at his caravan on a Friday tea time when he is there along with J and B that's when the money is paid out and the fags and booze are there as well."*

Now going back to the stake out on B we found that he was lighting a bonfire on a Sunday evening and a Wednesday evening and it was kept going during the night with the aid of old vehicle tyres, exactly as he had been doing at Horsley's Chase in Lynn all those years before in 1967 when I wrongly thought he was disposing of stolen vehicles and put intelligence in on him. During that first week *"The SAS"* were disturbed committing a cigarette burglary at Clenchwarton and left without the property, on this night a Wednesday the fire was well alight awaiting them.

During the second week Bernie had pre booked annual leave and The

Squad supervisory role was filled by another Detective Sergeant whose name is omitted to save any embarrassment to him. How a former Crime Prevention Officer can go straight into being a Detective Sergeant on a Regional Crime Squad and later in charge of Force Intelligence evades my powers of reasoning. Anyway into the second week we went and sure enough on this Sunday night around 2:00am a bonfire was merrily crackling away at the back of B's and all looked set for visitors and we settled down to receive them. Around 2:30am the lights suddenly went on in B's trailer park home and I said quietly to the Det Sgt and the other three gathered in the bushes, *"Tonight's the night lads."*

Sure enough about half an hour later, Pete Boucher called up from his position near the Village Hall, *"Black Austin Maxi and registration??? Two up, coming to target address."* Shortly after we heard and saw the vehicle approach B's and turn in the first driveway where his Nissan hut garage was, the lights of the car went out and we heard two doors shut and the doorway of B's home suddenly illuminated in the dark as it was opened and two figures went in and after this we saw people toing and froing, obviously emptying the car of its bounty.

This was also confirmed by the two lads staked out in the wood at the front. We waited for a signal from the Det Sgt to close in on the address and make the arrests but it never came. I kept saying *"Come on G, we've got them and the property there, let's go."* He kept saying *"I'm not sure."* So there we sat the seven of us waiting to be unleashed and one decision maker who couldn't or wouldn't make the decision. Twenty minutes expired and we saw the door again open, two figures came out, two car doors slam, headlights on and away they went back up the lane and past Pete's position who clocked them out. The lights of B's home went out and there we stayed until the first faint illumination of a winter's dawn changed the darkness to a faint, eerie and misty semi darkness and the Det Sgt gave the order around 6:00am to move off and we wearily decamped back to our waiting cars.

I was feeling completely demoralised at the thought that our whole existence doing this cross country trek was to nail this gang and we had let them slip through our fingers because of inept leadership. I must also add that at no stage whilst the burglars were at B's was anything put on the bonfire, so it was for him to later burn up anything identifiable from the stolen property which was now in his possession.

No sooner had I been dropped off at home than Therese who was early turn Control Room at Lynn phoned, and said *"You'll never guess what, Middleton Service Station strong room was burgled overnight and 70,000 cigarettes were stolen."* I said *"Yes and I know where they went."*

I then informed Kevan Coyle of the night's events in connection with the burglary. The Maxi stolen from Dersingham was later found abandoned with the rear seats down to make a storage area where the 350 X 200 cartons of cigarettes had been conveyed in, forensic examination revealed nothing.

I went back that night and the RCS lads had an air of despondency about them. Bernie came back on the third week and was livid that his job that he thought he had left in safe hands had been cocked up in such a manner. We went into the third week and there was another aborted attempted burglary so our quarry through bungling and luck didn't come to book. After that with British Summer Time approaching and the dawn coming much earlier to show us out the surveillance was knocked on the head.

It took a further 18 months before Lynn CID decided to have a further assault on closing down B's reign. In the meantime I decided to make him my number one priority and staked out his address at every conceivable opportunity and continued to build up a profile of his visitors and vehicles.

### *"The Dukes of Hazard"*

During the first week in July, 1981 I was on a week of night duty with AN Other and at 3:30am on Wednesday the 7th of July with him fast asleep in the passenger seat, I decided to do some observation on the approach to B's home and hid the police Ford Escort Estate up on the car park at the rear of the Village Hall, where I could clock anything that went down the lane. I was still there at 5:00am when it was a broad daylight sunny morning and it was time to check if Therese was up for early turn so I walked from the car the 100 yards or so to the telephone kiosk situated across the village green. As I was speaking to Therese from the kiosk I heard the sound of a high revving vehicle approaching at speed from the Cross Roads on the A148 road side of me.

This vehicle a Red Ford Capri with a Black vinyl roof then pulled up outside the kiosk, which was one of the red GPO ones with metal square framed windows. I saw and immediately recognised the driver as being O and his passenger as L. At this stage they hadn't seen me and L got out and walked round the back of the car intending to use the kiosk, obviously to ring B about the consignment of contraband on board the car; oblivious to the fact that a uniformed police officer was standing inside it.

Shock Horror! From L just as he tried the kiosk door handle he saw me and bolted back into the waiting Capri which tore off at a great rate of knots with O who was a bit of a Michael Schumacher driving furiously. I ran back to my parked vehicle whilst circulating the car and occupant details on the repeater set radio I had on me and on getting back to the police car, tore off in pursuit of it down Leziate Drove towards the B1145 and Ashwicken. Whilst AN other was coming around and out of what he thought was a nightmare. When we got to the B1145 King's Lynn to Gayton Road I saw dust coming up from a track that led into British Industrial Sand Pits at Leziate and together with other police colleagues who turned up checked the area.

The Capri roared around through Leziate and Bawsey Woods until it ran out of petrol and was later found abandoned, hidden up covered with branches and inside the boot and on the rear seat were three large brand new television sets and three top of the range video recorders, all still in their boxes. O and L had obviously got back to Lynn and the Fairstead Estate by walking along the British Industrial Sand railway track (this will feature further along during another "incident").

During the day the car was reported stolen but it was not until Thursday morning when Curry's of Fakenham, who had been closed on the Wednesday, reported a burglary and electrical property stolen, totalling over £2,000 which was what was recovered from the stolen Ford Capri, not bad for a night's work and when you consider that was about three months salary for me then and compare it on today's value. Both O and L were arrested and remanded in custody to Crown Court. Both later pleaded not guilty at a two day trial at Norwich Crown Court during April, 1982 and I was called to give evidence. The prosecution case was that a burglary had occurred at Curry's Electrical Shop at Fakenham overnight of the 7th/8th of July,1981 and three TV sets and three VCRs together worth £2,500 had been stolen. O and L had been seen by PC Clark in a stolen Ford Capri at Pott Row at 5:00am on the 8th which when found abandoned contained the stolen property and therefore had committed this burglary. Paint samples found in the Ford Capri by John Hansell SOCO, matched those of the point of entry of the burglary. There was no evidence placing either man in Fakenham or at the scene of the burglary, so everything rested on my uncorroborated evidence.

The Defence agreed that L was a passenger in the car out for a joyride with an unknown male and not involved in the burglary and L also gave O an alibi. O alleged a case of false identity that he was not the person that I had seen in the car. As you can imagine I was in the witness box for some considerable time with the Defence Barrister trying to undermine my identification evidence and credibility.

The Jury found both guilty and The Recorder told both before sentencing that the burglary had some hallmarks of organised crime. O was given three years imprisonment and disqualified for two years and L two years imprisonment and disqualified for two years. Altogether a good result and it felt really good to know that the twelve Jurors had believed me.

It's also strange that I was involved in two cases with O where paint samples were involved, the first in 1976 involving the Gayton Road house burglaries when paint from his car was left on a fountain and this case when paint samples from a shop burglary were in the car driven by him.

As a result of this episode, towards the end of July, 1981 Kevan Coyle asked if I would do some day time observation on B to see if he was moving stolen property and I was written off for a week hiding in the dense wood opposite. I observed B's comings and goings and all I saw was him putting potatoes into sacks and loading his tractor and trailer with them and driving off.

I did a discreet follow and saw him drop off some of the sacks at a South Wootton address owned by a mobile *"Fish & Chip"* proprietor who was known as a handler of stolen goods, the rest B dropped off at a supermarket/post office owned by another known handler in Kings Lynn. Not having hindsight I did not see or know that in the bottom of each sack before potatoes were put in, that cartons of cigarettes and bottles of spirits from burglaries had been placed inside each one, this would be revealed some time later. All I got for my pain that hot sunny week were numerous mosquito bites, nearly driven to distraction by swarms of flies and countless bloody scratches caused by brambles, which is what the insects were after.

## *"The Royal Wedding"*

Wednesday the 29th of July was declared a national holiday for the wedding of the Heir to the Throne HRH Prince Charles to Lady Diana Spencer later to be HRH the Princes of Wales. Therese and I were off duty and watched the day's events on television, we had the police house decked out with a Union Jack ribbon and I had planted red, white and blue, alyssum and lobelia in the flower borders for the occasion.

This occasion could easily have been overshadowed and marred by events some 6 weeks earlier if the circumstances had been different i.e. the gun had been loaded with live cartridges. On Saturday the 13th of June at just before 11:00am BST Her Majesty the Queen was riding past crowds during the Annual Trooping the Colour Ceremony in Horse guards' Parade when she was shot at by a young man who managed to fire six shots before being overpowered by a Guardsman and Police. Luckily the rounds were blanks but they startled the Queen's horse, Burmese, Her Majesty looked shaken by the episode, but soon recovered her composure and she comforted Burmese the 19 year old horse she had ridden for the past twelve years. The man arrested was a 17 year old a former air cadet. He was jailed for five years under the 1842 Treason Act on the 14th of September, 1981. The court was told that he at one stage had planned to kill the Queen, but had failed to obtain a suitable lethal weapon. He said later *"I wanted to be famous; I wanted to be a somebody."* The Queen was to endure further lapses in security just over one year later.

### *"Living Life in the Fast Lane"*

From Monday the 12th of October to Friday the 13th of November, Therese and I were on a Standard Driving Course based at Force Headquarters. Her Instructor was PC Mike Henry, and mine Norfolk's first Civilian Instructor a retired *"Met"* Copper and former Royal Marine Commando, Dave Brady, later to be the author of two books *"Yankee One And George"* and *"The Chosin Few."* The other Instructors were PC Don Greenwood and PC Pete Hadlett, Sgt John Chenery was in overall charge of the Force Driving School

Department. There were four cars each with an Instructor and twelve of us on the course, three to each car.

During the course I again became *"The Joker"* on several occasions. As Dave had let slip that he had been an explosives expert during the Korean War, Therese and I bought a packet of cigarettes the brand that Dave smoked and spiked several of them with exploding caps. Then one Friday lunchtime whilst Dave and the other Instructors were engrossed in playing cards in their office I switched the doctored pack for Dave's pack out of his jacket. On the way to our respective cars the unsuspecting Dave handed a cigarette to one of the other Instructors, who lit up and it went bang! He got the blame and then lit one up and that too went bang! That wasn't the end of that episode though. Dave came on duty the following Monday morning and kept muttering *"Bastards! Bastards!"* I said *"What's the matter Dave?"* He replied *"Picture the scene I'm sat at home with the wife, the cat's on the mat in front of the fire, all is peaceful and serene. I offer her a cigarette and when she lights it, it goes bang! The cat runs off and I get accused of being childish and to calm my nerves, I light up and that too goes bang! You Bastards!"*

Dave told us his two pet hates, one not politically correct to mention, the other *"Specials."* During another lunchtime I crept into the office on some pretext and nicked Dave's official Norfolk Constabulary jacket off the wooden coat stand and disappeared with it like a thief in the night. We had found some *"Special Constable"* shoulder tabs and Therese sewed these onto the shoulders of Dave's jacket and I returned it to the stand without raising any suspicion.

It was a hot day and after lunch Dave walked with his jacket neatly folded over his arm until we got to the car where he started putting it on as we drove out of Headquarters. As he did so he saw the flash of something white which caught his eye and roaring out *"Bastards!"* tugged the jacket off and spent the next few minutes trying to unpick the stitches of the offending articles in order to remove them. Dave still hadn't sussed out who had done this dastardly deed but concluded because of the neatness of the job that it must have been sewn by one of the two females on the course and wrongly suspected the other female officer B.

Fifty miles further away and one and a half hours later, he was still chuntering on about his jacket as we pulled into Dersingham Police Station where he spied one of the other driving school cars parked, the crew from this one containing the female officer B and they were in the canteen drinking tea and eating cream cakes that they had bought from Playford's Bakery. As our crew entered the room Dave went straight over to the other crew table picked up a cream horn from amongst the assortment on the plate and rammed it straight into poor innocent H's face! To the amazement of everyone gathered.

The place then went into uproar and Pete Hadlett the other Instructor thought that Dave had flipped, when it calmed down I informed Dave who the real culprits were and he was quite embarrassed and apologised to H. Apart from these incidents Therese and I studied hard on theory and drove consistently on the course and on the

final day we both passed as *"Grade One Drivers."*

A big thank you Mike and Dave it was the best course that I have ever been on. As a token of our appreciation we bought the Instructors a tin of *"Rover Assortment"* biscuits but I couldn't resist one last wind up, I undid the sellotape seal and placed a note inside the lid saying *"This tin will self destruct you have five seconds to clear the room. Bang!! Too Late!"* and re sealed it. At lunchtime of our last day I knocked on the Instructor's Office door where all five were and walked in saying *"Excuse Me"* and walked slowly and carefully with the tin of biscuits to create maximum effect towards their table and placed the tin gently down and then ran out of the room slamming the door!

I then got a chair and peered through the fanlight window above their door and took in the scene. Most of the Instructor's had got up and were standing as far away from the tin as they could because of what had happened with the cigarettes and there was brave Don Greenwood on his knees carefully cutting around the sellotape seal with his penknife. At that moment he popped the lid off and they all saw the note and laughed with relief.

Three years later Dave wrote his first book *"Yankee One And George"* which is a humourous look at his life in "The Met", inside the copy we bought he had written *"To Therese and Chris Clark, I forgive you for sewing Special Constable to my jacket – but only just!! Your mate Dave Brady."* Sadly Dave is no longer with us having died during 2013.

The Laughing Policeman

*Pete Hadlett Dave Brady Therese Mike Henry*
*General Order 16/76 Item 5: A Grade 1 Driver is authorised to drive Patrol Cars and all other Force four-wheeled vehicles.*

# This is to Certify

that

P.C. 409 CLARK

attended a

Standard Driving Course

at the Headquarters of the

Norfolk Constabulary

from 12th October, 1981     to 13th November, 1981

and successfully completed the Course being

classified as a Grade I driver.

Chief Constable

## *"Olympic Standard but not a Pheasant Plucker"*

I had no sooner got back to Gayton when my new driving skills were put to the test. At about 4:45pm on Saturday the 21st of November I was driving along the B1145 in Lynn Road in the village and heading towards home and as I was rounding a right hand bend by The Rampant Horse pub this estate car came flying round the bend in the gathering dusk from the Gayton Thorpe direction towards Lynn containing two men.

I did a U turn and went off in pursuit achieving 80mph to keep up with this vehicle with my headlights and blue flashing light on, the vehicle in front did not slow and was trying to get away. It took a further five miles of furious driving before I managed to overtake it on Gayton Road at King's Lynn close to Gaywood Cemetery where I pulled it. As I was doing so I saw in my rear view mirror the driver jumping out with the car which was still moving and the bloody thing ran into the back of me. Thinking that he was doing a runner I leapt out stick in hand just in time to see him throwing something over a hedge into the park. I then grabbed him and pinned him against the rear of the estate car and then looked in the open hatch and saw 6 dead cock pheasants which were still warm and numerous live 12 bore cartridges strewn around.

I then searched the area where I had seen something being thrown and found and expensive up and over Browning double barrel shotgun which had recently been fired. I arrested him for poaching and found that he was J aged 18 years of King's Lynn, who was the current British Open Skeet (Clay Pigeon) Champion and a member of the British squad for the Olympic Games and who held gold, silver and bronze medals for team and individual shooting at World and European level.

None of this cut any ice and he was dealt with the same as everyone else who had the misfortune to come my way. His solicitor made a big thing about it when it came to court the following January on a guilty plea and

I was not called, he implored the magistrates not to confiscate his £1,000 shotgun. Although he was fined £50 for using the gun and cartridges to kill game and a further £25 for taking pheasants without a licence he was allowed to keep the shotgun. The story was featured in the local Lynn News and Eastern Daily Press newspapers and even made The Sun. The Chief Constable also allowed him to keep his shotgun certificate and not revoke it.

### *"It Wasn't Santa Claus"*

Just before Christmas 1981 there was a knock on the front door at my Gayton police house home and there was B my Archenemy with a large metal butcher's tray full of meat which consisted of joints of pork, pork chops and sausages. He said *"These are for you Chris."* I declined his offer as it was obvious that he heard about my earlier surveillance of him and the arrests of O and L and was trying to buy me off. Also I would not have taken anything from a villain apart from a cup of tea and a biscuit as it is the start of a slippery slope and then the villains have got you. He said *"I always have a couple of pigs slaughtered at Christmas and I give some to…."* and he named three Detective Sergeants.

Later when I was Deputy Collator I researched the cigarette and spirit burglaries and none were occurring in the areas that the aforementioned had responsibility for, but were in other Divisions and surrounding Force areas. Obviously B and the three Det Sgts were keeping each others backs scratched.

Going on to nailing Bob that came about when Ted Worby took over as DCI in 1982 and decided to see what truth there was in Bob's involvement following O and Ls convictions and put a team in. On the first night one of the officers Roy Daynes from training school days and my predecessor at Gayton, sat down on a pile of sacks to carry out observation and found something hard and lumpy underneath. Upon lifting the sacks up he found a load of bottles of spirits and cigarettes hidden underneath. B was arrested and the property was identified as coming from a burglary at Sheringham, some 40 miles away.

He went to Crown Court and was sentenced to a term of imprisonment. This was the only time in 25 years that this old scoundrel had been brought to book. After his release I used to go and see him regularly and have a cup of tea with him. I decided that this was the best way to keep tabs on his movements, rather than cruising past and noting his vehicles, visitors, etc.

On Thursday the 24th of December, Christmas Eve, I completed a night shift duty at Gayton and at 6am went to King's Lynn Police Station to help Therese cook a full English Christmas Breakfast for "B" Relief; in two sittings. Little did I know that they were soon to become my new colleagues. In the photographs are newly promoted Chief Inspector Terry Finbow (my former Inspector at Dersingham) Inspector Mervyn Clingo, Sergeant Dick Curtis, Sergeant Bob Funnell, and Constables: Roger Lord, Matt Sharman, Neil Adams, Tom Neill, Mick Chipperfield, Paul Chapman, Andy Claxton, Kevin Reeve and Mark English, most of these would later be promoted.

Chris Clark

I had spent four happy years at Gayton and it would appear that I had been popular with the community and big wigs judging by the amount of produce which mysteriously turned up at my back door, including pheasants, turkeys, sacks of potatoes bottles of spirits, etc. Apart from actual duty time I had always made myself available to the public, when off duty, to both callers at the door and on the telephone. I never turned anyone away or fobbed them off, even though at times it was inconvenient, being asleep after night shift or on rest day.

Sadly all good things have to come to an end and due to a further Force Reorganisation; I was on the move back to King's Lynn the following March with happy memories and mixed emotions. I had quite an eventful four years but as I had handed in my diaries for that era I only have sketchy details of some things I dealt with.

I know that I dealt with the suicide of an Agricultural Scientist from Cambridge, on a Christmas Eve, early Christmas morning possibly in 1980 at his friend's address. I think that there had been a *"Gay"* falling out and the friend was elsewhere. He had pooned Cymag, an agricultural cyanide poison (originally used to gas rabbits and vermin and banned since 2004) into a cup of coffee to mask the taste and gone to bed with it, put a towel over the bed and had a washing up bowl in case he was sick. But the suddenness of it had even taken a scientist by surprise and the convulsions had thrown him out of bed onto the floor still holding the bowl and he died instantly.

On a New Year's Day probably 1979, whilst on early turn I had driven down a village lane to check any activity at B's and on the way out came across a Ford Consul car containing 5 teenage local up and coming villains, a PNC check revealed that the vehicle had been stolen from London during late December. All did a runner from the car upon seeing me, but as I knew them all I was able to later pick them up one by one and take them to Dersingham Police Station to be charged. Two were other nephew's of B another H became another labourer burglar of *"West Norfolk Mafia"* and several years later in 1986 was arrested for Rape another case I was involved in.

On another occasion probably the summer of 1979 the *"Golden Fry"* Fish & Chip shop plate glass window in Gayton was broken. Outside at the time were ten local teenagers involved in horseplay. I walked them all back to the police house and left them in my *"office"* the dining room to decide between them whether they were going to be reported or reimburse the victim, whilst Therese and I listened by the serving hatch in the kitchen. They chose the latter and ten lots of Gayton parents were relieved that their *"Bobby"* had dealt with it in such a sympathetic way and not *"crimed."* On another occasion, probably 1978 Chris Dann and I were on night Section Motor Patrol and we were called to a road traffic accident on the A148 Road at Hillington. An articulated lorry had jackknifed and partly demolished a house a wall and the *"Rager's Garage"* filling station shop. When we got out of the police vehicle we realized why, the whole road for about a quarter of a mile was nothing but sheet black ice we had to don wellies to stand up.

During another night shift with a regular colleague who was fast asleep in the passenger seat and reminiscent of a previous saga, I drove out of Bawsey Woods onto the B1145 and stopped a van being driven towards Gayton from King's Lynn. I quickly ascertained that it had just been stolen and arrested the offender E. I then had to wake my colleague up so that he could drive the van to Lynn while I went with the prisoner in the police car!

One further thing springs to mind, one weekly rest day during the autumn of 1982, Therese and I were returning home from Dersingham when this car came bombing from the A148 into the B1153 in front of us and being driven by a prat. I followed it and it went to an address on Spring Vale in Gayton and out stepped M the only one of *"The SAS"* that I hadn't arrested and this was only a few months after O and Ls convictions for the Currys burglary. I cautioned him about the manner of his driving and he said *"I'm not talking to you; you sent two of my mates down."*

I never did get M as he moved away to Cambridge and became a big time drug dealer, like the others I had previously put away did, in the mid 1980's and into the 1990's. I continued to keep tabs on them and put intelligence into the National Crime Squad who had target packages on them; which was of valuable assistance to achieving an eventual result.

### *"Gunpowder Plot"*

During 1982 Therese and I decided to do a repeat of our famous exploding cigarette trick on one of our policewomen who was always running out. This particular night A drove for the first half and as I got in placed the pack on the dashboard and said *"These are for you"* she became immediately suspicious but for the wrong reasons and refused to touch them. She thought wrongly that I had some intention on her body and would make some sort of advance. You could cut the atmosphere with a knife in the car and it was a really foggy night and A hadn't been back off her standard driving course long and the fog and rural windy roads which were also unfamiliar and her tenseness soon caused her to run out of cigarettes.

We went for mealbreak at the Queen Elizabeth Hospital and Alison decided to open the spiked pack in the safety of the staff canteen. She lit one up and that went bang! And she fell about in hysterical laughter with relief that it was just a stitch up and nothing more sinister much to the annoyance of medical staff on their break.

A couple of years later A became the innocent victim of another stitch up which wasn't meant for her. C who was transferred onto the Relief because she was idle and the Guvnors wanted her sorting out started having children like they were going out of fashion, taking full maternity leave, then coming back and immediately getting pregnant again.

This went on for several years and four children later we then got lumbered with her in the Control Room and she was not a nice person at all. One night I crept down the first floor corridor with a roll of cling film and doctored the rim of the bowl of the ladies loo and waited in gleeful readiness for her to answer the call of nature. There was a downstairs separate ladies and gent's loo near the back door for patrol officers to use and we expected the female patrol officers to use those facilities so hadn't warned them.

But this night A came in and went to use the upstairs ladies. The first thing we knew that our windup had misfired was when she walked into the Control Room with soaking wet culottes and had to go off to shower and change! She took it well though. This reminds me of what I did to J another woman on another occasion during a night shift sometime prior to this when the Control Room was still downstairs. It had been snowing heavily and she and A came in and stuffed a handful of snow down the back of my shirt and had a good laugh about it.

Whilst J was standing by the radiator to warm up I crept up behind her with a can of menthol air freshener in hand and sprayed most of the contents upwards into the legs of her culottes, she cried out in shock *"Oh you've wet my knickers!"* Well that brought the room down and we were all hysterical with laughter.

## *"Knot Funny"*

During 1984 when a new PC joined the Relief we decided to see what he was made of. On one Sunday night shift I devised the following scenario: A suicidal male was thought to be heading for King's Lynn in a named vehicle we used a private car again and it was placed in readiness in County Court Road close to the edge of The Walks. At a predetermined time one of the lads "spotted" the vehicle heading into the town centre near to The Walks and lost it. In the meantime B who was dressed in civilian clothes was rigged up in a tree in the park adjacent to the police station to appear that he had hung himself, to complete the effect of looking *"dead"* he had flour daubed on his face.

The new PC was sent into County Court Road to search for the vehicle and came across it; and confirmed this over his radio which was on *"talk through"* so that all the Relief could hear blow by blow. I then instructed him to search the immediate area and shortly after his torchlight picked up the eerie figure of B who looked like a corpse dangling by its neck. On seeing this the PC ran across to the five foot high park railings topped with spikes and vaulted them and ran to the front door of the police station calling *"10/9! 10/09!"* The urgent assistance requested call sign and upon reaching the internal doors shouted out *"Let me in let me in I've found a body!"*

I then instructed him to return to the scene and cut down *"the body"* which he did and just as he was reaching up to free the noose around the stiff's neck. B suddenly moved and went "Boo!" The PCs fear immediately turned to anger and grabbed B around the throat and we nearly did have a dead body on our hands, another windup which worked a treat.

Chris Clark

## *"Radioactive Fall About"*

There was another time when a Sergeant was on the shift and I owed him a wind up as we had had a couple of run-ins together whilst he was with us. He was due to go on secondment and on his last tour of duty with us a Sunday of late turn I devised a devious plan to get him. I typed out a telex purporting to have come from Headquarters to the effect that a radioactive isotope had fallen from a train on the branch line between British Industrial Sand at Leziate and King's Lynn Railway Station and that secrecy was to be established in order that it didn't fall into the wrong hands. I then informed the Relief accordingly without the Sergeant's knowledge knowing that once he knew he would jump in with both feet and want to take the glory.

I then called the Sergeant into the Control Room and showed him the telex; he swallowed it completely and called the Relief in for a briefing. I produced a large scale map I had showing the branch line and its journey to British Industrial Sand. He then armed himself with a powerful seek and search torch and went down to King's Lynn Railway Station where he started to walk along the branch line the some two miles to BIS. The other personnel that he had deployed to start from BIS, knowing that it was a wind up, ignored this command and positioned themselves on top of the railway bridge on the King's Lynn Bypass some mile and a half outside Lynn and waited.

Eventually they saw his torchlight flashing about and it started getting closer to them, they had some difficulty in not bursting out laughing. Just before he went under the railway bridge he suddenly heard an audience clapping and upon flashing his torch saw the rest of the relief and knew that he had been had: he took it in very good heart though.

One thing more before I leave our telephonist who was always crossing this Sergeant and couldn't stand him called him JAFO (Just another F…ing Observer) from *"Star Wars"* behind his back. Later in the year the Miner's Dispute kicked off and at short notice and this Sergeant was deployed to South Yorkshire with a King's Lynn contingent of Police Support Unit Officers. Coaches were laid on and somehow in the melee his suitcase containing changes of clothing and toiletries got left behind in the Control Room. I simply addressed it to *"JAFO South Yorkshire"* and it got to him! Such was his reputation.

### *"Pyscho Sam"*

Not all windups went so smoothly however and I remember this one vividly. Again we were on nights and there was this Station Sergeant and he was one of those who just couldn't hack nights and stay awake. The Patrol Inspector had contracted the same sleeping sickness only he was a *"psycho"* with a short fuse who should be given a wide berth at all costs. On this occasion the Sergeant was asleep in his office which was adjacent to the Control Room where another PC and I were working. It was around 3am and most of the lads were either in for meal break or having just completed one on their way out. The Inspector being more discreet and unbeknown to anyone but me who knew his habit was also asleep in an upstairs office.

Our Patrol Sergeant of that time (who later went on to greater things) said *"Let's wind B up by setting off the fire alarm!"* I said *"I'm not sure about that as "pyscho Sam" will be asleep somewhere in the building"*. He went and checked the Inspector's Office and other parts of the building and then returned saying *"No he's definitely not in the Nick and his cap and radio are nowhere to be seen."*

I said *"I'm still not sure about this you know what he'll be like if he gets disturbed without good reason."* The Sergeant then said *"Go on Clarky set the damn thing off!"* I then went into the corridor and set the fire alarm off which was situated near the Charge Room and with this loud siren going off at points all over the building the PC and I hid crouching behind the Charge Room counter to await the fruits of our labour. Whilst the Patrol Sergeant and the rest of the Relief hiding in the passageway to the cells which were empty.

After a short time this PC and I slowly rose to peer above the top of the Charge Room counter expecting to see the yawning rueful looking Station Sergeant; instead we saw the dishevelled figure of the Inspector with hair awry shirt buttons and epaulettes undone and flapping, looking like an angry bear that had just been disturbed from early winter hibernation. On seeing us two he made a lunge over the counter at us but luckily at that moment heard the rest of the shift giggling like school kids and his attention was diverted towards the cell corridor.

He roared *"Come here you bastards! I'll f…ing kill you"* and off he went in that direction and upon seeing that it was him and not the Station Sergeant they scattered in all directions like rats out of a barrel. The Patrol Sergeant ran into one of the female cells and slammed the door shut which had a self lock and couldn't be opened without the key which was safely in the Station Sergeants' key safe. Another PC wasn't so fortunate the Inspector chased him and caught up with him in the parade room where he set about nearly throttling him before calming down. In the meantime my Control Room PC and I had slunk back into the Control Room and hoped that the Inspector had forgotten about us.

A short while later he came in still angry and in his former dishevelled state muttering to to Station Sergeant who had by this time awoken, about the Patrol Sergeant and the lack of discipline on the shift, with the Station Sergeant having a self satisfied look on his face. In the middle of all this I said *"Actually it was me who set the fire alarm off to wind B up not you"*. With that the Inspector's mood changed completely like the sun coming out from a thunder cloud and we all had a good laugh.

The Inspector wasn't the sort of person to cross, a couple of examples of how he became aptly named as "Psycho" it was common knowledge that if a prisoner was brought in for knocking a policeman about, he would get the cell keys and go down and *"have a talk"* with him about it. On another occasion a knife wielding mad man was causing havoc on North Lynn Estate and the entire Relief was up there with riot shields trying to contain him in the street. The Inspector came into the Control Room to find out from me what it was about and a few minutes later he was at the scene. The lads up there said that he just appeared from nowhere and pushed past them walked up to the armed fugitive punched him knocking him out and then left them to arrest him when he came to. He turned out to be a good *"guvnor"* he left us to get on with the job but was there if advice or help was needed.

### *Bomb Disposal Squad*

This windup occurred in the mid 1980s and I feel it appropriate to add it here. We had this new recruit who clearly was not up to the mark he was very gullible, lacked common sense, observation skills and had poor judgement and one who we clearly could not rely on to watch our backs in a rough house or applying the *"ways and means act"* when necessary.

One Sunday early turn during the summer the same Relief Patrol Sergeant mentioned with "pyscho Sam" located an old WW2 250lb general purpose empty bomb casing minus its detonator and filling in the property store and at first light took it down to where a granary was being demolished to make way for a town centre development. There it was placed in an excavation with a rope tied around it and the rest of the Relief hiding up inside the granary holding the rope.

# Chris Clark

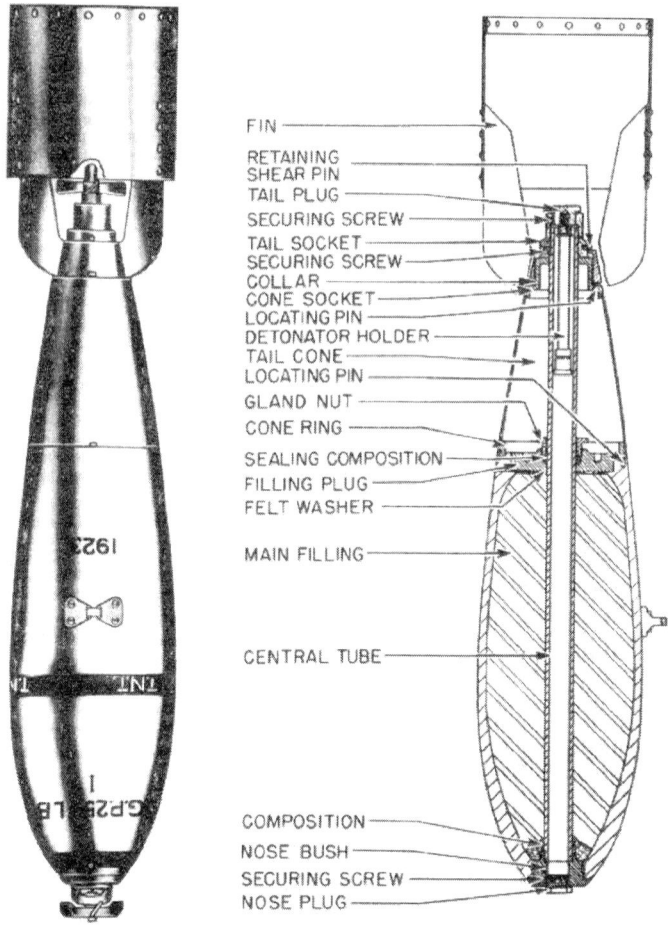

At the pre-determined time the Patrol Sergeant informed this recruit that a UXB (unexploded bomb) had been found and that he would have to go down and with a rope pull it out of the crater with the Sergeant so that the workmen could get on. As they got to the scene and located the UXB the Sergeant fashioned the rope into a noose and placed it tightly over the fin of the bomb and instructed the recruit to keep his back turned in case the thing exploded! The rest of Relief then pulled tightly on their rope like a tug-of-war competition whilst the Sergeant #instructed the lad to pull hard on his rope.

The lad said *"Sergeant what about if the thing explodes?"* and he was told *"Just keep your back turned and if it goes off stick your fingers in your ears!!"* With that he pulled with all his might one way with the combined strength of the Relief pulling the other to make the weight seem authentic and at that moment the Sergeant raised his arm and the Relief let go of their rope. The result was that the bomb casing flew out of the hole and with a resounding metallic thud crashed onto rubble behind the recruit. He was then told to run as far away as possible in case there was a delay mechanism fitted and the thing exploded! It should be quite clear to the reader why this particular recruit didn't make the grade. As a footnote I bet that neither of these last two stories were broadcast in the upper echelons by the Sergeant in question when he rose to dizzy heights of office.

I hope that you have found this first part offering of my police service autobiography enlightening, entertaining and funny in parts. If so I look forward to providing you with my sequel entitled *"The Urban Spaceman"* which portrays the last third of my service in a much sombre setting of the 1980s and into the 1990s when political correctness became the rule of the day.

Chris Clark June 2016.

## FOOTPRINTS IN THE SAND

One night I dreamed…

I was walking along the beach with the Lord.
Many scenes from my life flashed across the sky.
In each scene I noticed footprints in the sand.
Sometimes there were two sets of footprints,
Other times there was one set of footprints.

This bothered me because I noticed
That during the low periods of my life,
When I was suffering from anguish, sorrow or defeat,
I could see only one set of footprints.

So I said to the Lord, "You promised me Lord,
That if I followed you, you would walk with me always.
But I have noticed that during the most trying periods of my life
There has only been one set of footprints in the sand.
Why, when I needed you most, have you not been there for me?"

The Lord replied, "The times when you have seen
Only one set of footprints in the sand, is when I carried you."

— Mary Stevenson